Advance Praise for
THE ONE DECISION *by Judith* Wright

"*If you knew that* one *decision would drive and govern every other decision, would you be interested? This is the significant power of this book.*"

—STEPHEN R. COVEY,
author of *The 7 Habits of Highly Effective People* and
The 8th Habit: From Effectiveness to Greatness

"*Most people sleepwalk through life without a clearly defined direction and purpose. Judith Wright has helped thousands break the spell and awaken to a life of zest and fulfillment. In* The One Decision, *she shows how.*"

—LARRY DOSSEY, M.D., author of *The Extraordinary Healing Power of Ordinary Things*

"*It's simple—and life-changing.* The One Decision *is right! I love the fact that an entire book is dedicated to this profound truth, so 'obvious' that it is more often than not ignored.*"

—TOM PETERS, author of the *New York Times* bestsellers *In Search of Excellence* and *Thriving on Chaos*

"*Have you read a lot of useful books but not found the one that really puts you over the top? This one will show you what's been missing. Judith Wright's* The One Decision *is inspirational and practical, visionary and down-to-earth. Don't miss it.*"

—LES BROWN, author of *Live Your Dreams* and *It's Not Over Until You Win!*

"The One Decision *is part inspiration, part motivation, and part wake-up call. This book embodies a powerful opportunity for each of us if we're willing to embrace the greater MORE in life that is right in front of us at all times. Judith's stories and real-life examples remind us that MORE is not just for the lucky few, but for all of us. Judith, and her book, are definitely the real thing.*"

—SONIA CHOQUETTE, bestselling author of *Your Heart's Desire* and *Trust Your Vibes*

The One Decision

Make the Single Choice
That Will Lead to a Life of MORE

JUDITH WRIGHT

JEREMY P. TARCHER/PENGUIN

a member of Penguin Group (USA) Inc.

New York

JEREMY P. TARCHER/PENGUIN
Published by the Penguin Group

Penguin Group (USA) Inc., 375 Hudson Street, New York, New York 10014, USA • Penguin Group (Canada), 90 Eglinton Avenue East, Suite 700, Toronto, Ontario M4P 2Y3, Canada (a division of Pearson Penguin Canada Inc.) • Penguin Books Ltd, 80 Strand, London WC2R 0RL, England • Penguin Ireland, 25 St Stephen's Green, Dublin 2, Ireland (a division of Penguin Books Ltd) • Penguin Group (Australia), 250 Camberwell Road, Camberwell, Victoria 3124, Australia (a division of Pearson Australia Group Pty Ltd) • Penguin Books India Pvt Ltd, 11 Community Centre, Panchsheel Park, New Delhi–110 017, India • Penguin Group (NZ), Cnr Airborne and Rosedale Roads, Albany, Auckland 1310, New Zealand (a division of Pearson New Zealand Ltd) • Penguin Books (South Africa) (Pty) Ltd, 24 Sturdee Avenue, Rosebank, Johannesburg 2196, South Africa

Penguin Books Ltd, Registered Offices:
80 Strand, London, WC2R 0RL, England

Most Tarcher/Penguin books are available at special quantity discounts for bulk purchase for sales promotions, premiums, fund-raising, and educational needs. Special books or book excerpts also can be created to fit specific needs. For details, write Penguin Group (USA) Inc. Special Markets, 375 Hudson Street, New York, NY 10014.

One Decision™, with its related trainings and materials, is a trademark of Judith Wright and the Wright Institute, Inc.

Library of Congress Cataloging-in-Publication Data

Wright, Judith, date.
The one decision : make the single choice that will lead to a life of more / Judith Wright.
p.   cm.
ISBN 1-58542-481-1
1. Self-actualization (Psychology).   2. Decision making.   3. Spiritual life.   4. Quality of life.
I. Title.
BF637.S4W74   2005   2005053879
158.1—dc22

Printed in the United States of America
1   3   5   7   9   10   8   6   4   2

Book design by Claire Vaccaro

While the author has made every effort to provide accurate telephone numbers and Internet addresses at the time of publication, neither the publisher nor the author assumes any responsibility for errors, or for changes that occur after publication. Further, the publisher does not have any control over and does not assume any responsibility for author or third-party websites or their content.

To the students of the Wright Institute,
the inspiring warriors who fight the Good Fight
in the name of their One Decision

Contents

Introduction

*There is One Decision that can change your life for the bet-
ter, forever. When you make this One Decision, you step into the
life you yearned for—a life of adventure, commitment, and fulfillment of your heart's desires. You probably do not know at this
moment what that decision is or what your life will look like once
it is made. You may be uncertain of your worthiness to attain it.
No matter: The One Decision will bring you into the life you
yearn for! The One Decision will form the basis and context for
all the decisions, big and small, that you will make in all the days
to follow. As you take this step and make your One Decision, you
will see the abundance of the universe, the inexhaustible gifts of
spirit, flow in to support you. Your One Decision will be your
map, your compass, your North Star, and your challenge as you
chart your life course. Let your One Decision be the light of your
heart that guides you to a life of MORE—more of everything
you truly desire.*

Have you ever wondered why relatively few people lead great
lives while most people lead average lives at best? <u>Like it or
not, we each live the life that we decide to lead.</u> Having a great
life requires making a great decision—the One Decision™. The One Decision is a commitment to pursue MORE in life—more love, fulfillment,
purpose, satisfaction, meaning, abundance, contribution, intimacy, and
spirit. And pursuing the bigger MORE will also bring you more of the

worldly things you desire—more money, great relationships, better health, and career success.

Everyone *wants* MORE out of life, yet not everyone has *chosen* MORE. We have chosen what we *think* will bring us MORE—we've gone to the right schools, changed careers, lost weight, accumulated money, done yoga, taken a class, joined a gym, gotten a makeover, bought lottery tickets, taken up art, meditated, jumped on the fast track, dropped out of the rat race, gotten married, ended relationships, bought bigger houses or fancier cars— or even gotten rid of it all.

Yet our attempts rarely deliver the results we hope for. The satisfaction doesn't last. We make random improvements, and as a result, we lead only partially successful lives. We achieve at work but fail at important relationships; we have a great family life but suffer from poor health; we enjoy great health but experience career problems.

Sometimes, for a few brief moments, we may touch the greater MORE—a sense of rightness with ourselves and the world, a feeling that we are a part of something larger. But despite this momentary high, the real, enduring MORE eludes us, and for a very good reason. No matter how many "good" activities or behaviors we add to our life to try to get MORE, we never truly experience MORE until we make the One Decision. Making this decision, we choose MORE directly. We learn to use this profound decision to guide us in making all the many choices we face each day in our lives.

This book will present you with the pathways, vision, insight, and perspectives that will help you to understand the greater MORE of life. It will show you how to create it in your life through making your own very personal One Decision. In this book, I share what I have gleaned from twenty-five years of coaching and training people who have wanted MORE in their lives—and have gotten it. It incorporates the experiences of thousands of our students and faculty at the Wright Institute, where we have pioneered and refined a process that helps people not only understand what their personal MORE is but also helps them achieve and maintain it.

Discovery of the One Decision

I first discovered the One Decision almost by accident. Looking back, I see that I had already been living according to my One Decision, but I didn't have a clue that I had made such a choice. In fact, I didn't even have a name for it. It was only after several of my husband's advanced students began coming to me for my consciousness and spiritual development courses and I began helping them to find the deeper meaning they yearned for that I discovered the One Decision. Most were unusually successful in marriage, parenting, and business. More than half of them had advanced degrees, many from top schools. Through my husband's parallel business, they were exceptionally trained in a wide variety of personal development arenas—communications, teamwork, project management, and even intimacy skills. Their lives were exemplary, but they were still lacking something.

I realized that while they had decided to learn and grow, they had not dedicated themselves, or given themselves over to, the greater MORE in life. As I began to work with them, they began to have exponential breakthroughs. And these breakthroughs all began with one very singular shift. It was as if all the work they'd done previously was just a dress rehearsal for the making of one very important choice. I began to identify and recognize this shift for what it was: the One Decision.

After these students had made their One Decision, all their activities and efforts had an amazing synergy, impacting all areas of their lives. Where they might have had marriage or business success before, now both were flourishing at new levels. And this was true for all areas of their lives— from their body and health to relationships to finances to career to family. These successful people had made a leap to an entirely new way of living, and their commitment, their One Decision, was what took them there. I recognized this commitment only because I had chosen it for myself earlier in my life.

My One Decision

Before I made my One Decision, my life was filled with exceptional achievements but not the greater MORE. Externally, everything was picture perfect. As a child, I had pursued as many extracurricular activities as possible and had been a leader in most of them. I was an "A" student, a drum majorette, a student leader—you name it, I did it. In college, I lost the extra weight that I had been carrying around for most of my life. Shortly after graduating from college, I had risen to national prominence in my field and married my college sweetheart, an intelligent and good-looking man. I was attractive, successful, and "happily" married. But my life felt empty.

The meaning and truth I yearned for in my relationship was absent. My husband was drinking too much and my career success did not make up for what was missing. I kept trying to do good things—working hard and playing hard—but then zoning out pretty hard, too. I felt unfulfilled, distracted, and empty. It seemed as if I couldn't get enough traction to really move in my life. The results of all the things I was doing kept falling short of my desires, even though I was externally succeeding. I took classes and dance lessons, read good books, saw a therapist—but I still didn't feel like I was getting what I really wanted out of life. My attempts seemed disjointed; success in one area didn't transfer to other areas. Even if what I was doing was "kind of working," given all the effort I was expending, I thought my life should have been better.

This was really upsetting to me, because I had put together all the ingredients I could think of for a great life, and it wasn't working. I still felt empty, as if I didn't fully exist. It was a very dark time for me. I was at my most desperate because I was running out of options. I couldn't figure out what else to do.

It was from this point of desperation that I made my One Decision. I decided that I was not willing to live my life dissatisfied, sleepwalking, and unfulfilled. I made a decision: I am going to feel my life. I am going to be awake and conscious and surrender myself to spirit. I didn't fully know what this meant, how to do it, or even if it would make things better, but I was going to find out.

I started to orient my life differently. I kept doing many of the same things I was already doing—but for different reasons. When I exercised, I began to revel in the sensations of my body—enjoying feeling graceful and strong instead of focusing on the calories I was burning. I discovered how joyful physical activity could be. I started adding things to my life so that I could feel and experience my life more fully. I read great literature to keep me inspired. I sought out and connected with all kinds of interesting people, people who thought in different ways and challenged me. I planned personal getaways in nature and spiritual travel to restore myself. I lessened my Soft Addictions, the mind-numbing activities that ate up my time and left me empty.

I began to demand more of my marriage and woke up to my husband's resistance. After putting a tremendous effort into our relationship, I reoriented to my One Decision and realized that if I was going to be in a relationship, I needed a partner who was aligned with my commitment—which eventually led to our divorce. After entering more consciously into the dating arena, I used my One Decision to choose whom to date and how, and met my husband, Bob. He is the ultimate truth-teller in my life, who honors and matches my dedication and reminds me of my One Decision even when I don't remember it.

On the career front, I deepened my work developing model programs for families of handicapped children, until my One Decision took me out of the university setting and led me to establish my own business, coaching and training others on the quality of life.

Now my life has synergy. I have a touchstone to guide each decision that I make. I can focus much more easily on what matters to me and design my life to meet my deeper desires. It is easy for me to rule out activities, including spending time with some people who are not in alignment with my One Decision. I don't have to go into an endless internal debate. I know which activities, thoughts, and situations serve my One Decision and which ones don't. I am more satisfied, my life has depth, and I feel my life more fully. I have more intimacy and more satisfaction. I make more contributions, and I have more creativity—more than I ever knew existed.

It doesn't mean that everything is perfect or that I don't have hard times or upsetting moments. In fact, I may have more of these episodes because I am engaging in life more fully, living it as an adventure, and taking more risks. But I also have more rewards, more satisfaction, and more victories. My One Decision is about being alive, conscious, engaged, and devoted to a higher purpose—it's not about being perfect. I continue to learn how to live it more fully and how to realign to it when I get off course. It is a constant adventure, a constant state of becoming more me.

What Is the One Decision?

The One Decision is a personal commitment about how you are going to live your life. It is not a small step or a nice idea or a good decision. It is *the One Decision* you can make that will completely change your life. It is a compelling dedication to a way of being, a quality of life, or a higher principle or higher power. It is a decision so powerful that it becomes a touchstone you orient to when making every other decision. It is a personal commitment and is different for everyone. For one person, their One Decision might be "I stand for truth." For another person it might be "I choose to live as if every moment matters." For still another it might be "My One Decision is to be a vessel for spirit." The words a person chooses do not really matter. It is a commitment you make in your heart, not in your head. The words aren't as important as the feeling that you have inside yourself.

Making a One Decision and choosing a life of MORE is a definitive act, one that will separate your life into the time before and the time after. Like a sacred vow, your One Decision is not to be made, or taken, lightly. It is, after all, the One Decision that commits you to a way of living that leads you to MORE. It fuels the fire in your belly and feeds the flames that drive you to pursue MORE. It awakens you to the deep yearnings you have for something greater. The One Decision leads you to be the very best you can possibly be, to live the life that you came here to live, to have the sense that your life counts, and to show you that you matter.

I may have coined the term "One Decision," but human beings have been making their One Decisions from the beginning of time. Buddha made it by sitting under the Bodhi tree. Moses made it and led the Jews out of Egypt to the Promised Land. Abraham made it and God responded. But the examples don't end with religious history. Even Hollywood recognizes the concept of the One Decision. From Scarlett O'Hara in *Gone With the Wind* to George Bailey in *It's a Wonderful Life*, many characters make a life-altering decision. In the movie *The Shawshank Redemption*, Tim Robbins's character says, "I guess it comes down to simple choice, really. Get busy living, or get busy dying." Probably the best-illustrated example is in the movie *City Slickers*. The trail boss (Jack Palance), leading the urban neurotic character (Billy Crystal) on a trail drive, raises one finger in the air and says, "One thing, just one thing. You stick to that and everything else don't mean S**&T!"

While we get inspired seeing these powerful decisions at the movies, we often don't realize that the reason we are captivated is because these examples call to something within ourselves. We don't realize that there is a choice for us to make, and we don't see ourselves as the hero of our own life.

Sometimes it takes a near-death experience for people to realize the value of their life and commit to live it purposefully. Tour de France champion Lance Armstrong became a committed, service-oriented person after surviving cancer. For Buckminster Fuller, father of the geodesic dome, it took the loss of his daughter. For Saint Francis, it took illness. For others, it takes a serious accident. You don't need to wait for a catastrophe to decide how you are going to live your life. You can choose a life of MORE, however you personally define it, at any time.

The Exponential Effects of the One Decision

Students usually come to the Wright Institute to solve a specific problem or achieve a particular goal. And they generally accomplish their original aim fairly quickly. But in the process, they realize that there is a much bigger journey for them. We invite them into a larger vision for their life. When they make their One Decision and begin to live this vision, they are surprised to discover positive effects in every area of their life, a journey to even MORE. With this book, I would like to extend the same invitation to you. I can't tell you exactly how much MORE you will discover, but I can tell you that it is virtually impossible, having made the One Decision, to simply improve one skill or in one domain. The results are exponential.

My husband Bob and I have now seen this exponential effect with countless students, many of whom now teach others to live lives of MORE in their relationships, businesses, health and well-being, and all other aspects of their lives. The story of one of them follows.

Joe describes his One Decision as a moment "when I felt spirit moving inside of me . . . While I don't remember everything I said regarding my One Decision, I felt energy surging through my body in a way I had never experienced before. I felt clear, focused, and deliberate in every word that I spoke. I said, I want MORE out of life. I want 'Genuine Joe'—the real me—to manifest all the time, and to never, ever be denied the expression of myself in the world." Not the words you'd expect to hear out of this MBA and former partner and chief financial officer in a top international financial firm.

For many years prior to making his One Decision, Joe had been on a powerful journey of growth and development. He had defined his values, learned to live with principles, and identified his personal mission, purpose, and vision. But despite all Joe's efforts, there was still something missing. He lacked the clear focus he sought. He was making progress and growing, but he didn't feel like he was moving forward—he wanted to release the power locked inside him. He felt a calling for an indefinable MORE.

At one of my weeklong intensive trainings, Joe made his One Decision and found the focus he needed. Suddenly his personal power and influence began to manifest in more fulfilling ways. It was as if all the work he had been doing finally came together, and he gathered even more power behind his life purpose. "My One Decision is making a difference in all my roles—as a husband, father, grandfather, adviser, citizen, student, athlete, investor, and spiritual being." He is pursuing a deeper level of connection in his relationships, asking more difficult questions, telling harder truths, and holding people accountable. "I am actually looking forward to people telling me I am too gung ho! Not bad for a recovering passive-aggressive!"

How Does the One Decision Relate to Life Purpose?

Joe had understood his life purpose but hadn't yet learned to live it—and he's not alone. Your purpose gives you the Why of your life, and your One Decision gives you the How. Purpose gives your life focus, and the One Decision gives you the guiding principle for living every day. It becomes your core way of being. But you don't need to worry if you haven't identified your purpose; the One Decision, by its very nature, leads to purposeful living. Get to a good, solid One Decision and your purpose will take care of itself.

Bringing MORE to Life Commitments

Life-changing commitments are part of almost all religious orders, cultures, and faiths. Members go through rites of passage such as baptism, communion, naming ceremonies, bar or bat mitzvah, confirmation, marriage, vision quests, initiations, and even last rites. Alcoholics in recovery make a decision to stop drinking and then find strength in a higher power. Christians accept Christ as their personal savior and Muslims have faith in and follow the teachings of Muhammad.

Whether you're Muslim, Buddhist, Christian, Jew, atheist, agnostic, "born again," or simply a believer, the One Decision can help you deepen the lifelong and life-changing commitments you have already made, or it can independently give you a concrete way to claim this momentous turning point in your life.

The One Decision does not replace other life commitments, yet it will strengthen and deepen them. For example, a recovering alcoholic has acknowledged that his life is unmanageable and that he is powerless to change it alone. So he turns his life over to a higher power in order to stop drinking—powerfully altering the course and direction of his way of living. For many alcoholics in recovery, however, this does not necessarily indicate a total One Decision, because they have not aligned their choice with a commitment to living the highest-quality life they can, and to become the type of person they most respect.

While there are many Evangelical Christians who are "born again" and see a clear division in their lives from before they found Christ to after, there are many other people of faith who have made deep spiritual commitments or turned their lives over to God or spirit who don't feel they have a powerful way to fully claim and share this commitment. With the One Decision, these individuals now have a way to mark their lives— "Before the One Decision" and "After the One Decision."

A One Decision—whether it relates to declaring Christ as your savior or giving yourself to God or shifting your behaviors—is a fundamental decision about how you want to live your life. It is a commitment to pursuing total quality, satisfaction, and fulfillment in all aspects of our lives. Each of us faces a choice about the kind of life we want to live. For those who make it, the One Decision consistently brings them closer to the heart of their faith. Christians declare a personal relationship with Jesus for the first time, Muslims come closer to Allah, Jews rediscover their faith, while atheists find greater meaning and a sense of oneness and wonder. With the One Decision, it is common for unbelievers to believe and for others to discover love, peace, and belonging they never thought possible.

In this book I will be using the words *God* and *spirit* to indicate the source of all life, as I see it. If you are an agnostic or atheist, please interpret the term to mean life, love, the intelligence behind all that is, or whatever works for you. I do not believe you need to declare or believe in God as I do to reap the love available to us all. I have faith in the spirit of God throughout the universe—you do not need to see things this way to benefit from the One Decision. It is your decision and declaration that matters. I believe that how you live your life, aligned to a great good however you perceive it, is the most important thing you can do.

The stories you will read in this book are from students of the Wright Institute, who come from different walks of life, different religions, or no religion or spiritual beliefs at all. What they have in common is an alignment to something higher—their One Decision.

How to Use This Book

The One Decision is an invitation for you to consider or even choose a life of MORE of what truly matters to you. It is one of the most unconventional and potent "how-to" books because it doesn't ask you to do the exercises at first, or even at all. Your job is really to discover, recognize, become aware of, and use the insights in each chapter. That *is* the how-to. It's how to live, *really*. And a life-transforming approach like this can't be trivialized with ten easy steps. That is why the book is written in two parts.

In the first ten chapters, you'll explore different aspects of the One Decision to have MORE in life. Then, and only if you choose to, you can use the practical and applied section called *30 Days to Your One Decision* to explore how it leads to MORE and how to choose a One Decision if it feels right to you. Remember, this book is a gift you give yourself, an experience for you to savor and immerse yourself in. Any one of the chapters, if you embrace it, has the power to completely transform your life. But only you can be the navigator, the adventurer on this expedition.

The Chapters

The One Decision, like a diamond, has many facets. Each chapter of this book represents a different facet, or pathway, to the One Decision. You'll notice that the chapter on the One Decision is the third chapter in the book. I've done this because the concepts in the first two chapters,

"The Adventure" and "The Desire," are integral to understanding and making the One Decision. Without learning to live life as an adventure and heed your deep desires, you are less likely to make a potent One Decision. As you read all the chapters, you will begin to ask yourself some rudimentary questions about the way you want to live your life. Each chapter asks you to make a choice—to step a little closer to making your One Decision:

Will I live my life as an adventure or as a series of familiar routines?
Will I fulfill the desires of my heart or leave my yearnings unheeded?
Will I live a life of truth or illusion?
Will I be present or checked out?
Will I live a heartfelt life or a heartless one?
Will I find people to support me or go it alone?

Making the One Decision means that you choose between these kinds of opposites—a deeply felt life or a barely felt life, a consciously chosen and experienced life or a life that just passes by, a life of MORE or a life of less. The question really *is* to be or not to be.

And even though I don't know the specifics of *your* One Decision, I can tell you that if you've made it, it is certain, or very likely, that you will reap the benefits not only of one of these areas, but of all of them. You will have learned to live a life that is full of adventure, where you are following your deepest desire, living with heart, telling the truth, learning how to be present, transforming every area of your life, orienting to higher principles, and creating a powerful team of allies who will support you to live the life you were born to live.

Each chapter begins with an Invitation, expands on a core concept, and ends with a Send-off, encouraging you into your life of MORE. You may want to reread the Invitations and Send-offs as a way to remember the concepts, to brush up, or to recall and recapture the essence of the chapter. If any of the phrases appeal to you, write them down and use them to inspire you. Revisit the Invitations and Send-offs at any time to inspire you and remind you of the possibilities that await you in life.

30 Days to Your One Decision

30 Days to Your One Decision is the final section of the book. In this section you will go through three phases—Awareness, Action, and Application. There are lessons, life assignments, and reflections for each of the thirty days, designed to help you apply everything you have learned, choose your One Decision, and discover its power in your life.

Keep in mind that making a One Decision is a different experience for everyone. Some people may choose to "date" the idea of a One Decision for a number of years until they feel like they have the solid foundation they want in order to choose it. Others are ready to make an immediate declaration of their One Decision and jump in. Some make a decision when they're twenty, others when they're sixty-five. There is no right or wrong way. The One Decision for a life of MORE is a very personal journey. You will have your own unique approach and style. What is most important is that when you choose, it comes from you, in the way that feels right to you. This book is meant to be an exploration, an opening of doors and possibilities, to use how you choose.

Support and Inspiration

Living your One Decision requires support, encouragement, inspiration, and training. You deserve support to help you shift your life, and you deserve to experience the thrill and satisfaction of working with others who are committed to transforming their lives. In addition to the resources and support you will learn about in the book, please visit my website at www.judithwright.com where you will find tools, inspiration, and a special limited-time offer just for reading this book. You'll find information on forming or joining One Decision Groups, coaching to help you define and operationalize your One Decision, a complete database of sample One Decisions, inspiring stories of people who have made One Decisions, bulletin boards, and more. To take advantage of the special limited-time offer, go to my website, click on the information on the One Decision, and look for the "For Book Readers Only" link. Enter the code 774748Q, and you'll find a special limited-time offer just for puchasing the book.

What to Expect on Your Journey

As you start on a journey toward a life of MORE and consider the possibility of making a One Decision, be prepared to be alternately challenged, inspired, invited, confronted, thrilled, upset, and reassured. The greater MORE of life is not a cakewalk—it is a thrilling adventure of a fully lived life, with highs and lows, real truth, full engagement, all feelings, and all possibilities.

At different points during this book, you may find yourself confronting old beliefs and conditioning, feeling your routines threatened, and being invited out of your comfort zones. You may also feel excited, inspired, and ready to transform your life. Be aware of how you feel, what you respond to, and what you choose, for this awareness is part of your journey.

Be gentle with yourself as you raise your awareness and learn to live a full life oriented to your One Decision. Know that while you are either living your One Decision or not, moving toward it or away, your progress will not be a straight line. You will go forward and back, two steps toward and one away. Just keep reorienting and using your One Decision like a compass, leading you to the greater MORE of life.

And to learn to live a life of MORE, you'll need training, practice, support, encouragement, and skill. The people I've worked with who have made their One Decision are deeply committed to continually learning the skills of MORE, to getting coaching and training to hone their skills, and to keeping themselves connected to others who will cheer them on their way. There is a challenge to continually learning, growing, and evolving. Yet the rewards are a richly lived life, satisfying, thrilling, alive—MORE!

Welcome to MORE

You are being invited to experience the real enduring MORE—having life and having it more abundantly in every moment. It does not require transcendent moments or complete happiness at all times. The real MORE isn't even an action or a step. MORE is a decision, a shift in perspective that completely transforms the fabric of your life. It is living life as an adventure, living every moment, engaging in what's in front of you as fully as possible. MORE means having more life, more love, more fulfillment, more satisfaction, more joy, more feelings, more awareness, more self-esteem, more intimacy, and more than you ever dreamed possible. Living MORE means designing a life where rich moments are the "norm" of your experience, not the exception. Oh, and by the way, it tends to lead to more money, time, love, and worldly success as well.

Open up to the possibility of MORE in your life. The Adventure awaits.

There is a road before you, beckoning you to embark on your journey. It is the road that leads to your future, an adventure of becoming. On it you will find incomparable riches—inside you and in the world around you. You will experience adventures as you pursue your heart's desires. You will open your heart and determine truth. You will uncover the power that resides within you

and embark upon your personal quest. You will discover magical keys that open the potential of every moment and experience the camaraderie of allies on the journey. On this noble quest, you will fight many a good fight. It is not an easy journey, but the rewards are great. Step upon the path and claim the prize that belongs to all who journey here—a life of MORE. MORE is just One Decision away. What awaits you is a bigger, more meaningful, challenging, rewarding, and vibrant life—a life that is yours, and yours to have abundantly. This is the moment you've been longing for; celebrate as you take this next step.

The Adventure

A rich, wonderful, never-ending Adventure awaits you—it has been calling to you from the very moment you were breathed into existence. With the gift of life came this invitation to explore worlds of awe and wonder—to experience all that life has to offer, to feel every feeling, to take risks and be challenged, to learn and grow, to develop. Living every day as an Adventure, you are reborn; you reconceive and re-create yourself. To embark on this glorious challenge, you must leave the known and jump off the familiar, the status quo, to discover who you truly are and can be. As you continually step into the unknown, you become your most magnificent, sensitive, courageous, creative self. Through the Adventure, you will learn faith and discover divine will as you explore your destiny.

Pack your bags, buckle up, and get ready for the Adventure of your life.

Your life is meant to be a glorious Adventure! You were given the magnificent gift of life so that you could explore and discover yourself, your potential, your gifts, and the infinite possibilities in the world around you. As a child you knew this, but as you grew up, the adventure dimmed, and you limited your destiny. You are destined for MORE, but you must choose a life of Adventure to reach it. And if you do, a destiny beyond your wildest imagination awaits.

Your One Decision will require you to venture into new territory in all areas of your life, from career to relationships, from love to worship. You will face new challenges and risks. Though the risks are great, the rewards are greater—the spiritual and material treasures of deep connection, fulfillment, meaning, satisfaction, energy, financial success, intimacy, and health. In the Adventure of life, you discover not only who you are but who you can be. Each step of this journey opens new vistas of possibility.

Your greatest destiny will not just come to you; you must pursue its infinite possibilities. As you stretch your limits and redefine your your capacities, your body, mind, and soul will open to reveal treasures within you—talents, abilities, and capacities you never knew existed. Not only will you *do* more, but you will also make your One Decision to *be* MORE.

The alternative, of course, is to live life on the sidelines, watching other people's adventures, wishing and hoping that things would be different, and being only partially engaged in—or, in the extreme, completely numbed to—what's happening in your life.

Too often in our culture, we watch adventure rather than live it. We watch the newest sports star live out our fantasies of victory, or we follow soap operas to substitute for our own drab relationships. The vibrant kitchens and hilarious living rooms of sitcom families blare from the televisions in our own dull kitchens and lifeless living rooms. Television cops, doctors, and lawyers have the career success we are afraid to pursue. We waste the gift of our life gossiping about and watching others rather than engaging in and embracing our own experiences.

But, when you frame your life as an Adventure, everything

> *Never forget that life can only be nobly inspired and rightly lived if you take it bravely and gallantly, as a splendid adventure in which you are setting out into an unknown country to face many a danger, to meet many a joy, to find many a comrade, to win and lose many a battle.*
>
> ANNIE BESANT,
> *social reformer and freethinker*

shifts. You become the creator of your life, not an observer or victim of circumstances. Rather than feeling victimized by the vicissitudes of life, you see them as challenges. Your mistakes are no longer indictments. You honor steps and missteps as part of the journey, and begin to see life as a rich tapestry of wide-ranging experiences. When you live your life as an Adventure, you expect ups and downs, victories and losses. When you resist change in order to feel safe, you make life much harder than it needs to be. You miss out on the richness of MORE.

My Life as an Adventure

My own life has become an immense Adventure of the heart, of spirit, of risk-taking, and of consciousness. But it wasn't always that way. Early in my life, I sensed that there was something bigger in life—something MORE—but I didn't know how to go about getting it.

I am a butcher's daughter from Flint, Michigan. Growing up in a factory town where the norm was waiting for the day to be over, I sought out a different way of life. I was valedictorian of my high school class, held student government positions, won state-level awards, and spent my after-school hours in dance and music classes and volunteering. In short, I became an achiever, thinking that worldly success alone would bring me what I was searching for.

With everything I did to try to find something bigger in life, I was often ridiculed and teased for being different. Every nasty thing said about me hurt to the core, and, while I was brave, I also suffered a lot. I used food or television to numb my pain. Although I was outgoing and well-known in my high school, I was afraid of boys, avoided dating, and buried myself in my studies. I hadn't realized yet that even my pain and fear were part of the Adventure.

I finished both my undergraduate and graduate studies summa cum laude and engaged fully in a wonderful career developing programs for people with disabilities and families of children who were developmentally disabled. Those programs won multimillion-dollar grants, and in my twenties I rose to national recognition in my field. After six years of marriage to my college sweetheart, I had to face the hard truth that we were not on the same journey of engagement and consciousness. We divorced, and I moved to Chicago and subsequently started my own business. Though my work was fulfilling and exciting, and I had major gains and losses in relationships, I still wasn't living life as an Adventure. Every time I failed or made a mistake, I thought I was a bad person. It felt as if I were being punished because what I was doing wasn't right.

Then it hit me. *This is the Adventure*. This. This up and down, back and forth, succeed and fail—all of it is the Adventure. All the time that I was looking for a life of MORE, trying to figure out what it was that I yearned for, I was learning what it was to live a life of Adventure. It wasn't about being perfect, doing things right, and having wild success with no downside. It was risking humiliation, falling down, and falling short of my expectations as well as enjoying and building on my successes. I was learning to honor the real Adventure. For me, it is to do what feels right in my heart even if my head might tell me it is foolish or futile. It means feeling everything—love and despair, joy and grief, anger and peace.

I met my current husband, Bob, and started on a completely new adventure of intimacy. From our first date, we set a context for straight truth and accountability, exchanging both mutual appreciation and criticism. I discovered what it really means to be a woman in relationship with someone—the power in vulnerability, the power of total honesty, the power of openhearted living. I discovered and continue to explore my own spirituality and mysticism, and I have traveled around the world to sacred sites of world religions, willing to be led by spirit in my relationships, business, and daily life.

As a result of my journey and those sharing it with me, I have found vast resources within myself and others that continually surprise me. I understand things I should have no way of knowing. I am discovering how to live life differently from how I was taught. And through it all, I feel, I experience, and I keep taking steps. I keep growing and exploring, reaching and stretching—I expand and my life expands.

Lately, I'm choosing to reach out to more people and step into the public eye, taking strong and often unpopular stands for open, honest communication in relationships, taking risks for greater satisfaction and service at work, and orienting toward higher consciousness in all we do. As in my youth, I am sometimes ridiculed, attacked, or ignored, but I am also loved, cared about, and respected. That is my Adventure: to turn myself over and follow spirit to the best of my ability, to live a different kind of life—a better life than what I grew up thinking life had to be—and to support others to do the same. My Adventure is to strive to bring all the beauty and gifts of heaven to earth.

> *"A man practices the art of adventure when he . . . has the nerve to move out of life's shallows and venture forth into the deep. When he keeps his heart young, his expectations high and never allows his dreams to die.*
>
> —WILFRED A. PETERSON,
> *author of* The Art of Living

The One Decision and Adventure

Of all that you have ever been given and will ever have, there is no greater gift than your own life. How, then, are you living it? Are you treating your life as something to endure? Are you sitting interminably in the waiting room of life, expecting someone to call your name? Or are you fully engaged, ready to make the most out of what you have been given, to explore, stretch, challenge, and expand your life and what you believe is possible?

Your One Decision is a choice between opposites: Will you live your life as an Adventure or will you be a bystander in life, vicariously living through the adventures of others? Will you take risks or stay mired in what is familiar and comfortable?

A Life of Adventure Begins Right Here

To live a life of Adventure doesn't require moving to a new town, becoming an astronaut, plunging into the rain forest, or joining the Peace Corps. True Adventure is available regardless of your circumstances, financial status, health conditions, constraints, and responsibilities.

Listen to your heart and accept new challenges—wherever you find yourself right now. As an adventurer, you take delight in what is in front of you—being excited about or even afraid of the next moment. You wonder what is in store, and you take the opportunities that life presents all the time, big and small. Adventure is available in everything you do—from greeting other people in the morning, participating in a business meeting, scheduling your day the way you want, improving the quality of a product at work, sitting down to dinner, learning from your children and setting clear limits with them, expecting enough out of your marriage, to having a home that really works. These are the every-moment adventures we often miss, waiting for the big Adventure to come. Thousands of small missed opportunities for Adventure add up to a lifetime of less, not MORE.

Travis was a struggling freelance artist who rebelled against what he called "a mindless nine-to-five." Considering his innate skills and talent, his life and his art were dull and lifeless. He seemed to be going nowhere. He resented having to work—an attitude that came through in his art.

When he did find work, he refused to work longer than

eight hours in any day. At that he was marginally productive, with only short bursts of focus and productivity, followed by longer and more sustained slumps of inactivity and complaints. He snuck in breaks when he thought his latest employer was not looking. The idea of hard, rewarding work and nourishing rest and recreation were unknown to him. He often felt tired and drained, and he frequently overslept, a habit he rationalized as his need to "take care of himself."

Finally, Travis took a seminar in which he explored the idea of making his One Decision—of living every aspect of his life as an Adventure. As a result, he ended up developing an entirely new vision about how his work, not just his art, could be creative. He was amazed at how every aspect of life, even work, could be an Adventure.

He started with small things to make his work more effective—setting time goals he'd aggressively pursue, allowing himself to really engage with the painting in front of him, and taking great breaks rather than sneaking them. To his amusement and the amazement of his friends, he even began seeing himself as a businessman, viewing his sales as an opportunity to connect with new people rather than a burden he had to go through to get freelance work. As a result, he increased his sales activities many times more than he thought possible. He expected to feel drained from the new activity, but he found new sources of energy and stopped oversleeping as he felt more sustained and excited about his days.

For Travis, the simple yet profound choice to make his "same old work" an adventure has completely transformed the quality of his life—not to mention that in a few short years, he moved from being a starving artist to making a six-figure income.

Risks and Mistakes: Key Ingredients for Adventure

For most of us, the biggest barrier to living life as an Adventure is our fear of risk and, more important, our fear of making mistakes, looking stupid, or being humiliated. If you are going to do something you have never done before, what are the odds that you will do it flawlessly and without making mistakes? Living life as an Adventure means that you take risks, do new things, and make lots of mistakes. What matters is *that* you play. Success is no more important than failure in the Adventure of life.

> *Living life as an Adventure means getting on the playing field. In fact, in a life of MORE, that you play is more important than how you play. You may strike out, or you may hit a home run, but what matters is that you keep swinging.*

Although I love the excitement of Adventure and am pretty brave, if I can't do something well, I don't want to do it. But that means that I get caught in repeating familiar routines because they're safe, and with this safety I can feel competent. But feeling competent isn't the primary state for an adventurer! You are more likely to feel alternately incompetent and triumphant.

If you try something new—whether you do it brilliantly or awkwardly—hurray! That's the Adventure. If you speak up and make a dumb remark, that's the Adventure. What is important is that you step into new territory. This change in mind-set is a completely new way of looking at your days and your moments. In fact, from this mind-set, when I look at my life, I see that I should actually celebrate some of my most embarrassing moments and reward myself for taking big risks.

Sam was sitting in a meeting listening to the heads of the holding company plan a worldwide strategy that could save—or cost—the company more than a billion dollars. It could even mean the difference between life and death for the company—or at least the livelihood of thousands of people.

Sam, a junior staff member, spotted a key flaw in the plan but hesitated to say anything, reassuring himself that others more senior to him would soon recognize the same problem. He wasn't absolutely certain; he could be mistaken. As the discussion continued, though, he became increasingly certain that he needed to speak up.

Sam's mind raced and his stomach churned. He realized that not saying anything was the same as not speaking the truth—an important aspect of his One Decision. Time was running out in the meeting, and he had been backing away from the Adventure. So he spoke up—the only person in the room to voice opposition to the plan. There was dead silence as he began to talk. He felt like his body had been plugged into a light socket as his words filled the silence in the room.

When he finished talking, he was certain that the next words out of the CEO's mouth would be "You're fired." But when the CEO did speak, it was to declare that Sam had a greater grasp of the material than all of his superiors. The CEO turned the responsibility for managing worldwide strategy over to Sam. Had Sam not risked making a mistake, there might have been no worldwide strategy to manage.

The Illusion of Security

Helen Keller tells us, "Security is an illusion. Life is either a daring adventure or nothing. Security does not exist in nature, nor do the children of men as a whole experience it. Avoiding danger is no safer in the long run than exposure." Helen Keller is one of my personal heroes. Most people are familiar with her achievements, but when you compare her Adventure to what most of us face each day, the comparison is staggering. We try to create security for ourselves by not taking risks. Yet Helen Keller was willing to take the platform as a public speaker as part of her personal mission. She didn't say, "No, thanks, haven't you noticed? I'm deaf. My voice is distorted. Please find someone else to speak." No, she was willing to use every capacity she had, to allow her distorted voice to be amplified to multitudes in order to leave the unique mark she was destined to leave. Many of us are unwilling to speak up to a spouse or in a business meeting, and she was willing to not only speak up but also be recorded by television, by radio, for millions.

True Security in the Unknown

When life is an Adventure, things don't have to be predictable in order for us to be okay. We release our attachment to the external and focus on the internal reality. As an explorer, you expect challenges. Paddling on the river in your dugout canoe, you would expect to encounter shallow water, rapids, mosquitoes, hostile and forbidding conditions, and unfriendly people who are different from you. And you may discover new friends who delight in your freshness and who want to help you and share your adventures with you. You find the true security of engagement rather than the illusory security of a small life, a life unlived.

By detaching yourself from traditional notions of security, you open yourself to the MORE of everything, from danger to comfort. You begin to understand that security lies in engagement. Things don't need to turn out a particular way. All that needs to happen is that you engage.

> *All life is the exercise of risk.*
>
> —WILLIAM SLOANE COFFIN,
> *clergyman and peace activist*

An Attitude of Opportunity

As an adventurer, you need to develop an attitude of opportunity, looking for possibilities rather than problems in events and circumstances that previously you may have viewed as unfortunate. Everything that happens can be a blessing and an opportunity to learn and grow, to deepen your relationship with yourself and others, or to expand your ability to serve and be served. To live this way, you will need to be vigilant for your limiting thoughts that make you see life as a burden to be endured.

History is full of heroes and heroines who have seen possibilities where others saw only failure and loss. Mother Teresa saw opportunities for love and service where others fled disease and poverty, Abraham Lincoln saw freedom and unity in the face of division, and Nelson Mandela saw hope for the future of democracy even while in prison.

And you have the possibility for that attitude every day, right in front of you. For example, if your boss comes in and says you have a new project and you need to do a, b, c, d, and e by 4:00 P.M. the following day, how do you respond? Is your reaction "Wow, what a creative challenge and opportunity. What would it take for me to do this thing that feels impossible?" Likely those aren't the first thoughts that pop into your mind. Of course, you'll have a range of feelings and reactions in situations like that, but what if you chose an attitude of opportunity? What if you could take the energy of your fear and anger and direct it to solving the problem? What if you chose to shift your attitude and take on the challenge? What would your next twenty-four hours look like?

> *This is the true joy in life, the being used for a purpose recognized by yourself as a mighty one; the being a force of nature instead of a feverish, selfish clod of ailments and grievances complaining that the world will not devote itself to making you happy.*
>
> —GEORGE BERNARD SHAW,
> *Nobel laureate in literature*

Adventure or burden, opportunity or impossibility—the choice is yours. That is the One Decision. And it is a choice between opposites. There is no middle ground or shades of gray. The ability to see opportunity in loss is yours to develop. The challenge is given to us every day in life. Will you rise to it? Of course you will. Why would you want to live any other way? Turning defeat and pain into opportunity is key to the Adventure.

"Isn't being a physician enough?" Mandy complained. Divorced for more than ten years, Mandy had blindly accepted society's stigma for a single woman getting up there in years. Despite her deep resentment at "being too old," she had resigned herself to her fate of being single and miserable but putting on a brave face for the outside world. After all, she did have great satisfaction at work taking care of patients. "How many other women my age can say that? They're all just doing a nine-to-five and waiting to see the grandkids." Glib as she sounded, Mandy was mired in self-pity and resented everything but her professional life. Dating and relationships outside of work were just a burden. She "gave at the office."

But then she made her One Decision to live her life as an Adventure rather than a burden, and things started to shift. She expanded her circle of friends to include other intelligent professional women. With their help she began to see dating as an exciting undertaking— a great opportunity to get to know herself whether the men she dated were energetic, ridiculous, exciting, or boring. She also dated more and took more risks. She'd cut to the chase

> *The basic difference between an ordinary man and a warrior is that a warrior takes everything as a challenge, while an ordinary man takes everything as a blessing or as a curse.*
>
> —CARLOS CASTANEDA,
> *American shaman, anthropologist, and author*

and ask her dates about their dreams, their mission, their purpose. She realized that even rejection could be celebrated as an opportunity to learn and grow.

And suddenly she liked being with herself a lot more—traveling alone, going to movies alone. With or without a date, she was in great company. She discovered an ease and grace about being single that she never even dreamed was possible. Burden had been replaced by Adventure. By embracing an attitude of opportunity, she found herself, and she found MORE.

The Adventure of Being Human

The Adventure of being human means embracing the full experience—the highs, the lows, the sadness, the joy, the victory, the defeat, the beauty, and the ugliness. Reject the Adventure and you miss out on your humanity and deny essential aspects of yourself. Embrace the Adventure and you are in for the most extreme roller-coaster ride you can imagine—excruciatingly slow ascents, terrifying descents, turns that rattle your insides, and a deep satisfaction and excitement between rides.

The Adventure of being human happens whether you recognize it or not, and the "roller-coaster skills" definitely apply—relaxing rather than tensing, keeping your eyes open, taking in the scenery on the way up, and screaming your head off on the way down. And being human has its own unique skills—feeling deeply and experiencing broadly, allowing the full range of emotions of joy, despair, love, pain, fear, and bliss.

Your life is meant to be outrageous, overwhelming, thrilling, exciting, and full of challenges. You are supposed to work too hard, try too hard, stay up too late, eat too much. You then cut back and do too little, only to do too much again. You learn to live a life you love—constantly learning and growing, to experiment, succeed, and fail. If we avoid the Adventure of being human, we avoid being fully human, fully ourselves. We avoid MORE.

> *If we were supposed to have limited experiences, we would have been given a day, not a lifetime, to learn how to live.*

Stepping Off the Map

The Adventure requires stepping off the map. In a scene from the movie *The Fellowship of the Ring*, Samwise Gamgee and Frodo Baggins are heading off on an adventure that will take them into new territory:

Sam: This is it.
Frodo: This is what?

Sam: If I take one more step, it will be the farthest away from
home I've ever been.

Frodo: Come on, Sam, remember what Bilbo used to say: "It's a
dangerous business, Frodo, going out of your door. You step
onto the road, and if you don't keep your feet, there's no
knowing where you might be swept off to."

Living life as an adventurer, you will go beyond the territory you have previously mapped and explore uncharted territories of feeling, thinking, and
doing. You will find adventures to be lived in every area of life that can
take you far beyond what you have previously experienced or even
known existed.

Traveling in these new territories, you can question and test the beliefs
you were taught. Where you once feared offending people, you now test
relationships by sharing the truth. At work, you ask for honest feedback
from coworkers while you consistently give it in return. You take a class
in a new subject, try a new recipe, apply for a more demanding job, and
expect more support from your friends and family.

Breaking Your Own Record

Just as athletes continually break their own records, and the best athletes also break world records, living the Adventure, you can continually break your own "record" and can set new standards for others to
follow.

The four-minute mile was thought to be unbreakable, but once broken,
it was broken many times in the next few months. What if rather than 50
percent of marriages ending in divorce, instead 99 percent of marriages
could succeed? What if careers could really be vehicles for self-expression,
development, and high compensation? What if worship and spiritual dis-

cipline could nourish and develop our fullest connection to creation? What if you could break your own record in any of these areas and pave the way for others to follow?

With the Adventure guided by the One Decision, all of this and more is possible. Singles discover the excitement of getting to know themselves as they get to know others, and can establish their standards for dating while living a wondrously fulfilling life. Couples, rather than just staying together, discover the huge possibilities of flourishing and growing together in communication, intimacy, parenting, and love. Instead of asking if this is the right marriage, they ask if they are being the right partner, the one they would want to have. The Adventure of career and business opens up new possibilities of partnership. People discover the synergies and satisfaction available when aligning toward a vision and operating a business based on higher principles.

"I never thought we'd be here," Jane remarked to her husband, Michael. Only a handful of years ago, Jane was just "helping out" as they tried to extricate themselves from mountains of debt. She would book a few gigs and bring in limited business to her husband's struggling DJ and video firm.

Now here she stood, side by side with him at a highly prestigious event in downtown Chicago, their DJs and videographers recording the glitzy affair she had designed for their client. They had quadrupled their revenue, become full partners in the business, and now led a staff of employees and interns learning and growing with them in the business.

And on top of the business, Michael and Jane had become partners in their marriage. Before making their One Decision to have Adventure in every area of their lives, they had reserved their excitement for nights on the town. But once they committed to the Adventure, they found it lurking in every corner—in this new business, in their marriage, in how they hired, fired, and trained employees, in what clients they took on, and in what sales goals they set. They didn't have the full vision when they made the commitment, but constantly setting new standards and breaking records has become their vision at work and at home.

The Power of Adventure

You can find power in all parts of the Adventure—not just in the successes, but in the setbacks as well. You tap the power of Adventure when you honor your struggle as part of the journey. However, when you struggle against the adversity rather than accepting it as part of the Adventure, your energy and power are dissipated. Suffering is one of the most common ways to resist the Adventure. You are disempowered when you suffer or feel victimized by circumstances.

You have a choice when things don't go well—either to punish

> *A man's life is interesting primarily when he has failed—for it's a sign that he tried to surpass himself.*
>
> —GEORGES CLEMENCEAU,
> *French statesman and prime minister*

yourself with a litany of criticisms or to gain power by analyzing what happened in order to strategize better for the future.

This way of living is powerful. You become stronger as you accept and honor all aspects of your experience and learn from them. You treat yourself with immense respect, as a resilient person who can take on new challenges. Rather than shrinking from the tasks before you, ignoring your feelings, or hiding out in numbing addictions, you courageously step into the situations ahead.

An Adventure of the Spirit

The Adventure is also a spiritual adventure. Whether you align with God, spirit, a higher purpose, the universe, or nature, or are simply exploring, you can open your heart and care more deeply. You can learn to live with greater faith, to open to the infinite realms of spirit, to live according to your highest vision. Choosing a life of MORE means engaging in the continual creation of new possibilities, expanding capacities, improved skills, and new resources. Your pursuit of outward adventure will also lead you to voyage deeply into your inner terrain, the exploration of the vast uncharted territory of your internal frontiers. Of necessity, your faith, your alignment with something higher, all become part of the Adventure.

> *God comes to us only as we reach for him.*

I am learning more about faith each day as we grow our business and expand beyond the comfortable existence we had before we decided to stretch. I am now living beyond what I had previously known, expanding my territory. In doing so, I can no longer rely solely on my own resources or on things that worked in the past. I am forced to rely on the universe's help, because I don't have it in me alone. My Adventure would be impossible without faith and God's grace. If the challenges we take on are beyond what we think we can do—and they should be!—they will require some kind of faith. Be it faith in God or in the universe, no matter. You must trust.

The Adventure Begins

You are meant to have life and have it more abundantly. You were created for MORE. It is your heritage, if only you will claim it. You were not meant to settle for less but to enjoy the greater MORE. Do not seek the illusion of security; have hope and strength in the knowledge that MORE is possible. You can be surrounded by love, majesty, and beauty every day. Seek, pursue, be curious, learn, grow, feel, and use all the faculties that you have been given to experience your life and your world.

Your life is meant to be big, rocky, and full of unexpected challenges and rewards. It is appropriate for you to be terrified, exhilarated, sad, and joyful. You are supposed to feel out of control and overwhelmed at times. You will feel that you are not up to the tasks before you. Only then will you be forced to stretch, to reach beyond your previous capacities, and to see things differently. Only then will you become who you are supposed to become—who you are meant to be. When you make your One Decision to live life as an Adventure, you grow, you evolve. You ask yourself, "What are my talents? What are my gifts? What could I possibly do with my life?" That's the Adventure, opening up to what is possible in every moment of every day.

May you awaken to the possibility of your life as an Adventure. May you embrace the joy and love, laughter and tears, excitement and fear, that lead you toward a greater experience of

*your life. May you explore the possibilities of a life of MORE
every day. May you turn to spirit and others for your security and
guidance. Trust in divine will, your own resilience, your ability
to learn from everything and grow, and the love and support of
your fellow adventurers. May you learn to see your life from a divine perspective—honoring all of your life experiences.*

Welcome to the Adventure!

The Desire

You are meant to hunger, to yearn, to Desire. Cherish this Desire, for it has been encoded in you, written into your very soul. Your heart throbs with deep and powerful urges, yet they often remain unheeded. Learn to tend to these inner urges and your Desire will lead you to the life you yearn for. It is only through activating these deeper cravings that you learn to live your One Decision, pursue your heart's desires, and discover the treasures in store for you. Heed your lust for life; avoid false substitutes. Know that you deserve to experience the exquisite delight of satisfying your deeper hunger. Reawaken these inner cravings, this beautiful hunger for the divine. Surrender to your yearning, and delight in the very wanting, the Desire for MORE.

Satisfaction and fulfillment are available every moment of your life if you honor and follow your Desire. Your deep yearning will lead us to everything that is powerful, meaningful, and loving in life.

Each of us is encoded with the Desire for MORE, whether we are consciously aware of it or not or even if we don't feel entitled to MORE. Yet no matter how much money, happiness, social position, or even love we have or pursue, we still desire, and deserve, MORE. Now is the time for you to uncover, explore, and celebrate these longings—your Desire for MORE.

What Is Desire?

Desire is the manifestation of the universal longings of the human heart. I've often described these expressions of Desire as spiritual hungers to reflect their sacred nature. These deeper hungers—to connect, to serve, to experience beauty, to be inspired, to express our creativity, to learn, to grow, to be seen, to be heard, to love and be loved—are encoded into our very beings. But when we deny the wisdom of these longings, when we try to meet this Desire indirectly— through the latest media fad, a bigger house, a superficial relationship, mindless gossip—we miss out on the biggest, most potent formula for living heaven on earth.

> *Deep within you is encoded the Desire for MORE—the ancient calling of your soul to pursue all that is wonderful, all that is beautiful, all that matters in life.*

The formula is right here in front of us at all times—and that is simply to pursue our Desire directly. Having made the One Decision, we can go straight for the deepest longings of our soul. In any moment, there are infinite opportunities to fill these hungers and satisfy our Desire. If we hunger to connect, we can follow our Desire and call a friend, risk sharing an opinion with a boss or coworker, or reach out to a neighbor and ask them how they're doing. If we hunger to be seen, we can excel on the job, upgrade our appearance, or participate in community theater. If we long to feel inspired, we can listen to a stunning piece of music, savor a well-prepared meal, or read poetry or sacred writings.

The opportunities are endless. But the yearning for MORE calls you to seek all things that are of spirit in your life here and now. There is no waiting for a different job, a different situation, a new relationship, the afterlife. We are living in a world that is ready and waiting to help us meet our Desire and our deepest hungers. But you must choose, make your One Decision, and learn to follow your Desire for MORE.

My own choice to follow my Desire has given my life a richness I had never imagined, but it wasn't always this way. Growing up I was a good girl. Ironically, this meant suppressing my Desire. I did what I was supposed to do; got good grades, did my chores, and played well with my friends. In adulthood I did good work and received significant recognition, but it was only when I made my One Decision and learned to recognize and heed my Desire that I discovered the fulfillment I craved.

While I have always longed for MORE in my life, it wasn't until my marriage to Bob that I really began to understand, recognize, and fulfill my Desires. Bob was much more certain about his wants and Desires, which both let me know what was possible and also gave me an example to follow. But even more importantly, he listened to my Desire and honored my urges. This helped me to learn to cherish my own Desire, to know that I had the right to want MORE, and to listen to the urges of my heart. I've since learned so many lessons in Desire, both the ethereal and the concrete.

By understanding what I am really hungry for, what I truly Desire, I can design my life to fulfill my Desire. I can now recognize and listen to the longing in my heart and let it guide me moment to moment. I am no longer as willing to accept the false substitutes of my surface cravings when I can meet the Desires of my heart. I realize that my deepest Desires are to know that I matter, to make a difference, to love and be loved, to connect with others, to be part of something bigger—and that these beautiful and blessed spiritual hungers are shared by every human being. We are all meant to desire MORE because it makes us the most human—and the most divine.

The One Decision and Desire

Your One Decision will be founded on your Desire. It is a powerful focusing of your deeper urges. Acknowledge your Desire as the extraordinary gift it is intended to be, and your One Decision will follow. Rather

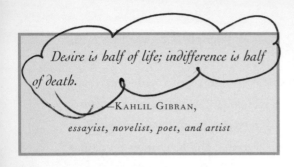

Desire is half of life; indifference is half of death.

—KAHLIL GIBRAN,

essayist, novelist, poet, and artist

than being embarrassed by your hungers, dismissing them, or appeasing them with superficial solutions, heed the impulses of your soul and your spirit flourishes. If you deny your Desire for MORE, the essence of your soul fades, just as your body would grow fainter if you denied its hunger or fed it the wrong things. Your One Decision will help you stay focused on Desire, and your Desires will empower your One Decision.

So what will it be? Heed your Desire for MORE or ignore your yearning? Accept your Desire as a divine impulse implanted into you to pursue the riches of the kingdom? Or be embarrassed by your yearnings and numb them or hide them? Fulfill your heart's desires or settle for indulging your superficial cravings?

Will you sense the urges that pulse forth from your heart's desire and follow them to fulfillment? Or will you misinterpret them and try to pacify them with distractions? It is your One Decision—pursue your Desire or leave it unheeded.

Desire Is Part of the Grand Design

As you pursue your Desire, you discover that it is sacred and spiritual. In fact, it is part of the grand design. Just as we are encoded with physical hunger to prompt us to nourish our bodies, we are also encoded with spiritual hunger to guide us to feed our souls. It is encoded into our bodies, our minds, and our emotions. We are designed to desire, seek, and enjoy the inexhaustible gifts of physical, emotional, and

Desire is the very essence of man.

—BARUCH SPINOZA,

seventeenth-century philosopher

spiritual nourishment—all for our taking and our pleasure when we make our One Decision for MORE.

And not only are we given appetite, we are provided with everything we need, in abundance, to satisfy it. The earth offers up its lush bounty—fruits hang from the trees, vegetables and grains spring from the soil, flesh and fowl roam the earth—to feed our physical appetite. And the universe provides the infinite gifts of the spirit—limitless opportunities for love, connection, nourishment, service, creativity, inspiration—to fulfill the yearnings of our heart.

You may not know yet how to find these provisions, just as you might not know how to forage for food in the forest. But nevertheless, everything is available and is right in front of you in every moment, if you learn to seek it. People often think that this Desire for MORE is about achieving transcendence, experiencing a spiritual epiphany, or floating on the clouds with angels. But in fact, it's just the opposite.

Learning to orient to your deep Desire is the opportunity that is right in front of you, and it shifts your entire life. When you design your life to meet your Desire directly, you no longer need to be left feeling empty, distracted by your temporal wants or your surface cravings. When you are in touch with your desire for connection, you take the risk of reaching out to others, of hugging, of deepening a conversation with a coworker. Yearning for beauty, you fill your home and your office with flowers and artwork you love. Hungry to make a difference in the world, you operate from higher principles and values wherever you are. You experience MORE and bring MORE to others.

"As long as Morgan is happy, that's all that really matters," proclaimed Benson about his fiancée and their upcoming wedding ceremony. "Wait a minute," said Bob as he was helping them create a vision for their marriage. "You need to be satisfied too; what do you want?" "I guess I really want to see our friends have a good time too," he responded. "Still not enough," said Bob. "With that limited of a vision you are setting yourself up for a midlife crisis where you will look back resentfully and think that you've sacrificed everything for your wife, children, and friends. Then you'll likely start looking to have an affair to make up for all the years you deprived yourself. Is that fair to you, your wife, or the children you will probably have?"

Thus began Benson's inquiry into his Desire. By the time the wedding rolled around, he had made some progress— helping plan the ceremony, select music, and vision for the evening—but he was still having a hard time recognizing anything more significant than the urge to watch television, drink a beer, have regular sex, and be left alone.

It took a great deal of work and introspection before he awoke to his deeper Desire, but a breakthrough came several years later when he was feeling left out with his own family. It began when he started noticing that he really longed to be greeted when he came home from work. This small urge kept expanding into a Desire for new and more creative ways to be with and feel closer to his wife and children.

Benson's expectations continued to build and now he is a

far cry from the man who wanted so little at his wedding. When Benson talks about how his kids rush to greet him at the door and his wife warmly greets him at night, the excitement he feels being with family and friends, and the love, intimacy, and connection he has created, he actually tears up with the fullness of his life and the Desire fulfilled.

Benson has succeeded wildly as a vice president of sales for a major consulting firm and opened his own company. But more and more, his greatest pride is in discovering the richness available in every moment of his life when he can tune into his deeper Desire and now his life is about sharing that through his family and his business.

Sacred Emptiness

When you don't understand the nature of your deep Desire, you may think there is something wrong with you when you sense a void or feel the stir of divine dissatisfaction. You seek to fill the void with the wrong things or even the right things at the wrong time or for the wrong reasons—relationships, degrees, jobs, money, clothing, food. And when you can't fill it and they fail to satisfy it, you try to squash it, to minimize the void by avoiding it. You may despair or think you are being ungrateful or that you want

> *Man is characterized by a hunger for the infinite, for an eternity of life, love, and joy.*
> —ALAN WATTS,
> *philosopher and writer*

too much, but the hunger you feel, properly interpreted and met, will lead you to the ultimate reward of MORE.

This yearning is not an indication that there is something wrong with you. On the contrary—it is proof that there is something very, very right with you. You were designed with a spirit-shaped hole in your heart—sometimes it is a sweetness, sometimes it is an aching void—and it can only be filled with divinity.

I used to feel a great emptiness that I now know is an altar, a sacred infinite space for spirit to enter. I have had to learn to embrace this void, to cultivate my ability to be comfortable with the ache. It was not until I gave myself over freely to the pain that my tears could wash away the despair and open my eyes to the beauty of the void. It felt so pure to embrace the space—it did not feel right to fill it with anything other than spirit. I realized I am meant to be alternately filled and unfulfilled, just as I eat a meal and become once again hungry. How else would I once again seek fulfillment and connection?

As I continue on my journey, I feel more fulfillment than I ever thought possible. By being in touch with my deepest Desire, I have learned how to reach out for true nourishment. I remember when I first realized this: I was leading a pilgrimage to sacred sites of Greece.

At the powerful site of the Eleusinian mysteries, where Greek and Roman leaders had been initiated for centuries, I caught a glimpse of the profound truths I believe they received in their initiations. Walking up to the ancient site, I felt a shiver go down my spine and closed my eyes. I felt a profound awareness of the incompleteness of myself and all of mankind. I cannot tell you how, but I became acutely aware that, no matter how concrete the world seemed, the only reality that was truly solid and immutable required both heaven and earth. Earth without heaven was a mere illusion. I saw that God held a part of me, and that I was not complete until I connected with the divine. I was meant to seek God so that I would be complete. And I was meant to be empty and bereft until I found my completion in spirit.

"My physical weight does not weigh as heavy on my heart as my concern about my marriage," said Howard. Despite his 334 pounds, Howard came to the Institute's Men's Training not seeking weight loss, but seeking skills that would improve his relationship with his wife. "Instead I discovered that the Desire I felt inside me, the one that I had been trying desperately for years to fill with food, is actually sacred and something everyone has. When I mistakenly try to meet my hungers with food, the result is weight gain and poor health. But when I respond to my desire for interaction with others or with spirit, these hungers are met. Now I have changed my whole life not only spiritually and emotionally, but also physically. As I meet my deeper needs and touch that void inside me, I feel more fulfilled and nourished, and the pounds are disappearing."

It has been eight weeks since the end of Men's Training and not only is Howard's marriage transforming but he has dropped to 305 pounds, a weight loss of twenty-nine pounds with no effort! "Now, that's a diet that makes sense and I can live with."

Accessing Desire:
Learning to Want MORE

If Desire is such a powerful tool then why don't we orient to it all the time? Our reasons vary, but the essence is the same for most of us. We have trained ourselves to not want enough, to close our access to Desire. We have invented a wide variety of rational-sounding reasons that over the years have become our core beliefs.

We tell ourselves that we don't deserve it, that we are greedy if we want MORE, and that MORE is only for lucky people. Or we tell ourselves that we have already achieved more than we thought was possible, so how could we want still MORE? And besides, what if we had MORE and our friends stopped liking us? What then?

Many of us settle for small improvements or superficial change rather than the greater MORE of life. We seek magical solutions that appear to have the potential to feed spiritual hungers, but don't work because they are done for the wrong reasons. With the wrong motivation, these activities repress deeper hungers—like focusing on making money instead of making contact with loved ones, or getting cosmetic surgery instead of adjusting our internal attitude. Instead of taking risks and telling the truth at work, we pin our hopes on a lottery ticket. Some of us simply numb ourselves and sink into what we consider reasonable wants, such as losing weight instead of becoming fit, or having a nice date with our spouse rather than creating true satisfaction in our relationship. And some of us scale the corporate ladder when we really yearn to climb the heights of heaven.

Learning to want and seek MORE can be a difficult task, yet it may be the only really rewarding pursuit there is. This magic

> *The biggest human temptation is to settle for too little.*
>
> —THOMAS MERTON,
> *Roman Catholic monk and author*

source of motivation that is encoded into your very being will lead you to MORE.

Much of our work at the Wright Institute involves helping people open up to wanting MORE. We work with our students on envisioning possibilities of MORE, thinking the unthink-

> *If you limit your choices only to what seems possible or reasonable, you disconnect yourself from what you truly want, and all that is left is a compromise.*
>
> —ROBERT FRITZ,
> *consultant and author*

able, expanding their horizons, and developing broader visions for their lives. They go beyond having merely a vision of either/or to having a vision of both/and. When they see other students living MORE, they begin to understand that they can have it, too. They realize that they don't have to settle. They can have a great relationship and a successful career. They can become an outstanding leader, follow their creative pursuits, develop a spiritual life, and become healthy and fit.

Two of our students, Doug and Lucy, had hired an au pair. Shortly before she returned to Bosnia after a year with them, she said, "When I came to live with you, I thought I could have either a career or a family, but never both. After living with you, I see love, work, family, worship, and learning actually go together. There is no either/or I can have everything I desire." The same holds true for you. Whatever you want in this moment, whatever Desires, dreams, and goals you have, you may have that—and MORE.

I first met Kevin when he came to me for career coaching. An executive in his firm, he told me he had taken himself out of the running for vice president. When I asked why he didn't bid for the job, he gave a pat answer about wanting to do well in the job he was in. Yet his boss had repeatedly given him positive feedback on his performance, and had even expressed surprise that he wasn't pursuing the promotion.

As I probed for his deeper Desires, I could see the spark of wanting MORE burning more brightly inside him.

As we talked, Kevin revealed that he was the son of a factory worker who worked two jobs during the week and one on the weekends. He was the first child in the family to go to college. It hadn't occurred to him that he could be a vice president—he was already more successful than he had ever imagined. He couldn't allow himself to want MORE. His firm's holding company was European, and he knew that any promotion would involve foreign travel. He admitted that he had never been out of the country before and couldn't fathom traveling to Europe. It had seemed beyond him, so he denied his desire to do it. As I explored the possibilities with him and gave him permission to envision, it was like his Desire was suddenly activated. He became increasingly excited and said, "I can't wait to go back and talk to my boss and tell him I want to be considered a candidate for the position!"

Living with Desire: The Urge for MORE

The Desire for MORE begins in us as an urge. We are literally bursting with urges, yearning to live lives of MORE, and yet too often our very life force is spent repressing these powerful impulses. We frequently don't recognize the urges because we haven't been trained to feel them or to act on them appropriately. In fact, we have been conditioned to ignore our Desire, to view our urges as impositions on our lives of comfort, or as an embarrassment. And yet these urges can be like a compass guiding us to true fulfillment—if only we heed them.

> *There is a vitality, a life force, a quickening that is translated through you into action. . . . You have to keep open and aware directly to the urges that motivate you. Keep the channel open. There is no satisfaction whatever at any time. There is only a queer, divine dissatisfaction, a blessed unrest that keeps us marching and makes us more alive.*
>
> —MARTHA GRAHAM,
> *dancer, teacher, and choreographer*

You may be out of touch with your moment-to-moment urges. The problem, however, is that the longer these urges go unmet, the more they build up. Then we attempt to meet them all at once with a fantasy solution. As difficult as the fantasy solutions may be to achieve, they are often shallow, hollow attempts to sate the soul-deep Desire with the equivalent of a crumb, leaving us just as hungry.

Like most people, you have been conditioned to ignore or repress your urges. Nonetheless, they are still there, aching to be met all the time. No one has the urge to be bored to tears in a business meeting. Rather, you're bored to tears because you've ignored, suppressed, and negated your deeper urges. You're sitting on them and pretending that they don't exist.

What if you let yourself go? You'd probably hop on the boardroom table during a business meeting and belt out a song, spin around in the swivel chairs, and eat all the sprinkles off the donuts. I'm not suggesting that you actually indulge in these behaviors at your next business meeting. But as you start to unearth these impulses, you can find appropriate ways to satisfy them anywhere, at any time—whether at a business meeting, at lunch with a friend, on a blind date, at a family gathering, or being home alone on a Sunday morning. You can reach out and call a friend for comfort, seek acknowledgment, express yourself, date a different kind of person, take a risk in your next job interview, or share a truth with your partner. In other words, take actions that respond to those urges to put you on the path of the Adventure of life!

Translating Your Urges

It takes skill to recognize true Desires and urges. Urges are signals birthed by our greater desires. Urges reflect deeper or higher needs. They tell us when our inner self is making a demand, or that something is lacking. But we don't often recognize the true need beneath those urges. We misread the cue, thinking that it is an urge for a cup of coffee when it is really an urge to feel alive. We misread the impulse for connection as a compulsion to share some gossip.

> *Only when we constantly feel the force of our Desire, and the pulse of urges it sends through us in the moment, will we be guided to right action. It is not our goals that bring us MORE; it is heeding our Desire.*

When we first feel our Desire, we are often only in touch with it long enough to think of a very specific goal or solution—usually a magical solution or a soft addiction, not the fulfillment of our Desire. We lose touch with the Desire and become attached to the solution, whereas it is the Desire that we should stay connected to. Without staying connected to that Desire, we latch on to a particular outcome, a specific version or brand, and if we can't get it or get it now, we get agitated, upset, and anxious. We get addicted, not sated. We will never be satisfied if we misinterpret our urges as surface wants, rather than heed our deeper Desire.

As I write this, I am feeling an urge. I'm toying with the idea that the impulse is to eat a cookie (chocolate chip, of course). But I know that this urge is really pointing to a deeper desire to be nourished, to remember why

I am doing what I am doing. Feeling pressured by my schedule and a little daunted by the task ahead of me, I call in to my office. My assistant tells me how important my work is, and what a difference it has made in her life. She reminds me that I have an obligation to share these concepts with more and more people. My true urge met, I'm ready to turn back to my writing.

When you learn to recognize and follow them, your urges direct your attention, stimulate you to action, give you momentum, and drive you to relationship. They make you real and spontaneous, rather than rehearsed and sterile. They are essential elements of the life force pulsing within us.

You may have a Desire for your company to do better, and an idea for a possible solution sparks within you at a meeting. Rather than stuffing it, afraid of offending someone, speak up. You may long to to develop yourself but are afraid of failing. Rather than squashing your Desire, follow the urge and try something new. If you have the impulse to challenge your date instead of sitting silently, follow the urge. If you have the urge to point out a self-defeating behavior in your partner, point it out, rather than be afraid of hurting his or her feelings. Engage, listen to your heart, and follow it.

I asked Kirsten to notice what she really desired and what she truly felt. I watched as this executive who had driven herself to perform mercilessly at high levels transformed before my eyes. Her visage shifted, she sat up straighter, her expression softened, her voice lowered, her eyes became clearer, and color rose to her face. Her eyes moistened. Her presence became compelling. She said she felt tingly all over, as though she could start singing or dancing at any moment. Tears and laughter seemed equally available. For the first time in her life, this career performer realized that her true power came from asking, "What is within me?"

Kirsten had come into coaching because she wanted a promotion and was wary of making a wrong move. She thought she had to know everything and impress everyone with her self-assurance and unerring ways. She drove herself to conform to her picture of what she thought others expected her to be.

As Kirsten began focusing on her inner urges, she relaxed at work. Her conversations became more fun and she was surprised to discover how much more she learned about her coworkers. However, she was certain that with this shift in herself, she had lost any hope of the promotion and had resigned herself to her current job, in which she was actually experiencing much more daily satisfaction.

She got the promotion, but she was shocked by the feedback she received. She was told that she previously had been removed from consideration because her hard edges were making it difficult for the rest of the staff to relate to her. But as her boss noticed that her contact with others had become more genuine, more pleasant, and more powerful, she was a logical fit for the promotion.

Following the urges that stem from your Desire is your guide on this exciting adventure. You take risks, say things you wouldn't have said before, do things you would not have allowed yourself to do before. Your life becomes less predictable, more spontaneous, and more fun. You have more feelings, energy, and sense of life. It is not all rosy, but it is alive! Rather than suppressing your urges and muffling your desires, you give them voice with your actions. You become more passionate. Your creativity surges. You are unleashed!

Keeping the Fire of Desire Alive

Stoke the fires of your Desire by continually seeking what inspires you. When you are moved to tears by a powerful piece of music, when you are touched by a story, or when you get chills after hearing an uplifting quote, something has touched your Desire. Surround yourself with beauty, encouragement, and inspiration—music that swells your heart, great friends who believe in you—and it will activate your Desire and uplift you. You are more likely to interpret your urges correctly when you have been raising your spirits with inspiration. Don't wait for inspiration to occur—make it happen.

Living your One Decision for MORE is not just having one desire and meeting it. You are never done, because there is always MORE. Sense the urges that bubble up from your deepest desires and express them. Learn to act on the guidance of those urges, bringing you MORE every day. Celebrate wanting MORE. Recognize that the source of the Desire is from your heart, the deep tug of your soul to desire spirit and the things that are of spirit. Learning to live with the candle of Desire lit inside you provides the foundation for MORE.

You know now that your urges will give you clues to your deeper desires, the longings of your heart. An infinite universe is your playground. There are no limits to where your Desire may take you. You have an entire planet to explore, to touch, to understand, to love. You have an inner world that is as vast as the cosmos. Your Desire ushers you to the farthest reaches of the earth and the deepest corners of your soul. You will seek, find, and experience the full adventure of MORE.

May you experience your Desire as a powerful force, a great motivator driving you toward MORE. May you reawaken the Desire that is programmed into your soul and follow your urges to your deeper hungers. May you keep your hunger alive, knowing that you deserve to be satisfied in every moment. May you live with the kindled flame of your Desire. May you design your life to express your deepest desires, tending to the divine void and ignoring the false more. As you celebrate the life force flowing through you, you claim your birthright of vitality and fulfillment. Desire, desire, desire, and demand that this inheritance come to you. It is your sacred duty to summon the universe to respond to your holy Desire and allow the universe to answer. Desire MORE and MORE and MORE.

The One Decision

There is One Decision that determines the quality of your life—the love that you will experience, your spiritual fulfillment, your worldly success. It is your choice—will you choose to be the you that you were intended to be at the moment of the inception of your very soul? You were sent here to manifest an aspect of spirit that will never be manifested unless you do it because you are the only you that ever was and will ever be. It is your destiny to become the you of you. Will you accept that destiny and step into it choice by choice? Will you make consistent choices that will lead you to become who you were intended to become? Will you step into who God had in mind and heart when you were breathed into being? This is the essence of your One Decision—to use your free will to align with heaven's will and to allow creation to be expressed through the unique vessel that is you.

There is One Decision to make about your life that will guide every single choice thereafter. This decision will impact the quality of your life, transforming the very fabric of your being. Each person must come to their own personal crossroads and will have their own unique decision to make, but no matter what that decision looks like, it will, in its very essence, be a choice between a well-lived life and an unlived one, a meaningful life and a meaningless one, a deeply felt life and a barely felt one.

At its very highest, the One Decision is a choice to accept the gifts of the universe, to become the most "you" you can be, and to fulfill your potential. It is the choice to pursue and receive MORE in life. Your One Decision is an invitation to break your denial and to pierce the illusion that you are not worthy of a magnificent life, or that you want too much, or that you are not special.

The One Decision is a commitment—a choice about what you care about, what you value, and what matters to you. It is a decision that you will increasingly learn to live into so that, day by day, more of your choices reflect that overriding decision. You do not wait until you know how to live your One Decision to make it, because you can't know how to live your One Decision *until* you make it. It is your commitment that will help you explore more fully what your personal One Decision is and start learning how to live it. From your commitment, you enter the Adventure of following your Desire.

And at the same time, just exploring your One Decision will transform your life. You don't need to make your One Decision over the course of the book. You may choose to make it at another time or just to try on a One Decision. In this chapter, your adventure is simply to notice, be aware, and follow your urge to have a One Decision. You'll get to know the One Decision, what it looks like, and its ins and outs. If, later in the chapters that follow or at the end of this book, you choose to claim and name your One Decision, you can do that on your own or with the thirty-day plan provided. But for now, just open your mind and heart to the power and possibilities of the One Decision.

A Choice Between Opposites:
To Be or Not to Be

The classic One Decision was powerfully stated by Shakespeare, who may have said it best: "To be, or not to be. That is the question." To *be*—to be alive, aware, and to be yourself—or *not to be*—to be dimmed down, numbed out, unaware. To be conscious or to be unconscious.

Your One Decision can be worded in any way that seems right to you. But it is actually a binary choice, an on/off switch between two opposites:

To be or not to be
A life of MORE or a life of less
Awake or asleep
Deep or superficial
Substantive or vacuous
Real or fake
Light or dark
Spiritual or temporal
Fulfilling deep desires or surface wants
Truth or illusion
Adventure or suffering

Whether we want to admit it or not, there is only one choice. It is either one thing or the other. It is the only choice we have. To pretend that there is any other choice is absurd—and completely false.

Many wise people have echoed these truths. As Einstein said, "There are only two ways to live your life. One is as if everything is a miracle and the other as though nothing is a miracle." Buckminster Fuller asked whether life is to be Utopia or Oblivion. In the movie *The Matrix*, Morpheus offers Neo the choice between the red pill and the blue pill—the choice between truth and illusion.

The choice is yours. What do you choose?

Don't kid yourself about the

> *This is as true in everyday life as it is in battle: we are given one life and the decision is ours whether to wait for circumstances to make up our mind, or whether to act, and in acting, to live.*
>
> —Omar Bradley,
> *World War II Army chief of staff and chairman of the Joint Chiefs of Staff*

power of this choice. Don't hide out thinking it has to be complex. It is either on or off, adventure or suffering, miracle or no miracle, truth or illusion, awake or asleep. It doesn't mean that you live it perfectly. But it is this clear.

All the back-and-forth mind talk of *I don't know what to commit to. Will I do it right? What should I choose?* or *I can't decide* is unnecessary obfuscation and procrastination.

> *Making your One Decision is like drawing a line in the sand and then stepping over it, vowing never to go back. It's that big, that clear. And it's that powerful.*

Don't pretend that you don't know what the One Decision is. Don't layer it with fake complexity. If you are reading this book, you already know that you want MORE out of life. So that is the choice: Will you have MORE or less? That's it. It's that simple—and that profound.

A Complete Shift in Perspective

The One Decision generates a complete change in perspective on your life. It's not *what* you are doing that is so profoundly changed. Rather, what has changed is the context for *why* you're doing what you are doing. Your One Decision provides an overriding direction for your activities and unifies your life. It becomes a beacon, a guiding philosophy, for all the smaller decisions of your life. It has the capacity to end mindless internal "should I or shouldn't I?" chatter, never-ending lists of pros and cons, indecisiveness, or even rash or impulsive decisions. After your One Decision, activities and tasks—even the most mundane or routine—will be imbued with more meaning and have more synergistic effects.

After you make your One Decision, the only real question that matters is *What can I do right now that is in the service of my One Decision?* As all your choices come into alignment with this, your thought process no longer includes: *What's not going to get me in trouble? What can I get away with,* or *What's acceptable?* It's not even about avoiding doing something that's bad for you. Those are questions you stop considering or, if you do, you realize that

> *Making the One Decision is momentous and life changing—yet deceptively simple. The One Decision isn't about performance; it's a way of being.*

they aren't central to your motivation anymore. This new clarity makes it much easier to sort out the activities and ways of being in your life that don't fit.

Without making your One Decision, it looks like there are many good things from which to choose, but having made your One Decision, the choices narrow and the results become more powerful. There is greater direction and thrust in all you do. This sense of direction helps you make decisions more quickly and more powerfully, and gives you more time, more fun, and less confusion. Your life becomes more integrated. It's a truly adventurous way to live—energetically, peacefully, and organically.

A Guide to Make Small Decisions

Once you make the One Decision, it guides all of your actions. It helps you make the smaller decisions of life. It helps you synthesize different activities and initiatives. With your One Decision, you stop asking small questions and start asking the big questions that really matter. Not: *Will she like me? Do I look better with my hair up or down? What should I wear? Will I say the right thing? What's on tonight?* Instead, you consider deeper questions: *Am I being myself? Am I on purpose? What will help me live more in consonance with my One Decision today? How*

> *Life is the sum of all your choices.*
>
> —ALBERT CAMUS,
> *French novelist and essayist*

can I serve? What will fulfill me? What do I desire deep inside? How can I meet that hunger?

A One Decision is a powerful tool for the smallest of decisions, like what to wear or what to eat for lunch. Suddenly, your meal choice is no longer a running internal debate of push-pull, moralizing, beating yourself up, and engaging in rebellion; you simply choose. Having made your One Decision takes a lot of the drama out of your daily choices and simplifies your life to bring you more of what matters. It can guide you on how to spend your evening after work, with whom to spend your time, how to spend your money, and how to use your resources to have MORE in your life.

"I choose to love myself beyond measure as a unique gift of God's love." That was Andrea's claim at one of my trainings.

Andrea, a corporate officer in charge of training for 70,000-plus employees, had struggled with her weight her entire life.

> *We do not choose to be born. We do not choose our parents. We do not choose our historical epoch, the country of our birth, or the immediate circumstances of our upbringing. We do not, most of us, choose to die; nor do we choose the time and conditions of our death. But within this realm of choicelessness, we do choose how we live.*
>
> —JOSEPH EPSTEIN,
> *American lecturer*

She tried every diet and eating plan from Richard Simmons to Suzanne Somers, from the grapefruit diet to the cabbage diet, from Atkins to Jenny Craig.

Little did she know that by her choice to love herself no matter what, her next meal, and all the meals to follow, would never be the same. Gone was the usual moralizing—right or wrong, should I or shouldn't I. Instead she asked herself, "What would I feed myself now if I really loved myself beyond measure? What is the best possible food for someone I love?"

Little by little since that day, she has started uncovering deeper ways to take care of herself and really love herself. She knows that she won't be thin overnight, but she's lost twenty-two pounds so far, and her journey is no longer about losing weight but about finding herself.

A Guide to Making Bigger Life Decisions

In addition to guiding those smaller decisions in life, your One Decision will also be a beacon for making life's big, momentous decisions. Decisions like: *Whom do I marry? What career or job should I pursue? Where's the best place to live?* Some of these bigger decisions can dramatically influence the course of our lives, and we are more open to the fulfillment and satisfaction that is possible when our One Decision is our guide.

> *It is our choices . . . that show what we truly are, far more than our abilities.*
>
> —J. K. ROWLING,
> *author of the Harry Potter series*

Peter was facing a big decision. He had gone to the "right" school and gotten the "right" degree and now was perfectly positioned when the large consulting firm that he had been aiming for offered him a salary he just couldn't refuse.

But he had just made his One Decision, and so he looked at this career choice in a new light. His One Decision was to live a life where he was learning, growing, and developing himself as fully as possible. As he revisited the consulting job offer, he realized he would have a great salary and he'd be set on his career path, but the scope of the work was very limited and he wouldn't be developing himself fully. He would be advising people on running a business before he himself had even tried running a business, which just didn't feel right to him.

With his One Decision to guide him, Peter took a job that paid much less but offered a wider breadth of experience. It gave him the opportunity to learn every aspect of a business from the ground up. He became a sales manager, learned to manage people and resources, and then went on to manage bigger projects, learning and growing to the point where he was ready to launch his own business.

Now he's a successful entrepreneur and his fledgling business will do almost $1 million in sales in its first year! There was nothing right or wrong about the consultant position he turned down. For someone else, it might have been a perfect fit, but for Peter it simply wasn't aligned with his One Decision.

A Partial Commitment vs. the One Decision

Most of us have tried many things to give us MORE in life. Yet, without making the One Decision, our attempts don't have the full power that is available to us. While some areas of our lives may improve, our overall lives don't change. We add a few good things to our lives rather than having good lives. We add things that are supposed to help us grow rather than growing. We engage in a more substantive conversation every now and then rather than *being* substantive.

Or we make an "undecision." I made an undecision when I decided to lose weight. My decision to lose weight led to exactly that—I lost weight. So then I was thin . . . and still unhappy. Losing weight did not automatically lead to MORE. I had confused the cause and effect. I mistakenly thought losing weight, the cause, would bring me the effect I desired, a great life. But without the One Decision to have a high-quality life, I was only partially successful. It was only after I made my One Decision that I weighed what I wanted—and lived the life I wanted.

Otherwise, it's like condiments to a meal—a little parsley here, a little sliced pickle or a carved radish there. You add a spiritual thing to your life and sprinkle in a little growth thing on the side. You add a little consciousness, a mindful meditation perhaps, but go mindless the rest of the time. You add a little exercise here, but pig out the rest of the time. You are adding sprinkles on the top of the donut of your life rather than making a whole meal.

These fragmented attempts don't work, because they are not grounded in this greater contextual decision. At best, you feel as if things are kind of working but, for all the effort you're putting in, you should be getting more. And so you end up with new condiments on your plate, but the meal is still the same old stuff. It's a little tastier and it's got some spice, but it doesn't vary the daily diet of living. This is the result of a partial commitment. You achieve some goals but lack an overall synergy and direction for your life. Acting on intermittent bursts of motivation, you are not in touch with the deeper desires within you, so you do not follow your urges to satisfaction and MORE. It's as if you've found part of the solution but not the one big answer.

With a partial commitment, as soon as you hit a snag or a disappointment you start to doubt yourself. You ask: *Why am I doing this?* If your motivation is grounded only in a partial commitment, the reason probably isn't compelling: *Because I'm supposed to! Somebody will be mad at me if I don't. It seems like the right thing to do.* Rather than spur you on, this kind of thinking holds you back and makes you feel sorry for yourself.

With your One Decision, you can firmly answer: *I know why! I am committed to something that has deep meaning for me, to follow the desires of my heart. I know this is what is right for me and what will lead me to MORE.*

With the One Decision, in any situation, at any time, you can orient toward MORE in the activities, events, interactions, and relationships of your life. You aren't waiting for something to happen or someone else to come along. Living your One Decision changes the main course of your life from a sampling of condiments to a feast to feed your deepest hungers.

Making and living your One Decision brings about transformational shifts, not just incremental growth. It's the difference between doing spiritual things and living a spiritual life, between doing good things and living a good life.

66

A Tool for Breaking Through Blocks

In my coaching and training at the Institute, I frequently see progress and big changes occurring in people's lives. Yet often these same people get stuck in some stubborn patterns. They repeatedly receive feedback about their behavior, have been trained in the skills to change it, and yet they don't seem to change. You have probably noticed this in yourself— persistent behavior patterns that don't work for you. These patterns bring you less, not MORE.

One of the reasons for these patterns is that you haven't made the One Decision that would help you blast through them. It is not enough just to want to change something or to do it because it would be good for you. If you find that something is holding you back in life, chances are you have tried to do something about it in the past but your efforts didn't succeed. This is partly why we sometimes get discouraged or feel hopeless about the possibility of real change in our lives.

The One Decision gives you a compelling reason to keep unlocking a pattern, to keep learning the skills you need and garnering the support you deserve to shift this pattern. You don't expect to hit it with one attempt; you accept the journey. You are willing to do what you need to do to erode the pattern. This is why the One Decision is so powerful in helping to unlock long-standing Soft Addictions.

Lilly had an annoying pattern of tuning out in conversations, in meetings, or even at dinner with her family. Sometimes, she'd actually just shut her eyes and nod off. She didn't have a sleep disorder; she just tuned out. Her daughter was frustrated at Lilly's zoning out while she was talking. Her husband complained that she'd check out of a conversation at the dinner table. Her coworkers were tired of her spacing off in meetings. Everyone had pointed the problem out to her. She'd try to shake herself to get more present or get up and walk around, but it didn't work. She would just nod off again afterward.

Finally, after attending my workshop, Lilly made her One Decision. She chose to be alive, awake, and engaged—once and for all. With that very real commitment, she has done what she needed to do to change the pattern—not because others were nagging her, but because she had decided, from a place deep within herself, that she would no longer sleepwalk through her life. With her One Decision as a guide, she uses skills she learned to shift her behavior.

Now she doesn't need to walk around or splash water on her face if she feels herself spacing out. Instead, she is one of the first people with her hand up at a meeting. She actively engages or leads the conversations wherever she is. She has begun to state her opinions and feelings directly. Her creativity and aliveness are flowing. Her staff is motivated by this energetic and inspiring woman. Her daughter is much happier; her husband is thrilled.

Unlocking False Decisions

We have all made decisions about ourselves, our emotions, and the world around us that have some of the characteristics of the One Decision. These false decisions may come from our childhoods, when many of us came to believe certain things like: *I'm not lovable. There is not enough for me. I'm too much. I'll never be hurt again.* They color our perceptions and experiences and guide our decisions, even as adults.

These decisions had a purpose for you as a child, serving as a protective wall around yourself, to keep you from feeling hurt or to give you some parameters in an uncertain or scary world. The problem is that these early decisions are most often mistaken. They are a composite of beliefs that were formed from faulty or insufficient data, from a child's point of view.

These false decisions can work against every loving action toward yourself. They define and explain some of the struggles you may have felt and help you understand your thoughts of: *I can't do that. I can't have MORE. It's not possible.* According to your mistaken decisions, it may be impossible to have MORE—but not from the foundation of your One Decision.

Now it's time to let these decisions go so you can reorient to a true One Decision. As an adult, these false decisions no longer serve as a positive guiding philosophy. They are no longer relevant, and they no longer work. These phony decisions limit you and keep you from making a bigger, empowering commitment that is in consonance with who you are now and who you want to become. You must uncover and defuse these mistaken decisions that operate in the background even after you have made and committed to your One Decision. Otherwise, it's like driving with the emergency brake on. You'll be trying to move forward, but something will be trying to slow you down and stop you.

Test-Drive a One Decision

Despite the title of this book, you may or may not make your One Decision while reading it. Some people spend several years laying the foundation for making a One Decision. Others jump right in. Every journey is unique and personal. And that really is the point.

To make your One Decision, you must first dig deep and ask yourself: *What do I want my life to be about?* Put aside the "shoulds" and the ideals. Go into the deepest part of yourself and keep asking that question. What do you hear? If the answer doesn't come right away, that's fine.

If you are ready to take the steps to make a One Decision, you'll find a thirty-day guide at the end of this book that will help you do just that. If not, you may just want to test-drive some One Decisions and see how they feel. If you'd like to consider some possibilities, here are some One Decisions made by participants at a recent training I led:

I live my life as if everything matters.
I stand for truth in the world.
I choose to love myself.
I connect with people and lead wherever I am.
I stand for the value of human creativity as a direct expression of spirit.
I have decided, once and for all, I am alive, awake, and engaged.
I choose to honor my emotions as a gift from God.
I am a determined woman who makes things happen.
I choose to care and to engage.
I live my life as an adventurer, as a bold and vibrant leader.

What to Do When You
Fall Off the Path

When you make your One Decision, life doesn't become an old Hollywood musical where you burst out singing, everything is perfect, and all your confusion, struggle, and negative thinking magically vanish. What does happen, however, is that you receive a way to counter that negative thinking and silence those negative voices, to reorient toward your One Decision. You have a way to look at yourself and your choices with understanding and perspective. And when you do get off track, and you will, you simply use your One Decision to reevaluate where you've been, understand where you stepped off the path, and simply get back on. You ask yourself: *Was this in consonance with my One Decision? Do I respect who I was in that situation or not?* If you did, do more of it—and if you didn't, then you can shift.

The One Decision is never asking, *Did I do that perfectly?* You will never achieve perfection, and it's not the point. Perfection leaves no place to learn, grow, discover, and experiment. Perfection doesn't allow you to celebrate the brave act of just trying, taking risks, and stretching into new things. You're never one hundred percent conscious, or engaged one hundred percent of the time, but you can always navigate toward that goal. You can always see if you're improving or doing something that brings you more clarity or feelings or awareness or fulfillment. Use your One Decision as a gauge as you consider your choices and actions, and then use it to guide you toward the steps you should take.

Another powerful tool for getting back on track is compassion. With the One Decision, there is no loss, no regret, just learning and growing. You discover that there is nothing broken about you—you don't need to be fixed! Viewing yourself through the eyes of compassion becomes one of your main jobs. You acknowledge that you're going to fall down because you're risking more. You've made a big move, a big stand for your life, and facing struggles and challenges is simply a reminder for you of the bigness of your decision.

The Ultimate Surrender

Your One Decision means surrendering and giving yourself over to something. You have already given yourself over to something in your life, whether it is unconsciousness or greed, scarcity, pleasing others, or perhaps a mistaken decision you made as a child. Now it is time to take back your life and give yourself over to what your heart asks of you.

Your One Decision is giving yourself over to God, spirit, a higher calling, or a way of being that brings out the best in you. It doesn't matter whether you relate to God, Jesus, Buddha, Mother Mary, Allah, your Higher Power, the universe, or principles such as truth, love, value, or possibilities. Your One Decision is giving of yourself, an ultimate surrender in which you get yourself back.

We are meant to give ourselves to something. We are meant to be hungry for something and to give ourselves to the fulfillment of that hunger. Yet we have often been confused about what to surrender to. You are not surrendering your will; instead, you are using your free will to choose what matters most to you. You give yourself over to higher principles—whatever feeds your Desire.

There is an eternal moment of decision, unending, ceaselessly renewed, whether to join the vast act of creation, become again and once again an unfolding miracle, or let go, disengage, and drift away from becoming.

—JON FIELDMAN,
*attorney, chief information officer,
husband, father, Wright Institute student*

You do not lose yourself with this kind of surrender. You find yourself. You become bigger, more of yourself. With your commitment, you are making a vow, and you recognize the solemnity of what you are doing. You choose to honor this step, just as we celebrate other rites of passage where our vows are witnessed—whether it is a wedding, baptism, bar or bat mitzvah, oath of office, and so forth.

This great spiritual commitment you are making is no less momentous, and for some, it is more life altering than a wedding. It is important to honor your One Decision and keep it before you. The declaration isn't the most important part; it is actually living it that brings you MORE. People should be able to tell what your One Decision is by looking at your life.

Let your One Decision shine through you and become a beacon of possibilities for your life and those whose lives you touch.

Magic Happens When You Commit

Magic happens once you definitely make your One Decision. The very act of committing sends out a message to the universe, and then, and only then, can full resources come to your aid. When you definitely commit, unforeseen support, inspiration, and encouragement come your way. You begin to find synergies and synchronicities in events and things around you. You begin to attract the support of other people who have made deeper life commitments. It requires a leap of faith to make your One Decision, but once you have, resources will appear that you never would have expected.

Your One Decision is a powerful force that proclaims your intent to the world around you, drawing unforeseen resources to you.

Do You Want MORE?

Your true One Decision answers these questions: Do you want MORE in life? Will you accept the abundance that is your birthright and step into

Until one is committed there is hesitancy, the chance to draw back, always ineffectiveness . . . the moment that one definitely commits one's self, then Providence moves too. All sorts of things occur to help one that would otherwise never have occurred. A whole stream of events issues from the decision, raising in one's favor all manner of unforeseen incidents and meetings and material assistance, which no man or woman could have dreamt would have come his way. Whatever you can do or dream you can—begin it. Boldness has genius, power, and magic in it.

—W. H. MURRAY,
mountain climber and former POW,
quoting Goethe in a sermon

it and receive it fully? Will you step out of illusion and into what is real to the best of your ability? Will you accept reality? Will you admit that you are a child of God, of a loving universe, and worthy of all good things, and then live your life from that truth? Will you let yourself be a partner of other people? Will you let yourself be loved and adored? Will you turn yourself over to what matters the most to you? Will you let God, spirit, or a higher power be an active part of your life? Will you surrender and let go of your mistaken decisions and allow love to pour through you instead?

Are you willing to live a life that is alive? Engaged? Conscious? Satisfying? Delicious? Adventuresome and MORE? Commit, and the universe will deliver.

Your One Decision unites you to the bounty of the universe in new, powerful ways. When you decide, allies rush in to join you. It is almost as if these powers were waiting all along for you to claim your birthright. Your One Decision gives you a sense of security that allows you to relax and let the blessings of the universe pour into you. The abundance of spirit flows over and

through you. ~~Life itself shows you the way.~~ Say to yourself: I
choose MORE, I choose life, I choose love, I choose the best I can
be, I choose to be awake, I choose to feel, I am here to live my life.
See what the cosmos can bring as you jump into the Adventure.
That's the One Decision.

To live a full and
fulfilling life, to love
myself unconditionally,
to learn, grow and
develop myself fully,
to let my creativity
be an expression of
my spirit.

The Truth

Truth is love. Truth is power. Befriend it, for it is your essence. You need not hide any part of yourself any longer. Face the deeper truths you have feared and discover the peace of being your true self. Express Truth with full responsibility and enter into an exquisite dance of intimacy with your friends and others. Let yourself go and find your heart. Hold nothing back and offer your fullest self as you embrace life with the loving arms of your deepest Truth. Aglow, in touch with your core, you shine forth, and discern with increasing clarity the real from the illusion. Only with Truth can you be yourself, share yourself, know others, and be known. And only with Truth can you discover the very real abundance around you.

Truth is real freedom, real security, real peace, real love. When you make your One Decision and dedicate yourself to Truth, you are free to express yourself, to uncover your power, your energy, and your creativity. You are free to live the life you were destined to live. You are on a journey to a deeper level of authenticity, genuineness, and depth, to unmask your truest self, becoming more and more capable of deep intimacy and great love. And through your commitment to Truth, you regain boundless time and energy as all the thoughts, energy, and consciousness that you spent hiding the truth are now unleashed. You no longer scramble to keep someone from finding out what you have been trying to hide. You no longer invest in false illusions, but seek the truth of what is so.

No longer warring against yourself, you find real peace. With Truth, you are free. With Truth comes security. You can't experience freedom when you are defending your territory, trying to keep from being "discovered," or chasing after empty promises of the illusory MORE. Without the security and freedom of the Truth, you are always on the lookout for that one unchecked move, the slightest breeze that could send the house of cards tumbling down. You are afraid of being found out.

> *Have confidence in the truth, although you may not be able to comprehend it, although you may suppose its sweetness to be bitter, although you may shrink from it at first. Trust in the Truth . . . Have faith in the Truth and live it.*
>
> —THE BUDDHA,
> *The Dhammapada*

When you can face the truth about yourself and reveal it to others, you are free.

What Is Truth?

Truth is more than factuality; it is a personal journey to increasingly discern and show the truth of your experience to your highest vision, to the best of your ability. When you embrace this concept, you learn to tell increasingly potent, deep truth—helping you develop into your fullest self. The One Decision requires that you learn to express Truth and become more genuine and real.

Aligning to Truth means that you are not rationalizing. Rationalizations are abstractions we make up to justify our behavior. Most of us have pat answers for why we do what we do or superficial explanations for our behavior. We remain unconscious to what is really going on and are unwilling or unable to frankly assess and report on our actions, behaviors, and motivations.

As we grow in our commitment to Truth, our vision changes and we are able to discern and express more and more truths. We are able to go beyond our shallow excuses and knee-jerk explanations; we seek and give more conscious responses that reflect more Truth.

The journey of Truth is personal for everyone. Over time, it can include having no secrets from your spouse, becoming less defensive, having an increasing sense of integrity. It can mean that you feel more genuine and real, that you reduce lying and withholding information, that you develop honest friendships with straight feedback.

Like many others, I grew up in a family of secrets. On one hand, there was a lot of room in my family for play and expression. But on the other, I learned that there were territories not to venture into, other subjects that could only be approached in certain ways, and certain things you simply did not say to people. You just didn't tell the direct truth to others, especially if it pointed out something upsetting.

This pattern contributed to my experiencing less in life. I wasn't trained to responsibly express Truth—whether emotional or factual. I was accustomed to living with tension, rather than breaking it by acknowledging and giving voice to the Truth. I didn't know how to speak direct, unadorned truth with another person. I learned to compensate, and always tried to understand the other person rather than express what was going on inside of me.

My journey of Truth has led me to MORE—more spontaneity and less internal editing, more power to express my insight forcefully, more intimacy, more connection with others, more peace, more clarity, and more energy. I have begun to feel free in a way I didn't know was available to me.

I am still on my journey, and unearthing more ways I hide the truth from myself and from others. It is a blessed relief to keep coming clean. I experience the contentment and peace that are possible with Truth.

Truth and the One Decision

Truth is a powerful force for staying aligned with our One Decision. It is recognizing the true MORE from the illusory more. It is not being seduced by false promises of infinite ease, instant fixes, or magical solutions, but being able to discern the true MORE. It is not about being fake, hiding truth from yourself in an attempt to protect yourself, or accepting when people around you are disingenuous. It is about loving yourself enough to honor all aspects of yourself and tell the truth about them. It is about being willing to do the same for those you care about.

> *Everyone must decide whether he wants the uncompromising truth or a counterfeit version of truth. Real wisdom consists of recommending the truth to yourself at every opportunity.*
>
> —VERNON HOWARD,
> *author and spiritual teacher*

Living your One Decision requires you to express your deepest truth. What will your life be about? What will you choose? Will you orient to Truth or hide out in illusion? Will you be genuine or fake? Will you live with integrity or deceit? Will you reveal yourself or hide yourself? Will you speak up or hold back? Will you skate on the surface level of your life or consistently challenge yourself to go to deeper levels of loving yourself, telling the truth, and living the truth of who you are?

Dispelling the Illusion

The goal of most spiritual paths and philosophies is to pierce the veil of illusion, to see through the false promises of the material world, and to seek transcendent truth—the truth that exists outside the material world.

> *There is no greater disaster in a spiritual life than to be immersed in a false reality. We abandon the false reality for the sake of a greater reality. Knowing God.*
>
> —TED DEKKER AND BILL BRIGHT,
> *authors*

Vedic philosophy calls it Maya, the illusion of a limited physical reality in which our everyday consciousness has become entangled.

We often get caught in a web of consensual truth that we—individually and collectively—agree to. Think of the hype we see in the media, the false promise of advertisements, commonly accepted and unquestioned beliefs, or oft-repeated advice expressed as aphorisms. We hold as "truth" superstitions like the belief that walking under ladders or the number 13 are unlucky or we take folklore or popular relationship advice to heart. We accept generally held perspectives as truths when, in fact, they are not true.

If you immerse yourself in a false reality, you sacrifice the greater reality of having a more meaningful spiritual life, of accepting that you are a beloved child of a loving universe. This truth is the ultimate Truth. Wherever you are, transcendent Truth is available.

There is no formula for transcendent Truth. It is a living, breathing reality. As you learn to express your highest truth, you will see through the illusion of the false more. You embrace this reality more fully, and every day brings more truth and a greater experience of MORE.

The Illusion of the False More

One of the biggest illusions of societal truth—breaking through the illusion we buy into as a group, family, community, or world—is the false more. This persistent enemy entices you to believe in the fantasy instead of the real MORE. The illusory "more" presents societal norms as reality. Often, what is considered normal or even good in our society is the illusory more. We are led to believe that being rich, thin, youthful, famous, having Soft Addictions, or numbing our feelings is our ticket to acceptance and fulfillment. Too often, we persist in our belief that the hype is true, that there really is a magic pill for all our problems, that instant youth, beauty, power, or love are magically available—if we use the right products or do the right things. That illusion is a lie that leads us away from the Truth and MORE.

> *I seek the truth . . . it is only persistence in self-delusion and ignorance that does harm.*
>
> —MARCUS AURELIUS,
> *Roman emperor-philosopher*

"I've got $15 million liquid and I can't pull the trigger on the next deal," complained Craig. "What's wrong with me?" he asked.

The answer was simple—Craig had focused his whole existence on making money, but money hadn't fulfilled his Desire and this dawning realization was causing him to drag his feet on business transactions that used to be matter of course. He achieved his financial goal, but with $15 million to his name, three failed marriages under his belt, and grown children who would not talk to him, he clearly had missed the mark when it came to a life of MORE.

Growing up dirt poor, Craig swore he would never be poor again, and made good on his promise. But though he wasn't financially poor, he was definitely poor in relationships.

Luckily, Craig made his One Decision, discovered his purpose, and finally learned the difference between having more stuff and the greater MORE of life. He made peace with his children and found to his surprise that they wanted him, not his money. He found the thrill of giving of himself, not just his money, and he began training young businesspeople as a professor. And he mentored and developed his staff, who came to love and appreciate him. He still had financial success, but finally he was rich in relationships, not just his wallet.

MORE isn't more stuff, more success, more dates, more money—although it can result in all of these. It isn't meditating three hours a day, repeating affirmations, quitting your corporate job and moving to the mountains, or working less. In fact, it's not a formula at all. Once you make your One Decision, you might do yoga or meditate or even lose weight, but these things are an expression of your One Decision, your pursuit of MORE, not an end in themselves.

Be aware of the lure of the mistaken more. Resist the temptation of seductive, false versions of more. There is no substitute for MORE.

If you align to Truth, you are less likely to be seduced by false promises. You are skeptical of the promise of magical solutions and better able to follow your urges to express your deepest desires in the moment. You are less willing to accept anything that doesn't feel true to you. You even shop differently; you won't be so tempted by ads promising that their product will make you happy, give you a great life or instant sex appeal. You will discern sincere invitations and interactions from come-on lines.

As you stay focused on Truth, you engage in a deeper inquiry and recognize the Truth around you more clearly. You dispel the illusion of the mistaken more, see through its false promises, and you open the space to pursue the true MORE of life. Truth destroys the roadblocks on the way to MORE.

Your Personal Truth

Personal truth is the truth about you, your feelings, thoughts, concepts, ways of being, strengths, weaknesses, dark and light sides, gifts, and limitations. Personal truth involves factuality—what you know did or didn't happen—the truth of your feelings, and being honest about the judgments, hypotheses, or conceptions going through your mind. Sometimes people will tell you a factual truth but their emotions are dissonant. If they say in a flat, lifeless voice, "I'm really excited," it may be factually true but not emotionally honest.

We have all experienced times when our factual truth is disconnected from our emotional truth. Therefore, what we say, or what we say we feel, is partially false. We are not telling the whole truth. In a workshop, I asked participants to say to one another, "I'm really mad at you," with intensity and anger in their tone of voice and expression. After the exercise, one participant, a woman named Molly, admitted, "I have probably never in my life said those words with the impact that I just said them. I've absolutely always felt it, but I have never expressed it like I just did. I've always whitewashed it."

It was a shock to her, and it was also upsetting that she had never been that emotionally honest before. And she was honest in reporting on it—both factually and emotionally—which others could see in her voice, fa-

> *It is difficult to respect yourself if you are lying and withholding, or are out of integrity. Wholeness is experienced only by living with Truth, learning to love yourself as you learn to trust yourself.*

cial expressions, and demeanor. Since that experience, she has become determined to bring this level of honesty into her relationships.

You experience so much MORE—more power, connection, genuineness—when you express yourself honestly at the level you really feel it. Factual truth joined with emotional truth is powerful.

These levels of truth take training and skill. Most people are locked in patterns of defensiveness, hiding, and manipulating information to put up a good front or to have people think better of them. Learning to reveal Truth to our highest vision makes us more real and more whole.

Thoughts Masquerading as Truth

We all have these haunting doubts and self-limiting beliefs that try to present themselves as facts. These thoughts represent stinking thinking that distorts our reality by masquerading as Truth. This way of thinking can become so ingrained that it talks you out of your value, entices you into false substitutes, and creates the illusion of more.

Mistaken beliefs and assumptions spawn stinking thinking. It takes many forms: rationalizing, making excuses, being defensive, overgeneralizing, thinking you are unloved or unworthy, labeling, blaming, minimizing, projecting, being prejudiced, mind reading, being superstitious, obfuscating, all-or-nothing thinking—all ways of fudging or denying the truth, escaping from the deeper reality underneath.

Stinking thinking robs you of MORE. This false thinking keeps you from achieving what you could, and discourages you from trying new things, taking risks, and creating MORE. You may use these thoughts to talk yourself out of pursuing MORE before you even get a fighting chance. Stinking thinking lowers motivation and kills hope. And it's how most of us think and talk most of the time.

Falling into the loop of stinking thinking, you embrace what is false reality. You continually revisit your stinking thinking litany: *I can't. I'm too old, young, poor, fat . . . to do that. If only I were thinner, richer, or more attractive, everything would work out. It's his fault. It's her fault. I'll never be able to have MORE in my life. I already tried that and I failed, so it's no use trying again. I'm not smart enough. It'll never happen. This always happens. It will never get any better. I'm not okay. No one will ever love me. All the good men are taken or gay. Women only want men who are rich and successful. This is hopeless. I'm hopeless. I'll start my diet tomorrow. I'll never learn. When I win the lottery, I'll make my One Decision . . .*

None of this thinking is valid and keeps you mired in nonproductive patterns. Stinking thoughts may creep up on you, but you can learn to watch them rather than invest in them. You can even have a sense of humor and compassion about them. What you don't need to do is entertain these thoughts or accept them as real.

Aligning your thoughts to Truth—accepting yourself as a magnificent being, worthy of all good that life can bring—keeps you from the negativity of stinking thinking. You can bring light to these negative thought patterns and orient yourself to the Truth instead.

Finding Yourself in the Truth

Why is it that we resist the truth about ourselves, and that feedback is often difficult to take? Why is it so hard to hear that we are fat, or mean-spirited, or selfish, or loud, or whatever it is that we resist? If it is true, why do we resist it? Why do we so often get so angry? Because we are ashamed of or not at peace with these aspects of ourselves. We have decided that we are not supposed to be this way or that way.

> *If you do not tell the truth about yourself,*
> *you cannot tell it about other people.*
>
> —Virginia Woolf,
> *author*

As children, we had a wide range of emotions and ways of being. Yet our families didn't always appreciate, love, or even know how to handle our expression. If you were angry and started yelling at your parents, they may have let you know through their words, withdrawal, or physical response that it's not okay to be angry. And so you learned to hide your anger. Or maybe you got the message that you were too much, too full of energy, too outrageous, or too sensitive. So you decided to hide that.

You suppressed these parts of yourself and, for the most part, revealed only the parts that you deemed acceptable. You decided that nobody could see those other parts of you because if they did, you would be unloved, bad, or shunned.

The journey to Truth will help you get to a point where you make peace with these aspects of yourself and become whole. You accept these parts of yourself, recognize the hunger underneath them, and learn to meet those needs in a more appropriate and direct way.

Rather than just getting angry, hurt, or humiliated when you are exposed, your commitment to being genuine helps you to see yourself more fully. You realize that your feelings of anger, hurt, or humiliation are indications that there are aspects of yourself in need of healing and acceptance.

"I've been chubby, overweight, voluptuous, Rubenesque, and any other euphemism you want to use," spouted Elizabeth, "but it's taken until the last two of my fifty-one years to actually use the 'f' word." Elizabeth was fat, seventy pounds overweight on her five-foot-one-inch frame. Yet in the past eight months, she had lost forty pounds more easily than she ever thought possible, and she had kept it off.

The secret to her weight loss? She says that saying the "f" word, "fat," was the first step, and a big one for her. "It's true what they say—denial isn't just a river in Egypt. Once I broke my denial, then I could figure out what to do about it." Elizabeth's letting go of her false self, and the lie about the situation she was in gave her a strength and power she hadn't imagined. She's well on her way to letting go of her last thirty pounds, and she's thrilled to finally be telling the truth.

Truth-Telling

Truth-telling—and truth-receiving—are powerful skills for MORE. When you align with Truth, you count on those around you to tell you the truth and you do the same. When you are dedicated to being truthful about yourself and to another, you admit and disclose truth about yourself and actively seek feedback to help you remove your blocks to MORE. You give feedback as a way to empower those around you to live to their highest.

People who have made their One Decisions are more likely to recognize the value of Truth in a relationship and can call out un-truths as they occur. They aren't

> *When friends stop being frank and useful to each other, the whole world loses some of its radiance.*
>
> —ANATOLE BROYARD,
> *American literary critic*

interested in merely criticizing you but are invested in your highest self and can point out to you the ways you sabotage yourself—your nonproductive patterns, lapses in consciousness, rationalizations, and spin-doctoring—as well as what you do that empowers you.

The more you embrace and face the Truth, the more power you have. The more Truth and power, the more you can serve in the world. Truth unlocks your power and allows you to align more powerfully with others. It allows you to become your highest self and partner with others more deeply.

At the Institute we have a culture of Truth where students can get straight feedback on their strengths and weaknesses—what is facilitating their quest for MORE and what is blocking it. In your life, in your world right now, you can seek to establish a culture of Truth around you, where you give and receive feedback and your communications are powerfully honest. That is the freedom of Truth.

Alison, a nurse practitioner in her fifties from a large family, described the web of her family secrets as "a giant, invisible, yet palpable ball of unspoken judgments that divides our family and blocks our ability to connect with each other on any deep level." Her brother's financial irresponsibility was an off-limits topic for her family. Alison had distanced herself from him over the years, fearing she'd offend him if she shared her true feelings. Instead, she barely spoke to him.

Through a course at the Institute, Alison began learning the skills to take risks to tell the truth. At the next big family gathering, she pulled her brother aside and shared a resentment she had held about him. Rather than push her away, he opened up and revealed more about his circumstances—a first in their adult relationship.

For Alison, this experience was powerful and liberating—deflating a little the bubble of secrets and resentments between them and allowing her to feel much closer to him. This first conversation led to another where he shared his fears about providing for his family, and gave Alison another chance to tell her brother even more truth and clear away some things she had been holding on to. Alison is thrilled to be in the process of renewing a relationship that she had given up on long ago.

A Life of Integrity

Taking a risk to tell the truth where they had been avoiding it is a first step for many people, but as you live your One Decision consistently, you begin, step by step, to build a complete life of integrity. Your choices are in consonance with what is true for you. Truth becomes your way of being. People expect the truth from you and know that when you give your word on something, you will be true to it. You use your One Decision to be a consistent truthteller everywhere. This integrity and sense of wholeness permeates all areas of your life.

Hannah's heart raced as she sorted through her options. Mike wanted her to lie. Should she risk losing her job, servicing major accounts for a financial services firm, by refusing to change the numbers for Mike? She had already taken a major step toward her own personal integrity by choosing to leave a very prestigious firm where she had little room for growth and resented her work. But could she put this new job on the line? She didn't want to be disloyal to Mike. After all, he was the senior partner. But as she oriented to her One Decision, it clarified her path. She chose to tell him the truth and not make the changes he requested.

Her work environment continued to get very challenging as Mike undermined one of the firm's other major partners behind the partner's back. Hannah put her job on the line by confronting him on his bad faith. Things escalated further to the point where Mike wanted her fired. But, to Hannah's surprise, the partner she had been quietly backing stepped in and stood up for her. After more truth came out, Mike was terminated, and Hannah is in line for partnership. By living her One Decision, Hannah didn't simply tell the truth, but rather created a life of integrity, where truth-telling is simply who she is.

Diving Below the Surface: Deeper Truth

We can always dive more deeply under the surface into what's really true, what's really so. Each truth can lead to a deeper truth. You might tell someone, "I'm angry at you for not remembering my big event today." Once you've said that, you feel the urge to add: "I'm hurt and am afraid that I don't matter to you." And then you give voice to the deeper truth and what you really need to fulfill the urge: "I am feeling insecure about how I handled the event today, and I'm picking a fight with you rather than asking for what I really need. Could you please reassure me?"

> *The personal life deeply lived always expands into truths beyond itself.*
>
> —ANAÏS NIN,
> *poet, diarist, and feminist icon*

It is as if one truth creates a space for more truth, an opening for you to take another step. Then there is the moment of realization and relief: Your Truth was there all along, waiting for you to find it and express it. We may not know what is going on inside of us, but if we kindle our desire to find out, we can follow the urge to Truth, genuineness, and wholeness.

I have adopted a "no-secrets" policy with Bob. This has been quite a journey—and continues to be. Anytime I become aware that I want to hide something, not share fully, exaggerate, or withhold, I remember my contract with Truth and find a way to express it with him.

It's been fascinating to see what I haven't immediately wanted to tell him. I've learned a lot about what I am embarrassed by, feel guilty about, or am even afraid of in our relationship. Yet, by being willing to allow to the surface even the creepiest thought or smallest piece of information—or even my desire to fudge about how much something cost—I have

> *Truth begets truth.*

learned a lot about myself. And as my vision grows, I discover more that I can share with him. If I can't be myself fully with my husband, then what is the point? This creates immense trust, safety, and intimacy in our relationship.

Don't Shoot the Messenger: Accepting the Truth About Yourself

If you can't admit your foibles or face the parts of you that embarrass you, or if you can't tell the truth about your full experience, you will have a difficult time when someone else brings these things to your attention. You won't accept the feedback if you are trying to protect your false perception of yourself. You are likely to be defensive and reactive toward them. You may judge them as being mean; you may even leave a relationship because someone told you something that was true but too difficult for you to hear.

> *The truth will set you free, but first it will piss you off.*
>
> —GLORIA STEINEM,
> *journalist and feminist leader*

Yet, if we can accept truthful feedback without "shooting the messenger," we are freed from having to defend ourselves. It helps us accept ourselves and heal the parts we have been trying to hide.

Truth Tools: Consciousness, Compassion, and Humor

To experience MORE, we must be conscious and aware of what is true. Just as only ten percent of an iceberg breaks the surface of the water, much exists below the surface of our awareness in our unconscious mind. Our goal should be to become as awake and aware of our total experience as possible.

Our minds and senses process an amazing amount of material. Tor Norretranders, in the book *The User Illusion,* reports that we process some 11 million bits of data every second. Yet we are only aware of forty bits. In fact, studies show that we make things up after the fact to explain our actions and think we are reporting factual data. Because of this, we remain unaware of our blind spots. We are unconscious or blind to vast amounts of data about our behavior.

The journey to Truth is a demanding one. It takes skill and determination to constantly seek Truth, to follow your impulses to their source, to identify and express feelings, to accept feedback, and to respond responsibly.

Compassion, understanding, and a sense of humor are critical tools to live with more truth. When I have a tough time taking in feedback—which is most of the time—I try to ask, "What am I defending? What don't I want to know about myself or what do I not want to be seen?" This helps me to see which parts of my false self are being revealed and what parts of myself I need to integrate. I try to have compassion for myself and to see why I wanted to hide those aspects of myself. My One Decision involves being genuine, and I can't be genuine without Truth.

While I take in truth like medicine, recognizing that it is good for me, my husband Bob revels in Truth. He teases it out, calls out untruths, and confronts defensiveness with amazing accuracy and facility. When I interviewed him about his feelings about Truth for this chapter, he responded with "Truth is love." For Bob, Truth is love. So for him, the more Truth he experiences, the more love he has.

Oh, a great sense of humor helps, too. Think about the best comedians. They skillfully poke fun at themselves with incredible insight, revealing truth about themselves and others. A sense of humor about yourself and the human condition helps you live with Truth.

Lies and Avoiding the Truth

In a mistaken attempt to get what they think is MORE, people often lie, withhold, and exaggerate. In a survey of 1,001 adults in *Money* magazine (April 2005), seventy-one percent said they keep secrets from their spouses or tell outright lies to themselves or others when it comes to money. Nearly a third admitted to faking a lifestyle—telling tall tales, overstating a job, understating investment losses—to impress others.

> *Men occasionally stumble over the truth, but most of them pick themselves up and hurry off as if nothing had happened.*
>
> —Flannery O'Connor,
> *American author*

We're often not willing to see the lies that others tell, partly because we don't want to see our own deception. We're afraid to label ourselves as liars, so we couch our falsehoods and withhold or exaggerate. We try to hide from ourselves so that we can stomach the fact that we aren't telling the truth, the whole truth, and nothing but the truth.

At a seminar I led, we were discussing the importance of Truth. Patricia, one of the participants, became defensive and said, "This doesn't apply to me. I always tell the truth." Then she looked deeper, realizing that although she prided herself on telling the truth, her penchant to not tell people bad news and to withhold information that would cause her more difficulties at work, were actually forms of lying.

Other seminar participants admitted to exaggerating, minimizing, embellishing, editing information, and telling out-and-out lies. One person admitted, "I don't like that I am capable of delivering truth with some people, and shut it down with other people and then want to blame them because I wasn't honest."

We try to tell ourselves we speak the truth, but our falsehoods come in all shapes and sizes.

"My partner wasn't a thief, but his lies robbed us of the business and company we shared," said Bill, a driven and successful professional services business owner.

Bill's business partner was a very generous and talented man, but his optimism regarding the company's finances began to turn into blatant lying, and he didn't seem to be capable of changing. Despite his giving nature and abilities, he consistently fabricated business results that had nothing to do with reality. Bill spent three years in counseling with his partner trying to work on these issues. But, after a deception that turned out to be the straw that broke the camel's back, Bill was forced to finally face the reality of the situation. His partner was just plain lying and deceiving him with no intention to change, and he needed to move on. They ended their business together, and Bill now has his own firm. And he has learned a hard but important lesson about recognizing lies in all their forms.

Truth and Intimacy

There is no intimacy without Truth. It is only when we are revealed, open, and honest that we can experience true intimacy. And when you do express Truth in a relationship, the rewards of the intimacy are boundless. Your relationship becomes a powerful, exciting, ever-evolving work of art.

Many of us are afraid of Truth, mistakenly thinking: *He wouldn't love me if he knew the truth.* Or *I'm afraid to rock the boat.* Or *What will she think?* So we manipulate around the truth rather than be truthful. Yet the only true security lies in being truthful, genuine, and forthright.

In your relationships, you may try to be on your best behavior so somebody will like you. Think about when you have gotten ready for a date. Maybe you bought a new outfit or borrowed someone else's clothes because you thought what you had wasn't good enough. You wear your hottest ensemble, go to the tanning salon, and put on shoulder pads, a Wonder bra, or control-top panty hose. You don't order dessert. You may not even eat what you ordinarily eat. You pick at your salad, you have a drink so that you become less yourself, or you don't eat the bread. You act interested and nice; you laugh at everything your date says to you, even if you are thinking what a perfect dork or twit he is. Or the person says something that offends you but you don't speak up because you don't want to upset him; you want to be liked. You may be afraid to be the real you, because you think he wouldn't like the real you. But what if he does like you? If you are being fake and he *does* like you, then what? You've got to keep it up. But then he doesn't really like *you*—just the illusion of you. The pretense won't work for long.

My first date with Bob was the most interesting first date I had ever had. Rather than try to impress each other or pretend we were something we were not, we both were fairly honest with each other. We freely shared what we liked and didn't like about the other. We gave each other feedback, countered points of view, and challenged each other. We shared vulnerably and vociferously. It was so scary—and at the same time exhilarating and refreshing. There was no rehearsal. We related in the moment. We each found out what the other was made of and set a pattern of honesty from the beginning that continues today, twenty-some years later.

> *To experience true intimacy, you must begin with Truth and then build upon a foundation of honesty.*

To Thine Own Self Be True

Being disingenuous doesn't happen only in dating. We do it with friends, at work, at social gatherings—even with our partners and families—when we are being phony and trying to impress someone. There are many times, however, when we haven't consciously chosen to be fake. Instead, this way of being can become habitual. This is our knee-jerk reaction of being with other people.

At a recent women's training I conducted, one of the participants, Susan, lamented: "I've been so fake. At the end of the day, I really don't know who I am." She'd been acting and pretending for so long, she couldn't answer the important questions: What do I feel? What do I care about? What do I like or not like, and why? She had lost touch with herself and needed to learn to realign with the truth of her feelings and experience.

Fortunately for Susan and the rest of us, we do not have to be stuck with our old habits of phoniness, illusion, and delusion. Just admitting "I haven't been my true self," or even "I don't know who I really am," is the first step toward truth.

Becoming genuine, authentic, and whole is one of the great benefits of Truth. As you become more genuine, you experience the elation and relief of being yourself, sometimes for the first time in your life. It's like coming home again.

Dedication to Truth: Your One Decision

Your journey, your Adventure, is one of Truth-seeking—being more conscious, less mindless, more real and more substantive. As you become more honest with yourself and others, expect more genuineness from others, and reject false illusions, you become MORE.

As you know Truth, you know God and touch spirit. In touching spirit, you begin to see through the falsehoods, take away the facade of the false more, and recognize that nothing—whether TV or meditation—is a magic pill.

> *When in doubt, tell the truth.*
>
> —MARK TWAIN,
>
> *author, poet, and philosopher*

Only by understanding the ultimate Truth, that Truth is love, can you begin to love yourself enough to do what is truly good for you. You are able to discern the falsehoods within yourself and love yourself with understanding and compassion. You break through illusion to reality. You become more genuine and act with more integrity. You become a vehicle for others to discover the deeper Truth that you are learning. The deeper Truth lets you see through the false more and realize that the real MORE is available every moment in every area of your life. Learning to live that reality is why you are alive.

The Truth shall set you free. Free to experience MORE and the abundance life seeks to shower on you. Remember, there is no aspect of you that is unworthy of love. Nothing you cannot reveal. And there is nothing that can take that love away from you except your own denial. You need not look for magical solutions or quick fixes, because you are not broken. Align yourself to Truth, bring your shadowed places to the light. See the true MORE that is available to you. Open your mind and your heart to MORE and you shall be free. You are a magnificent child of

a loving universe that wants nothing other than for you to be the most you that you can be. May you seek the Truth within yourself, in those around you, and in your world. May you be at peace within yourself as you experience the resonance of Truth. May you be free.

The Way of the Heart

Open yourself to untold possibilities. Make the One Decision to live from your heart, in your heart, and with your heart. Discover the treasures of your emotions and feel life coursing through you. Vibrate with the blessings of life, pulse with Desire, dance to the beat of your spirit. Step into the embrace of love and the life you were afraid to wish for. Sing the song your heart is composing this very instant. Drop your guard and put down the shield that you mistakenly thought was protecting you. Find true security instead. No longer armored, you are open to feel, to freely receive and give love. Experience the relief of being real and the power of being potently authentic. Become your most wise and powerful self. Become MORE.

Living the Way of the Heart, you tap the infinite wisdom that resides within you, wisdom that transcends words. Living the Way of the Heart unleashes your joy, love, aliveness, emotions, creativity, and passion. You access the innermost recesses of your heart where your essential self resides—your deep desire, deep feelings, deep caring, deep knowing, and deep love.

Just as your heart sends life-giving blood throughout your body, your heart center sends forth pulses of aliveness to all aspects of your being to revive and feed your spirit. Your heart is a reservoir of emotions, caring, love, and intuition. It is the source of your creativity, your passion—the lifeblood of your soul's nourishment. Living the Way of the Heart unleashes these forces for you to fully live—and experience—MORE.

Learn the language of your heart and you learn its secrets, glean its wisdom, and express its essence—you translate the urges of your Desire into right action, for it is in your heart that you discern Truth and rightness.

And what is the language of the heart? Your feelings.

Feelings are the universal language of the human heart, connecting you with yourself, others, and spirit. It is through the language of the heart that we unite. Our feelings are the voice of love, hope, pain, passion, fear, and spirit.

When you live the Way of the Heart, you feel your feelings more vividly and savor the richness, power, and depth of life. You experience your life more fully, sensing the small tingles you normally miss. You inhale fully, expanding your lungs like a swimmer diving into a cool lake, only it is life, not simply water, into which you plunge, wholeheartedly, uncompromisingly. You engage in the Adventure of life, trusting your capacities, your resilience. You are spontaneous, open, and genuine. You experiment, go into the unknown, and live a life beyond what you previously dared—on the far side of your wildest dreams. This emotional richness transforms every aspect of your life—from relationships, to work, to conversations with friends, even how you get dressed in the morning or see a movie. Everything grows into something MORE.

"I can't believe it!" exclaimed Paul. "The colors are so bright and my heart hurts, but I feel full of joy." Managing director of a national financial firm, Paul described his breakthrough to me—getting to his heart, really feeling for the first time in as long a time as he could remember.

"I really thought my coach was nuts when he said I had emotional anesthesia, but now I understand. I really was a walking head. No wonder my wife complained that all I wanted to do was have sex and I didn't care about her. She was right." Paul felt sad about the wasted time and experiences with his wife. At the same time, he actually felt happy about feeling sad, because finally he was feeling! Paul had spent his career driving toward money. A bad year brought a mere million dollars—in a good year, he expected two to three million. But all the financial resources in the world could not give him the access to the emotions he needed to begin living the Way of the Heart. Finally, during a personal-growth activity, he had an intense experience that opened his eyes to what his wife and friends had been trying to tell him for years—that he was driving so fast through life that he was out of touch with himself, his feelings, his wife, and his children.

Paul still had a long way to go to realize his new vision of emotional availability, but now he had a powerful experience to orient to that would help him live the Way of the Heart, his One Decision.

The Way of the Heart and the One Decision

It is in your heart that you determine your One Decision. It is your heart that gets the final vote, for it knows best. Give language to your heart's desires and your One Decision will become clear. It takes your mind to apply your One Decision, and it takes your gut to will it into being, but it is your heart that knows what the decision is. And it is the One Decision that your heart asks of you.

The One Decision—will you choose the Way of the Heart? Will you choose a heartfelt life or a heartless one? Will you live a deeply felt life or a barely felt life? Will you tap your intuition and listen to the wisdom of your heart, or will you live solely by your intellect? Will you heed your heart and sense the rightness of your choices, or ignore its sensing? Will you use your feelings to express, to love, and to experience life, or will you numb them?

Ask your heart these questions and listen well. Your heart knows the answer.

The Sacred Gift of Emotions

Beneath each of the urges of your Desire vibrates emotion, God-given feelings meant to lead you to your highest self. Your emotions are designed to lead you to pleasure, warn you of danger, impel you to right action, keep you from unnecessary pain, inspire you to express, to share your glory, to love, and to serve. However, you miss their magnificence when you fear, rather than revere, your feelings.

Emotions help you seek nourishment, love, solace, and comfort. If you didn't feel the pain of missing affection or attention, you would never do anything to meet these needs. You wouldn't hug or touch, laugh, or be moved to tears. You wouldn't be you. Your feelings are the deepest

As we open our hearts and feel our feelings, we also nourish ourselves. We can feel the relief of releasing the bubble of joy within our heart, the surges of love, the energy of anger, the warning of fear, and the tenderness of pain. And we are bathed in the deep truth of our experience through our emotions.

essence of who you are. They are how you know that you exist. Repress them and you limit yourself; you restrain part of creation. Your feelings are part of the original plan—to experience MORE, to become MORE, to live MORE.

The Function of Feelings

There is a positive function for every single one of your emotions, and it is your job to restore them to their rightful place. Many of us have been taught, through family upbringing, fear or rejection, or other forces, to suppress and even deny the constant pulsing of our emotions. Each of us has labeled certain emotions taboo, whether they are anger, fear, hurt, or even joy. Far from being the internal enemies that you fight, control, stun, or hide, your emotions are allies that lead you to the greatest fulfillment, service, and love.

> *If it were only "I think, therefore I am," then God would have just given us heads.*

Feelings are the mediators of pleasure and pain, designed to allow you to feel more pleasure and avoid more pain. Fear, like pain, is designed to warn you of danger to keep you safe. Hurt signals you to shift away from the source of the pain, to alleviate suffering and move toward comfort and healing. Joy inspires you to share with others. Anger fuels your passion to attain desired outcomes, move away from danger and pain, and to make changes and right wrongs. Fear warns of danger and signals moves to safety, while sadness releases a hurtful loss and heralds a new opening and possibility. Each emotion moves you away from pain and toward pleasure. That is its primary function.

No Pain, No Gain

Pain has a function too. It opens your heart, inviting healing and succor. When you are in pain, you are open and vulnerable. Sadness and hurt flow. Pain is a sign that a situation or circumstance is hurtful and needs to change. It motivates you to learn and grow from your experiences.

> *Peace is not the absence of pain, but the acceptance and expression of pain.*

As your emotions move you away from pain, they also move you toward pleasure—hurt moves you to the pleasure of healing, sadness to relief, anger to accomplishing desired goals, fear to safety and security. Had you learned to use your emotions fully in childhood, you would have developed your capacities beyond your wildest dreams. However, that does not seem to be the plan. Rather, it is your job as an adult to reawaken your emotional life to its fullest, to develop your capacities and re-parent yourself. Reaching out with your emotions is reaching out with heart to your fellow man and to your Maker.

The Marriage of the Mind and Heart

Your mind is meant for knowledge, your heart for wisdom. Together you have it all. Wisdom doesn't come just from your heart, and knowledge doesn't come just from your head. When you learn to use your mind in the service of your heart, you

> *The heart has its reasons, that reason does not know.*
>
> —BLAISE PASCAL,
> *seventeenth-century mathematician,*
> *physicist, philosopher*

harness your true intelligence. You have been provided with a high quality life guidance system—logic and intuition in a powerful symmetry.

Three hundred miles deep into enemy territory in South Africa, a British officer is the only one of about sixty men to successfully survive an escape attempt from the schoolhouse prison where they were being kept. After scaling a wall in darkness, hopping on a freight train as a stowaway through the night, and escaping in daylight under cover of a bush through the next day, this prisoner of war reports he had "no strength . . . that could save me from my enemies. I prayed long and earnestly for help and guidance." Desperate, and at the end of his resources, he saw what he thought were the lights of a native village and felt called to them. After questioning himself, he felt the tug and followed his instinct. Instead of a village, he found a coal mine settlement, and, throwing caution to the wind, he walked up and knocked on the door of an imposing home. The door was eventually opened by its British citizen owner, revolver in hand. Imagine the relief of Winston Churchill as he was given cover by the only house for twenty miles where he would not have been handed over to the enemy.

Remarking on his choice to go inside, pray, and listen with his heart, he wrote:

It seemed to me that it would be very foolish to discard the reasons of the heart for those of the head. Indeed I could not see why I should not enjoy them both. I did not worry about the inconsistency of thinking one way and believing the other. It seemed good to let the mind explore so far as it could the paths of thought and logic, and also good to pray for help and succor and be thankful when they came. I could not feel that the Supreme Creator who gave us our minds as well as our souls would be offended if they did not always run smoothly together in double harness. After all He must have seen this from the beginning and of course He would understand it all.

Churchill's story reminds us that the Way of the Heart is more than an interesting concept. In my own experience, it would have been very foolish countless times for me to have ignored my inner voice and feelings and senses. The more I live the One Decision, the more I find that the Way of the Heart is indispensable and perhaps the most important element that has led me to a life of MORE.

Living the Way of the Heart

When we learn to recognize and validate our emotional life and look inside, we open our hearts. When our students learn to open their hearts and express their emotions responsibly, they begin to feel more secure and more powerful. They learn to tell the truth and face their fears. Even though it may disturb others, they learn to trust and express their feelings. They shift their values from comfort to openness, from seeming safety to the trust of honesty. They discover that living with Heart is a huge advantage in

> *God gave us tears so we could water our feelings and grow as people.*
>
> —NOAH BENSHEA,
> *poet, philosopher, scholar*

all situations—in business, at home, in relationships, in our leadership at work, and in our parenting.

Yvonne is artsy, hip, cynical, and sarcastic. Ever the social activist and creative urbanite, Yvonne thought she had little room for feelings in her life. She said, "I thought I knew what feelings were; they were these sentimental things people put on greeting cards that I had no time for. Why the heck would I want to get in touch with them?" For her, the thought of living the Way of the Heart was far from her cool, socially conscious image.

When Yvonne and her husband were struggling in their business, they began business coaching at the Institute. Yvonne wanted to live a healthier, more financially abundant, better life. When her coach proposed that a big part of her problem was that she was out of touch with what mattered—her urges and feelings—she mocked the coach, dismissing her feelings as the problems she had left behind.

Eventually, Yvonne admitted that there were things missing in her life. Even though she was madly in love with her husband, they weren't living a healthy lifestyle. Their marriage was more about partying than partnership. As she discovered the real function of feelings, Yvonne began to consider that living The Way of the Heart might be useful. Yvonne agreed to practice the skills she was learning, and what she found astounded her. Not only did she discover an entire universe locked in her heart, but she also found a highly functioning system of emotions and information that she had been ignoring.

She started to learn to recognize and interpret her feelings, and every aspect of her life started improving. She became a real contributor to her business, leading at levels she hadn't previously known. Her relationship with her husband deepened as they engaged in productive, profitable conflict, showing how much they truly cherished each other. As she learned to allow and feel her pain, her art took on an incredible beauty and depth.

The more she allowed herself to follow pleasure and honor pain, the more she could then differentiate and experience what she loved and what gave her joy. And as Yvonne continues to live the Way of the Heart, she is creating a life better than she ever imagined she could have—a life of MORE.

Quantum Leaps in Living

Opening your heart and learning to honor your emotions can trigger a quantum leap in how you live your life. Your greatest strength comes from keeping your heart open, staying grounded, and being in touch with yourself. If someone challenges you, or you are in danger, you can stay strong by accessing the truth of your emotions. In contrast, the various personas and defenses you use in an attempt to feel strong, powerful, and potent often have the opposite effect. They actually disempower you by cutting you off from your true self.

> *People may talk about living with Heart, but to truly live the Way of the Heart is to be transparent, to be vulnerable, to be honest, to live at risk.*

For all the time and energy you spend in keeping your guard up, you would think it would be getting you great results. But it doesn't get results; it doesn't really protect you. Chances are you still get hurt, you more readily lose confidence, feel humiliated, or even become shy or combative. Your defenses and armored heart don't help you, and they actually take away from your experiences, masking the evidence and suppressing the pain.

Sobbing, Alexis told Tim that she loved him, but if he wanted to continue living together, he had to stop lying around the house all day complaining about not having any money and how hard it was to find a job. After the seminar she had attended, she tapped her deeper feelings. She realized that she had built armor to protect herself from some of the hard truths she was ignoring. Once she faced these and opened to her deeper emotions, she realized that love was not "letting Tim be," as she said to herself. The truth was that by not saying anything she was helping him lead a numbed-out, meaningless life.

She had never believed his excuses when the landlord came looking for the rent money. She had given him her half of the rent only to find out that he had spent it on something else. She had become resentful and was forever angry and picking at Tim but doing nothing about it.

Through her tears she told Tim of her vision for the businessman she knew he could be. She outlined the fear, hurt, and anger that had built up in her. Tim began turning around immediately. He stopped lying around, sought coaching and training to get interview skills and launch his job search, and things began to improve immediately. Alexis's speaking from her heart not only saved their relationship but turned around Tim's life trajectory. And now Tim is beginning to empower Alexis to become a leader in her business.

Alexis finds that her emotions are becoming a trusted guide that she is learning to listen to and interpret with increasing effectiveness.

They still have a good deal of work to do on honesty and issues like conflict resolution, but they feel like the loving unit she had imagined when they first met. Turning the relationship around "is one of the hardest things I have ever done," Alexis said. "I'm learning that this is what it really means to have a fulfilling, powerful relationship and it is really worth it!"

Mistaken Beliefs About Heart and Emotions

When I first introduce people to the possibility of living the Way of the Heart, they often say, "You can't do that in the real world. People would take advantage of you. You would hurt other people's feelings." For most, it sounds too vulnerable even in a committed, loving relationship, much less at work or with friends. They are afraid of what others will think, that it will be too hard to do, or that they will look weak. They have been conditioned to believe that feelings are wrong or bad.

I come to four doors, closed at my heart: rage, denial, inertia, and loss. I believe most of us were taught to slam these shut, turn our backs, and lean up against them in fear. But I also believe that on the other side of these doors are passageways to our brightest fire, the choice to live fully awake and alive.

—Dawna Markova,
author

Our mistaken beliefs about the nature of emotions are the core of our repressed, denied, and deadened feelings. We all have mistaken beliefs about at least some of our feelings. We develop these beliefs by internalizing what we learn from family and our society.

And if you don't know how to deal with your feelings and you are around people who are expressing theirs fully, it can be upsetting. You are likely to think that people who show emotion are too sensitive or weak, or that something is wrong with them. The aliveness can also feel scary, unsafe, or threatening. Their aliveness is a reminder of who we could be or who we used to be. Rather than be that alive ourselves, we squash it in others. Sadly, society affirms our mistaken belief that emotions and aliveness are not okay.

If you are a parent, you have probably occasionally been irritated or threatened by the emotional expression of your children. Often, our discomfort stems from our belief that we do not have the freedom to express ourselves as freely as our children. At the same time, as a parent, your job is to socialize your children so that when they're thirty-five years old, they don't burst out singing at the top of their lungs at a board meeting! You need to train your children how to get along in the world while still teaching them that their feelings are okay and need to be expressed appropriately, not shut down or shamed.

The real job for each of us is to learn how to have that level of exuberance, spontaneity, and aliveness in our own lives, to feel our feelings appropriately, and to channel them into truthful expression. The first step is to be able to fully feel the energy and depth of your feelings. Then you can figure out how to channel them with aliveness and energy.

David screamed, "Shut up, I'm trying to work!" His five-year-old son stopped playing loudly and trembled in fear. David immediately felt terrible. He was working out of his home office and was scrambling to meet a deadline. Why couldn't he simply enjoy Sam's life and energy? He remembered getting the same reactions at Sam's age from his own father when he played loudly, and had learned to protect himself from his father's frightening anger by shutting down his natural exuberance. He had learned that it was too dangerous to feel in his own childhood. *Oh, God help me,* he thought to himself. *How could I be doing the same thing to my own son?*

He reached down and picked up the trembling child to hug him and apologize. His son seemed to understand when David told him how he needed to learn to sing and dance, too.

"Sure," Sam said. "I'd like to play with you."

Sam sang, "Ladeedadedah. My name is Sam, and Sam I am! Ladeedadedah. I want a cookie."

And David picked up where Sam left off. "I am mad I have this deadline. I am cranky and I want a cookie too. Ladeedadedah."

David still has moments of frustration with his son, but he is beginning to react differently as he learns to live the Way of the Heart.

Your Programmed Messages About Emotions

Think about some of the messages you have received about feelings. Most of us have received negative and conflicting messages with limiting beliefs behind them. We may have learned that crying and the expression of hurt are bad through messages like "Big boys or girls don't cry" or "I'll give you something to cry about." The belief that fear is bad

> *Our emotions are not the problem. The problem is our belief about our emotions.*

comes through in messages such as "You're a scaredy cat" and "There is no reason to be afraid. *I'm* not afraid."

The belief behind these messages is that hurt is bad: "You're too sensitive." "What do you have to be upset about?"

The belief that anger is bad and dangerous is behind these statements: "If you're going to be angry, go to your room." "If you can't say anything nice, don't say anything at all."

The belief that even joy is bad is behind these statements: "Why are you such a Pollyanna?" "Suzie Sunshine has arrived!"

If you aren't consciously aware of how much these messages and beliefs about emotions have limited your life, you can't examine them by asking yourself: "Do I think that? Does that seem right? Is that serving me? Do I agree?"

Listen to your heart and pick which messages you want to listen to and discard those that do not serve you. The choice is yours from now on: Which messages do you want to hear and live by?

Derek is a man's man. A highly accomplished businessman, former corporate officer, and an entrepreneur, he says, "I thought the goal in life for a man was to be stoic and even-keeled, making sure that no one could ever get to you, or at least not letting them know if they had."

He avoided pain and insecurities, and the underlying lack of self-esteem, by silently blaming everything on others and excusing himself. He admitted, "When I had a bad day at work, I might have thought about talking to my wife, but I would forget it as soon as I entered the house. When I opened the door and my wife asked me how my day was, all I'd say was 'Fine,' and then I'd withdraw. Little did I know that I was punishing her by withholding. I would get angry and seethe inside because she could not read my mind. She didn't know that I was upset, and yet I wondered why she didn't automatically comfort me. What really angered me most was her refusal of sex. She wanted to talk, and that was the last thing I wanted to do. So I spent the rest of the evening angry, picking on her and looking for ways to make her feel as bad as I did, to feel the pain that I felt."

On a journey I led to the sacred sites of southern France and northern Spain, Derek had profound experiences in which he opened his heart and allowed himself to express— and actually release—the pain he had been carrying inside. He was amazed to recognize the power of this expression. He realized that his withdrawal was actually an expression of anger and pain and understood that he had defined pain as bad, an indictment.

Derek began taking responsibility for his emotions, and to his surprise, he and his wife had better talks and much more meaningful sex. "I had no idea what we were missing." Derek realized he had a choice: "Expressing my pain and feeling the peace and joy that come after, or punishing my wife for not having sex with me so I could try to forget my pains from the day."

Derek's definition of manhood has altered radically. Now "being a man" means being responsible for his pain and seeking out the support he deserves. "Not only do I feel better, but my relationship has

> *Why are we afraid to go down into our pain? I'll go crazy, you think. I'll lose control. No one will understand or tolerate me. It'll destroy my family. Well, if you don't go into your pain, every single one of those things will happen.*
>
> —JOHN LEE,
> *therapist and men's movement leader*

never been better," he relates. "My wife and I feel closer than we ever have now that I am no longer blaming her. I am sharing my feelings with her instead."

The Costs of a Closed Heart

Closing our hearts and resisting our emotions cause us to suffer—which is much worse than any pain, fear, or anger we might feel. And while pain is necessary, suffering is not. When we open our hearts and express our feelings, they flow through us to completion. When we close our hearts, we remain in a stuck pattern of unexpressed emotions, which drains our energy and affects our outlook. We suffer when we resist feeling emotions, when we feel sorry for ourselves, when we feel victimized or put upon. Life then becomes suffering when

> *Don't be afraid to feel as angry or as loving as you can, because when you feel nothing, it's just death.*
>
> —LENA HORNE,
> *jazz singer*

we numb ourselves. Suffering is a choice that we make, not an inevitability of our lives. It is the opposition to pain, the denial of the natural functioning of pain.

A closed heart also leads to dead and lost friendships, unhappy careers, divorces, and estrangement from family. Add to that hurt feelings, avoided social situations, and a limited life, and the costs start to really add up.

And the costs have impact on our view of ourselves and of our own personal integrity. While learning to identify and express their emotions, people often tell me about these costs of closed hearts. They'll say things like: *"I really don't exist without my feelings." "I'm like a chameleon trying to figure out how to feel and respond." "I keep limiting my life so that I don't have to interact with people since I don't know how to handle my emotions. Pretty soon, I'm going to end up in a cubicle far away from anyone." "I'm missing out on life."*

"We all remember Mom in the kitchen, feeding our baseball team of a family. Nine kids were more than anybody should have to clothe, feed, and house. We said that she was a saint, but that wasn't fair. She was also a human being who knew loneliness despite the huge numbers of us around. We've all bragged about her ability to keep us in food and clothes, but more importantly, she showered attention on us to the exclusion of herself and her own needs. For her generation, that was a great act. But we can't say that we all turned out to be the happiest kids on the planet. She gave us enough, but we wanted more, and we didn't know how to get it." Thus began Chris's eulogy of his mother.

Chris grew up feeling hurt. The eighth of nine children, he had resigned himself to the fact that he had been a burden to his parents and family growing up, and that his feelings were, at best, a problem. After getting coaching in his career and launching his second marriage with a woman who was committed to communication, he started having more meaningful talks with his brothers and sisters. He was starting to practice the Way of the Heart. Some siblings liked it and some did not. He was experiencing and expressing all his feelings—hurt, anger, sadness, and joy—with greater freedom than ever before, and breaking a lot of his family's unspoken rules along the way. He heard all the comments again: "Why can't you just leave well enough alone? Just forget it. Leave the past in the past. Why do you have to dig up all those old feelings?"

But on that day of his mother's funeral, when he finished that eulogy, there wasn't a dry eye in the church, and even his toughest brothers came up and thanked him for his guidance, helping them say good-bye to her before she died and helping them deal with the transition once she was gone.

Chris's openness helped the family achieve a closeness through his mother's death that would not have been possible otherwise. Learning to live the Way of the Heart had tremendous payoffs in his life.

Imagine the cost to Chris and his family had he not learned to live with Heart. Closing your heart has immense costs to you and to the greater world around you. Closing your heart means you can't reap the gifts of your heart. Your creativity is sadly compromised. Your energy is lowered; you don't fully exist. You can't fully experience love, intimacy, or peace that you are meant to have.

The Skills for Living with Heart

There are skills you need to develop in order to live the Way of the Heart. Once you have accepted and honored your feelings, you need to identify them. You may not always know what you're feeling and it helps to be able to name them.

After accepting and identifying your emotions, you must learn to express your feelings fully and responsibly. You must learn to match what is going on inside you with genuine expression so that it's congruent and can be understood and seen by another person. For example, if you are actually angry but you are crying, that could send a mixed signal. When you're fully expressing, you learn how to have true emotional honesty—where your expression of the feeling matches the depth of the feeling itself. You learn to express the feeling at the level you're actually experiencing it.

And finally, you arrive at the natural state of your feelings, where they're flowing and can be completed, leaving you ready for the next experience. Think about a baby. Babies move from feeling to feeling as each one rolls through them. They cry at the top of their lungs, then coo the next minute, then giggle. You've

> *I've learned that whenever I decide something with an open heart, I usually make the right decision.*
>
> —MAYA ANGELOU,
> *poet, historian, activist*

probably experienced this after a big cry. Once you've finished it, it's gone, and you're ready for the next experience. You might even start laughing. Or you might get angry. We have the potential to be more like babies again. As adults, we can learn to restore the natural process of emotions within acceptable social limitations. On this journey of the Heart, you will learn to allow your feelings to flow, be expressed fully, and move on. It's daunting, but it's possible. And the benefit is a life fully lived—a life of MORE.

More Intimacy with an Open Heart

When your feelings are flowing and you follow the Way of the Heart, the possibilities for intimacy are remarkable. By dropping your guard and opening your heart, you are revealed, you are attractive, you are real. You connect powerfully with yourself and others. You are able to touch underbelly to underbelly, heart to heart, passion to passion, or anger to anger, matching in either vulnerability or full power. You are able to express truthfully and freely and use the power of your emotions to create more pleasure, to fight for quality in your relationship, to deepen your connection.

> As part of a couples' training, Ben and Kim engaged in an exercise where they focused on fully expressing their feelings to each other. They reported that they were blown away by their experience. Kim described the result as "a beautiful and powerful flow. We reached a level of intimacy we had never thought was possible. We cried, laughed, yelled, and even expressed pain with each other."

In fact, it was such a deep level of intimacy that they were almost uncomfortable with it. As Ben said, "We were so connected as a couple that it was actually scary. I've never experienced that kind of feeling and flow in relationship before. We would be yelling angrily at each other one minute, and then we would both be overwhelmed with love and adoration for each other."

Ben and Kim did not leave their newfound intimacy at the training. They continue to connect in ways that surpass anything either of them had ever imagined. And now they are teaching that training together, helping others to learn how to express their feelings to the fullest and reap the same rewards—the rewards of the heart.

A Conduit to Spirit

Just as the Way of the Heart creates intimacy in your relationships, it creates intimacy between you and spirit. You are able to express what is in your heart—your cares, concerns, joys, gratitude—and offer it up to spirit. Cry, stomp your feet, do whatever you feel moved to do. Just feel! You experience spirit directly through your heart. Your prayers become more spontaneous and personal, more heartfelt. You create greater openings for God to respond.

My prayers feel alive to me in ways I hadn't experienced before discovering the Way of the Heart. It is almost as if I am being prayed, rather than praying. Mystical experiences come to me through waves of unconditional love, visions of possibilities, or creativity, understanding, and wisdom beyond my own. It is difficult to explain the times I am moved to dance or cry, whether at healing sites like Lourdes, or places of ancient worship like stone circles, Egyptian temples, sacred mountains, or being with my loved ones, or coaching a couple, or on a walk in the woods.

I cherish the moments when our students begin to sense the truth at deeper levels, when they open their hearts and connect to others and the knowledge and understanding beyond them. Their spiritual experiences deepen whether they are Christian, Jew, Muslim, Buddhist, or in alignment with higher principles. They begin to believe in a universal intelligence and compassion because they experience it in their actions, deeds, and thoughts. They become more than they ever imagined possible, living the Way of the Heart.

You Have What It Takes

With the magnificent promises of the Way of the Heart, there is no excuse that justifies shutting your heart down. Whatever conditioning you have had, or hurt you have experienced, does not justify shutting your heart down and withholding yourself, not fully developing yourself, and contributing to what is wrong in the world.

We get hurt. That's what happens in life. If you want love in your life, you are going to get hurt. If you want to take risks, then you are going to get hurt, but you're also going to have a blessed, adventurous life that is worth living.

You are not fragile. You're just not. We all have pain. It's time to open up to it. You can do it. Joy and belonging await. To open to pain and to sorrow is to open to love and peace and bliss.

> *You don't have to worry about changing the world. Just follow the Way of the Heart and you will change yourself, and you will serve in the ways you were meant to serve.*

Care!

Open up your heart and allow yourself to care, really care. Let your love pour forth to all those whom you care about. Unabashedly share your caring. Let others know how much they mean to you. Compliment them, encourage them, comfort them, and exhort them to be their best. Let your feelings flow upon your face. Let your voice be filled with feeling. Share your passion; express your anger in the service of your caring. Share the truth of your heart.

> *Too often we underestimate the power of a touch, a smile, a kind word, a listening ear, an honest compliment, or the smallest act of caring, all of which have the potential to turn a life around.*
>
> —LEO BUSCAGLIA,
> *author and inspirational speaker*

Do not hold yourself back for fear of rejection or judgment. Do not hold back for fear of being hurt. Focus on your One Decision and know that you need not avoid feelings, for you are committed to the Way of the Heart. What is more important is to risk in the service of your heart. And allow your caring from your big heart to expand to encompass greater arenas—your family, friends, business, community, church or synagogue, service groups, and the greater world. Just care. And share your gifts with others. Be a guide to those who can use your expertise, and there are many.

The Way of the Heart is the way of love. Be the loving human being you were intended to be. Let nothing get in the way. Grasp the happiness that is available to you right now. Delight in being a child of God and share that delight as a loving agent of a loving God to those around you.

A World of Heart

Imagine our world if everyone lived the Way of the Heart, open to their feelings, allowing their feelings to flow through them, expressing emotions responsibly. Imagine if you could live the Way of the Heart, and through your example you led your brothers and sisters of humanity to express their hurt, their joy, their pain, their sadness, their anger. There would be no reckless expressions of suppressed pain or anger. It is in the withholding of our emotions that we turn to hatefulness and attacking. In the Way of the Heart, ultimately, there would be *no* violence, *no* war.

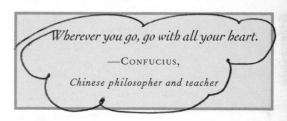

Wherever you go, go with all your heart.

—CONFUCIUS,
Chinese philosopher and teacher

We would have a planet where brotherhood and sisterhood are the experience of all, where we do not hide from ourselves or from our feelings. We would be at peace within, and so the world would be at peace. Where love is present in all of our hearts, we are able to see the truth—that Heaven is on earth, and that it is ours to experience. The choice is ours.

So let down your guard, crack the crust of your heart. The kingdom is yours. You are to dance and play in the fields of the Lord! Trust, take off your armor, and receive the gifts of spirit through the Way of the Heart. Embrace your emotions and sense the life force coursing through you. Open yourself to new ways of being and relating; finish past attachments, resentments, and unfinished business. Become your essential, most genuine self as you embrace the deeper truth of your emotions. Risk and reveal

your true self as you come together with others in the dance of the heart. Fill yourself with the love of the universe, radiate to others, and serve all whom you meet. You are open now, to pain and sorrow as well as love and peace. There cannot be one without the other. Love and peace are yours on the Way of the Heart.

The Power of Presence

Discover the infinite Power of Presence, the experience of being fully human, fully divine. Being present, you are conscious, awake, alert, available—you are the most You. Your heart is open, senses acute, creativity flowing, energy pulsing through you. And from this state anything is possible and everything is possible. Fully present, you command the resources of the universe. Expand into your Presence and feel the power available to you, the resources of the moment, as you ride the roller coaster of life. Float peacefully and rise joyously on the wings of possibility, as the Power of Presence stimulates, shaking you out of familiar patterns and ushering in the excitement of never-ending adventure. Open up all your channels to the gifts of the universe. Rise and shine and receive God's glory!

As you unlock the Power of Presence, you open a conduit to the infinite resources in the world around you. You are fully awake and alive, and have access to the vast information available from your senses, the wisdom of your heart, the energy of your emotions, the knowledge of your mind, and the wealth of your creativity and talent. When you live your One Decision, you are fully present. You bring yourself to bear in the world and receive the immense gifts the world has to offer. Also in this state, you make your best decisions, have the most power, and make the most impact. You attract support, love, and resources, and are able to make right use of all that comes to you. You become a source of inspiration for others. You are powerful, magnificent, creative, and the very most You you can be.

Tapping the Power of Presence is a decision; it is not dependent on a particular set of circumstances, years of training, or meditation. The Power of Presence is available in every moment—but you must choose it every moment. To unlock this resource, you must decide to be completely yourself—conscious and aware. Be alert, alive, and in touch with what is going on inside you and express it genuinely. With the Power of Presence, you are exquisitely aware of where you are, whom you're with, and what's around you. You are really able to see clearly because *all* of you is present. Your full Power of Presence is here, now, accessible, "plugged in." Through this power, you are able to use your senses and to have your feelings available, so that you are fully and genuinely manifesting who you really are and having significant influence in your world.

Limits or Infinity, Fog or Clarity

According to scientific research, in any given moment we are using only a fraction of our brain. How could this be, unless we are sleepwalking through our lives most of the time? The truth is that often we are not all there—we are overtired, hungry, stressed out, and spaced out. But there are moments of clarity when we wake up and become fully alert and alive. It can happen at any time—when we're in love, when we're full of rage, or when we're in danger. Suddenly, we're "on," and we discover just a little of our Power of Presence. Unfortunately, we don't stay there. We drift off, once again turning the "dimmer switch" until we feel shadowy, veiled.

Many people go through life allowing time to just go by, sometimes wondering to themselves where it all goes. Suddenly, you look and you've just been staring at the same computer page, writing that same paragraph. You're not focused and purposeful, not present, and certainly not powerfully present.

Our cell phones ring, our PDAs chime, our electronic calendars pop up with reminders. It's like a continual alarm clock trying to get our attention and yank us into the present moment, the here and now. But awakening to the present moment isn't enough. While the present is the only reality—apart from the past that no longer exists and the future that isn't here yet—this awareness is not enough. The present moment remains only a possibility unless *you* are fully alert, alive, and aware in that space, in that moment. The Power of Presence comes from your *presence*. You make "now" happen; you make this moment real and tangible; you empower the present with your energy.

Presence and the One Decision

When you make your One Decision, you choose to bring your full presence to bear no matter where you are or what you're doing. You choose to be conscious, to be awake and aware. The choice doesn't mean you won't zone out or avoid your feelings, but when you do get foggy, you can use your One Decision to reorient and tap the Power of your Presence. With the Power of Presence, you bring the other pathways to your One Decision to the forefront. Choose to be present to your Desires, present to your feelings, present to the Truth. Your consciousness is raised and your engine is revving so that you are open to experiencing MORE in the moment. You plant your feet where you are, claim your existence, and allow the unique gifts you were given to manifest right before your eyes.

Present and not present are an on/off thing. You are either present or not. Sure there are partial stages, the in-between zones—but if you consider life from the context of your One Decision, you understand that you are either "on" or you are "off." You choose to be either awake or asleep. You are present or you're not. When you are present, you can feel the universe flowing through you; you can feel your feelings, and you see things clearly, powerfully, and in Technicolor. You are aware and involved in the things that are there; your consciousness is reaching farther and farther, and

> *Life is what happens to you while you're busy making other plans.*
>
> —JOHN LENNON,
> *musician, songwriter, social philosopher*

your energy is flowing. Then—*whoosh!*—there is a surge of power, and you're cooking! You *know* you are present. You feel it. The difference between present and not is as discernible as day and night, cold and warm.

This is where true power comes from, because you can bring yourself to bear in these moments. You can bring your gifts into a situation only when you are really present. Only by tapping into your Power of Presence can you even exist. Only when you're really present are you really you.

Acting Present—But No One's Home

When you are not tapping the Power of your Presence, you aren't home. You may pretend that you are present, but you are not being authentic. If you are thinking self-deprecating thoughts or imaginative put-downs of others, if you are revisiting past hurts or imagining future catastrophes, don't pretend that you are all there, because you're not. If you are indulging in your Soft Addictions and are in a foggy haze, don't act like you are all there when you are obviously not.

Talking to someone who is not present or who is immersed in their stinking thinking is like arguing with someone who is under the influence

> *Presence is more than just being there.*
>
> —MALCOLM S. FORBES,
> *publisher*

of drugs or alcohol. The conversation can't go anywhere or get resolved, because they aren't really there. When both parties are using their Power of Presence, communication is clear and conversations don't get stuck in endless circles. Insight is increased, problems get resolved, and fights end in creative solutions.

I have plenty of evidence of this in my own life. Bob and I were having a rehash of an old fight. At least I think we were, because I didn't even know what the fight was about when I was in the midst of it. Bob said something to me and I went off, and I was saying the same things that I said twenty years ago! I was no longer really there.

The minute Bob says one particular phrase, it triggers a knee-jerk response from me. I spout off some familiar defense, but I am gone. I am not there. He's talking to me, and I'm talking as if I'm there, but I'm not. I keep responding as if I'm there, but I'm not. So the argument can't go anywhere. He can't reason with me to get out of it, because I am stuck on a track.

Finally, I admit it: "Wait a minute, I'm acting like I've got a full deck here, but I think I am only playing with one card, if that. I am not all here. I am not with you in this moment." Now I am back in the moment, living my One Decision to be conscious and feel my feelings and be a vessel for spirit, present fully on earth. I am back to myself, powerfully present and engaging in a real conversation. It's amazing what happens then. I become more vulnerable. I can see the truth more easily. I am clear. I share more truthfully and fully. I understand him and myself better. I feel closer to him, and my heart opens. We move from an immutable standoff to intimacy by embracing the Power of Presence.

Becoming more aware of when you are unaware is a first step to claiming your Power of Presence. Admit it when you are checked out. Don't pretend you are all there—it is actually more conscious to admit you are out of it. Even telling that truth can bring you more present.

Excuses Block the Power of Presence

Instead of taking on the responsibility to be present, we often blame our lack of Presence on distractions. We see something or someone else as the cause of the haze that envelops our brains, numbs our senses, and anesthetizes us into a stupor. How many times have you said to yourself, "If people would just leave me alone, then I could get some work done!" The truth is, even if people left you alone, if you are not fully present, you would still be frustrated and underperforming. You have misdiagnosed the problem. You blame too little time, money, and resources for your dissatisfaction, but not one of these is the primary reason for your underperformance. The real problem is that you haven't really shown up in your own life—you are only partly engaged. Instead of having access to your feelings, thoughts, and desires in each and every moment, you have unplugged your Power of Presence. All that's left is a very weak battery. No wonder you can't concentrate and nothing seems to get done.

Granted, being tired, being distracted, not having enough money, and feeling pulled in too many different directions at once does make it difficult to live your life to your highest sense of MORE. These conditions, however, do not need to defeat you. In fact, when you can harness your Power of Presence, then distractions and worries will not deter you from your One Decision.

Life, Presence, and the Present Moment

The Power of Presence is the power of life. Life happens one moment at a time. Life doesn't happen in the future, because the future doesn't exist. Life doesn't happen in the past, because the past is already done. Living your life happens in this moment—the Power of Presence is only available right now. There is no other moment than the one we have right now. This one . . . and then this one . . . and then this one . . .

When you are thinking about the past or imagining the future,

> *I have an existential map. It has "You are here" written all over it.*
>
> —STEVEN WRIGHT,
> *actor and comedian*

you can't be fully in the here and now, and your Power of Presence is diminished. This is not always a bad thing. Planning depends on the ability to review the past and project into the future. This, however, is different from the Power of Presence, when you are manifesting your total self in the here and now.

Our fullest potential of the Power of Presence occurs when we are present to what is happening right now. In the moment, you don't necessarily "know" things with surety; you sense. Genuinely sensing this moment is thrilling, like the feeling you get riding a roller coaster. It shakes you out of familiar patterns and ushers in the excitement of being present in this moment without knowing what the next moment will bring.

When you live in the full Power of Presence, with your emotions flowing and your senses activated, spontaneity happens—flashes of insight, creative sparks, solutions to problems, unknown resources, and heretofore hidden truths all burst through to awareness. You discover the source of a nagging feeling that you couldn't put a finger on before. You find new solutions to a problem. You make connections and associations that weren't previously apparent to you. You express truths that you might not have otherwise hit upon. When you are fully present, you don't know what you are going to say next—and then you are surprised at the wisdom that comes out of your mouth, or your rollicking sense of humor, or your amazing creativity. It's truly as if there is magic available at all times when you simply stay with this moment right here.

As you open up to the reservoir of the Power of Presence, life is full of enchanting moments and small epiphanies. You have revelations that can translate into life-changing actions. In these precious moments, you catch a glimpse of the divine, feel your feelings deeply, and feel connected and present. This connection might cause you to be inspired by a beautiful piece of music, spellbound by a magnificent sunrise, awestruck by the birth of a child, or simply soothed by gazing out a window at the twilight. You might be in a heated confrontation with your spouse, and truths pour out that you were not consciously aware of before. Or you blurt out the hard, but right, thing in a business meeting. Or you touch an undeclared yearning or receive a flash of insight. For the briefest of moments, you feel more like your true self. In that moment, everything seems clear. New things are possible and life seems impossibly rich because *you* are fully alive, fully engaged, and fully present in your own life. You have flipped on the switch, and your Power of Presence is flowing.

The majesty of MORE becomes apparent in these moments, but we need to pay attention to them. It is not an act of supreme will; it is a discipline of listening to and fully being yourself: present, conscious, and aware. By practicing being present, you begin to experience these moments, extend them, and replicate them. Even though the Power of Presence may seem abstract at times, the actual experience of the here and now is concrete—and profound. It is MORE.

"These were the days when I felt as if I was going to go insane, because I imagined that every day from here on would be as difficult as this," recalls Melanie, a working mother who was learning to tend to the constantly changing needs of her seven-month-old son. At first, she tried to keep everything under control and resented the time she was with him when he wouldn't "behave." He wouldn't eat something that he had previously liked. He wouldn't take a nap at his usual time. He wouldn't let her put him down even to get dressed.

But then she started realizing that her baby wasn't the problem. She was. She wasn't willing to really *be* with him. She wasn't presencing herself. She wasn't allowing her feelings to bubble to the surface. She wasn't talking about how upset she felt to herself or to anyone who could help. She was simply putting on a serious face and trying to brave it out, trying to be a supermom.

Once she remembered that her One Decision wasn't to be a perfect mom but to be herself, the entire situation began to change. She'd call another mom for support during the day, and she'd cry in front of her baby and not try to shield him from her upsetting feelings. In essence, she was more of herself. To her surprise, she started to notice that when she was more present, her baby was less agitated and calmed down more easily. She began to appreciate that, just like her baby, her needs and urges were constantly changing as well. She didn't have perfect storybook days with her new infant, but she did come to peace with the fact that perfect moments were not the point of her life. She realized that she needed only to engage and bring her full self to the moment to find the meaning and fulfillment she craved.

Energy and Productivity Come with Presence

With the Power of Presence, you can focus fully in the present without distractions; you will do things faster and with greater efficiency. When you are really present and conscious, you unleash great energy. You automatically have more resources; you engage with the world and overcome barriers. You are managing your life effectively, lovingly, with service for the greater good. Soon, you'll be looking for more and more arenas to challenge you. Your attitude to the world will be "Is that all you've got? C'mon, just test me, use me."

As you become more aware of the Power of Presence, you also notice that you feel the most tired when you are ruminating about the past or fretting about the future. You start feeling groggy, lose your energy, and feel powerless to do anything to get yourself going again. But you can make a powerful shift back to the Power of Presence. You just have to choose it. And then you have to rechoose it. In the here and now, you feel more alive, more awake, more conscious, more energized. The current is once again flowing through you.

"Closing two out of every three sales contacts! What a week," exclaimed Bruce. "But why do I wait until I'm completely behind and afraid of going broke to do this?" he asked rhetorically. Bruce had found that he could only tap the Power of Presence when he was in a terrified frenzy, scrambling to meet his minimum sales goals. Normally, he wasn't this productive—he allowed himself to get distracted, rarely making the number of sales calls he had planned to in a day. He was unfocused, slow, and tired. It was not until he made his One Decision and started bringing himself present that Bruce began putting more energy into his work, consistently closing a high percentage of his sales, even when he was ahead of his goal, and making more money than he ever dreamed he could.

Intimacy with Presence

Being fully present, we can experience intimacy. We don't need to be with "the one" or a romantic partner to experience this. We can feel closer to everyone with whom we have contact. Being present brings immense satisfaction.

When you go into the office and greet the receptionist, you will not be able to see her or engage her in conversation if you are only half there. If you see her at all, she will be little more than an object, and she will sense your distance and reflect that back to you. Your disconnectedness will be affirmed. But when you engage in the moment with full access to your mind, body, heart, feelings, intellect, and intuition, you will truly be able to see her. Even a simple "Hello" carries tremendous energy. A smile is electrified. Energy shifts and is transferred. What you receive in return gives you another energy boost, and so you connect in the moment through the Power of Presence.

In all the moments of your life, practice being fully present. When you tuck your child into bed, rather than trying to get through it quickly, open your heart to your precious child. Resist the temptation to focus on what you are going to do as soon as you turn the light out. When your spouse is angry about something, attend to him, be with him, see him. Be present and connect with him. Or, when you are feeling nervous before a date, be with yourself in that moment and acknowledge your fear. Be present to what may be making you nervous and attend to it or express your distress to shift the situation.

When you are praying, do your best to be present. Be with the experience of spirit, not just the rote repetition of words, to feel your connection with a power greater than yourself.

In all things and in all ways, experience the intimacy of the Power of Presence. I know it's a lesson I'm constantly relearning. Bob tells me he loves me daily. He is generous with his compliments, yet I don't always truly register his sweet comments. There are times I will look up and see him looking at me with an adoring look on his face, a slight smile on his lips, as he silently appreciates me. However, if I am not present, I miss these moments.

I frequently remind myself to catch these moments, to wake up, to see his look, to shake myself out of my reverie, disengage from my worries or my to-do list, and truly take it in. Then I am present and can accept his loving words or glance and let them nourish me. In turn, I feel appreciation for him and my heart opens. Love comes forth and radiates from my face. I experience love in the moment.

I am training myself to not offer a distracted good-bye kiss, but to be present and behold the man I love, my partner and my friend. Even in the early mornings when Bob leaves for work while I'm still sleeping, I'll respond to his good-bye kiss from my sleepy space, with a blessing for his day or a loving word. It is infinitely more nourishing to live this way.

> *The most precious gift we can offer others is our presence. When mindfulness embraces those we love, they will bloom like flowers.*
>
> —THICH NHAT HANH,
> *Vietnamese monk, activist, and writer*

Come to Your Senses

To be present, we need to use our senses—to see, hear, touch, smell, and taste. If you're not present, you can't smell the proverbial roses right in front of you. You can't even taste the coffee you think you crave in order to stay awake, or feel the chair you're slumped on. If you're not present, your senses are disengaged. Your nerve endings may sense something, but there is too much numbness between there and your brain for much to get through. It's like you've been given a shot of emotional novocaine. You know there should be some kind of sensation, but you don't feel it! Only when your senses are engaged can you smell, see, taste, touch, hear, and experience what is in front of you. Then you experience MORE. Then you feel more seen and more nourished.

> *The Power of Presence is something you experience, not just think about. To experience it, you need the powerful tools of your senses and your emotions.*

Learning to focus on your senses brings you more present. Stop for a moment right now. Listen. What do you hear right this moment? A hum in the background? Traffic noises? People talking? The whir of a motor? If it seemed quiet before you stopped to listen, the sounds will seem louder now.

It is calming to pay attention to your senses when you are present. It is almost as if the moment expands, and so do you.

I'm writing outside on the deck right now. I'm aware of a revving motor, birds calling to each other, a buzz from my computer, wind rustling dry leaves around my feet. Now I hear a plane overhead, a child singing far away. I'm more aware, more peaceful. I feel clear and present. It is almost as if time seems to stop and I become aware that there is so much going on! Amazing sounds surround me. I feel like I am part of them right now, in the swirl of life. No longer disengaged, separate, or removed from myself and the moment, I am here, now, alive, and plugged into the life around me.

Engaging in Experience

Accessing your Power of Presence is a goal of many spiritual disciplines and teachers who recognize its power. For many, meditation—a powerful tool with many benefits—is an all-around solution. I have often meditated to connect more deeply with myself. However, like any spiritual discipline or activity, it can become counterproductive when we

> *Each of us literally chooses, by his way of attending to things, what sort of universe he shall appear to himself to inhabit.*
>
> —MOHANDAS K. GANDHI,
> *political activist and*
> *human rights leader*

use it to detach from our experiences, to disengage from life, or to unplug from our Power of Presence. Then it becomes an escape from the Adventure rather than an exercise in deeper self-awareness.

Engaging more fully, rather than detaching, leads to the powerful experience of Presence—and you can access it anywhere, at any time, by fully engaging in your body, senses, and feelings.

Leading a workshop recently, I was trying hard to convey ideas and concepts that were important to me, and I was struggling to get my ideas across. My Presence was clearly diminished. I was painting a vision of the future when one of my students challenged me about the content being irrelevant to him, that it was too far out and impractical. Before I knew it, I was fully engaged in my experience. With no doubt in my mind, and tapping into the Power of Presence, I blurted out my real feelings for the message I was delivering.

My passion poured forth—my anger at how things have been in the world, my tears for the grief about how we have been living and how it must change, and my conviction and immense joy about the possibilities that lie ahead for all of us if we change. I felt like I was on fire. I couldn't have stopped the words that were flowing through me if I had tried. My real truth came pouring out in this unrehearsed Present Moment. The room erupted in applause. People rose to their feet, cheering.

The experience was powerful and energizing for everyone. Immense energy was flowing. It truly was a testament to the Power of Presence, fully engaged in my truth, my emotions.

Engaging in experience happens in ebbs and flows, and with our One Decision, we have a lot more flow. In the above example, it was not until

I was challenged and found the focus of my passionate message that I flowed and expressed my deeper truth.

Flow, Aliveness, and Truth (The New FAT)

When we tap the Power of Presence, we learn to communicate and connect with others on deeper levels. In this state of awareness, we solve problems, learn to share and listen, and become more intimate.

It's an amazing skill—to let go of storytelling and rehearsing old perspectives, and instead to allow yourself to discover the vast reservoir of wisdom and creativity that resides with presence. You'll be amazed to find how easily you can discern solutions to problems that have stumped you, to realize new possibilities, to clear emotional charges and discover treasure troves of information and ideas.

Welcome to the new "FAT"—flow, aliveness, and truth. Flow takes you out of your internal editor, aliveness takes you out of conventional behavior, and truth allows you to catch all the information, input, and data you had previously locked out of your awareness. This amazing communication technique unlocks the Power of Presence in your interactions with others.

Flow

When we are in the flow, we experience MORE. Flow occurs when we are fully present; it implies movement. Flow is a key element of our Power of Presence. It happens when we drop our self-consciousness and are more spontaneous and unedited. We are flowing when we are engaged in what is happening rather than trying to control events. We are in the present, not telling a story of the past. Flow means that we are dynamic.

To experience flow, you must tap into the Power of Presence in order to venture into the unknown where you are creating something new—a new thought, a new understanding, or a creative project. Your thoughts and feelings are flowing, and you are alive, feeling, and sensing.

Flow doesn't mean ignoring everything else in your everyday life. In fact, you only experience real flow when you are fully engaged in the world, in your work, in an activity for its own sake. The ego falls away. Time is suspended. Every action, movement, and thought follows inevitably from the previous one. Your whole being is involved, and you're using your skills to the utmost.

Flow happens only in the here and now. These will be some of your best moments, when everything feels like it is clicking. You are going with the flow; you are in that energized zone.

Aliveness

We are most alive in the here and now, when we are present and aware, feeling, smelling, touching, seeing, and hearing. Our senses are acute. Our hearts are open. Our thoughts are flowing. We are in our bodies, not just our heads. Through the Power of Presence, we feel connected to ourselves, to others, and to a greater whole. We feel vibrant, vital, and vivacious. Our life force is coursing through us. Our energy is flowing through us.

Aliveness can be expressed in high energy or movement, but it can be also be the quiet awareness in a still moment. It can be in rollicking humor, deep sobs, or creative expression. Aliveness unleashes your Power of Presence and brings you MORE.

Truth

As you tell the truth, you are present. Without Truth, you cannot experience being fully present. If you are not being truthful—if you are lying, covering something up, withholding information—you are concerned about the past and worried about the future. If you have a secret you don't want anyone to know, or if you're avoiding being caught or found out, you are worried about the future and maintaining your cover. You are not truly being yourself. You are faking and operating behind a mask.

Phil, a high-level executive, was considering leaving his job. He scheduled a meeting with his boss to clarify his role in the company, address some of his dissatisfaction, and decide how he could best contribute to the organization if he was to stay involved at all. To be fully present, heard, and understood, Phil relied on FAT—using flow, aliveness, and truth to achieve satisfaction and clarity.

Throughout the hourlong meeting, Phil consciously oriented toward flow, aliveness, and truth. He allowed his words to flow—he didn't edit what he was saying, he let himself express his thoughts and his truth and remained aware of his emotions. To increase his aliveness, he sat forward and straight in his chair, concentrating on his breathing, making eye contact, and heeding the clues of his emotions—the clutch of his gut, the thump of his heart, and the flush of excitement. It helped him stay clear and focused on the points he wanted to make. Several times, his boss became obviously uncomfortable and sought to redirect the conversation, but Phil kept flowing and went deeper and deeper into the truth of what was being discussed.

"What a ride! Rather than some predictable, managed, political conversation, we actually had a real and genuine exchange. I don't think he liked the conversation, because I challenged him and he was forced to take a stand," Phil admits, "but the outcome was great—not just for me, but also for the company. My boss is changing some of the policies that I felt were bad for the company. Now, I'm excited to be staying at my job, and I have also changed our company for the better."

A Childlike Spirit

When you are spontaneous, alive, truthful, and flowing, you are Present. You rekindle your playful, childlike spirit and experience MORE.

Children live so much more present, in the here and now. Children don't think: *When I get a million dollars in the bank or get that new job, then I'll be happy.* They aren't so concerned about the future and don't spend much time mulling over the past. They are fully engaged by what is happening now, and the thoughts, feelings, sensations, desires, and urges they are experiencing.

That is not to say that children don't get zoned out. It is just that we can see the contrast in them more clearly. The difference between a child zoned out in front of a video game and that same child's natural exuberant spirit when he is playing outside with his friends is unmistakable. It is children's lively, energetic, creative state that we want to emulate.

> *I tell you the truth, unless you change and become like little children, you will never enter the kingdom of heaven.*
> —MATTHEW 18:2–3
> *(New International Version of the Bible)*

Children are natural adventurers; they are curious and willing to explore and try new things. As adults, we need to reclaim our childlike spirit, to play more often, to be curious and aware, to try new things, explore, and experiment. Being childlike helps us be present and, as a result, step into the power of possibility. Rather than just rehashing past moments, we live the Adventure, following our urges, and we experience MORE.

Being present has a quality of play, where life is adventurous and happening in real time, right now! Children are growing and changing all the time. Their present isn't the same as their past. Likewise, our present doesn't need to be a repeat of our past. We can constantly grow and change and become MORE.

The Attractive Force of Presence

When you choose the Power of Presence, people will be drawn to you, attracted by your way of being and your energy. You become the kind of person that people want to be with, because they feel better after being with you and look forward to seeing you. Being present, you light up a room when you enter.

Your Power of Presence is an invitation to others to become more conscious. You can impact the state of general consciousness around you.

> *People with presence have an ineffable quality about them; they are "present," surprisingly attentive, and undistracted. A fullness, a centeredness, a wholeness radiates from them. We enjoy being "in their presence." You can build presence. It is the natural radiance of heart security.*
>
> —Doc Childre and Bruce Cryer,
> *founder and former president, respectively,*
> *of the Institute of HeartMath*

When even one person chooses the Power of Presence, it can elevate the entire conversation or activity. Yet the converse is true as well. Being out of it is catching, too. That is why it is critical to choose to be with people who are conscious and awake and to continually raise the baseline of your own presence. And it is also important to limit your Soft Addictions, mindless activities, and routines that mute your consciousness, because these ways of being are not in consonance with your One Decision and rob you of your power.

When you are present, it affects everything you do, everything you touch. The food you cook is more satisfying, the report you write is more powerful, and the loving gesture you share is more gratifying. Everything gets juicier.

Our presence is imbued in whatever we touch, including what we create. And whenever someone partakes of what we created, the Power of our Presence will be there, because it was part of the essence of it when it was created. This is true about all art, poetry, buildings, writing, and even food! If you read a passage that was written a hundred years ago by a writer who was present, it brings you more present. The essence is imbued into his writing, and you experience it when you read his words. You feel like you are having a conversation with the author, a hundred years later. If a painter was present when she created her work of art, and her creativity was flowing, you reexperience that when you see it. It is like when you see the Mona Lisa—there is a living presence, which is why we are all so fascinated by her.

As I visit sacred sites all over the globe, I am deeply moved when I touch the palpable Power of Presence imbued in these holy places. I think of the thousands or millions of people who have been present in these sites throughout history, opening their hearts—whether beseeching in prayer, being inspired to worship, desperate for healing, or offering up the

> *That which is created consciously retains the spirit of the creator. And so it is with us, created consciously in the image of God: We retain the spirit of the Creator. We are imbued with the consciousness of God, the embodiment of God's love.*

deepest cares of their minds and souls. That essence, that presence, permeates these holy sites. It is perhaps this that makes them holy—the imprint of all those who have been present, whether in ecstatic worship, deep pain, hopefulness, jubilance, or being moved by Spirit.

Being in the Presence of Spirit

Being present, we experience God. Our spirit. In this moment right now.

In this Power of Presence, we can sense that there is something bigger than ourselves, no matter how we may relate to it—as God or spirit, truth, consciousness, or love.

Through your Power of Presence, you access spirit and open yourself to that greater bigness that we are all a part of. The point is not just to think about God or spirit, or to engage in your disciplines, prayers, or meditation, but to experience the presence of the Holy Spirit, the Eternal, in this Power of Presence right now.

This is where mysticism comes from. A mystic has a direct relationship with God or spirit, the

> *Conscience is God's Presence in man.*
> —EMANUEL SWEDENBORG,
> *eighteenth-century scientist,*
> *philosopher, and spiritual explorer*

universe, truth, light, or whatever they align toward. In this moment, you experience your own relationship with spirit. You don't need to earn it, to study, or do good works. You don't have to go through another person. You can experience spirit right now, in your very presence—the moment of vastness, possibilities, and connection, where you are centered, peaceful, present, and alive.

In the Power of Presence, you can hear the whisper of spirit: "Be still and know that I am God." Be in the Power of Presence and know the essence of the Eternal. If we are made in the image of God, and God is awareness, consciousness, and presence, then any time we tap into our Power of Presence, we tap into the presence of God.

Step into the greater Presence—the province of the muses, divine guidance, the universal consciousness. Now you have access to the resources of the universe.

This, then, is home: not a place but a way of being—in the now, when all is well. You behold spirit in all its forms, from struggle to ease, joy to sadness. Imagine that God beholds you in your full Power of Presence, just as a loving parent sees the best in his or her child, just the way you are, right now; looking at you and seeing what's on your face and in your heart— seeing the little wrinkles at the sides of your eyes, the tear in your eye, and the delight in your smile. As you are present, you sense more of God's Presence and love for you. The Power of Presence is potent and beautiful. The Power of Presence is light. This is the divine emptiness, a sacred, infinite space, for you, in this moment, as you tap into the eternal presence, now and forever MORE.

May you enter the Power of Presence, a precious resource of boundless opportunity, of exciting adventure, new experiences, and MORE. To tap this energy, you must let go of the past, the

predictable, whatever has gone before, and give up your worry about the future, the what-might-happen. You must simply be present. Now. You only have this moment . . . and this one . . . as you will the next. Your whole life is a series of precious moments, as infinite and glorious as the stars in the heavens. How will you spend the infinite currency of your now? This is where true Desire resides and where all your urges originate and lead. Using your feelings, your emotions, and the sensations of your body, you arrive in your full Power of Presence. You connect genuinely with yourself, others, and spirit. You are here, now—powerfully present, and all is well . . . just as it should be. Peace, Joy, and Love to you.

The Life Quest

You are meant to be a hero of your own life. When you make your One Decision, you join the ranks of those who have done the same throughout history. As a hero, you embark on a quest that is yours alone—to seek, to discover, and to create yourself. To follow your Life Quest, you leave home—the comfortable and familiar—in pursuit of the magnificent destiny that awaits you. You are transformed on your Life Quest. Just as a seed grows into a plant or flower or tree, you transform to become someone new. The plant sends down deep roots while reaching for the sky, just as you go deep while reaching toward MORE. Do not settle for achieving goals or having incremental change or a small success in one area of your life. You are meant to transform your very being, to live richness in every area of your life! Your Life Quest ennobles you. Engage in it and step onto the path of becoming, the path of MORE, the path of your destiny.

A noble destiny awaits you as you embark on your Life Quest—the pursuit of your One Decision in every aspect of your life.

No longer dabbling, it is not enough just to enjoy the thrill of trying new things in the Adventure; you have now drawn a line in the sand. "I have made my One Decision! Once and for all, and from this day forward, my entire life is the quest for the fulfillment of my One Decision for MORE in life." This quest manifests itself in every moment, every day, and in every area of your life. It permeates your very being and becomes your way of being.

Your may have made a commitment for the pursuit of Truth, the Power of Presence, the Way of the Heart, Desire, or Adventure. However, in the Life Quest, you experience all of these aspects coming together in one powerful force.

Hero of Your Own Life Quest

A hero is one who commits acts of remarkable bravery and demonstrates strength of character. These are also the attributes of the Life Quester. By committing to live your One Decision in every area of your life, you show great courage—the ability to face uncertainty without being deflected from your course of action. Your character develops as you embark on your journey, as you engage with the tasks and challenges of the Quest.

Every hero has tasks to perform—whether it is to return the ring to Mordor as in *Lord of the Rings*, pursue the Holy Grail, or solve an ancient riddle. Your tasks, too, involve overcoming the source of darkness and distraction to your path, pursuing vessels of spirituality, and performing an alchemy similar to spinning straw into gold; you turn the mundane aspects of your life into meaningful, precious elements. However, as a Life Quester, you will not have one sole task to accomplish. Instead, every task of your life becomes an opportunity to solve the riddle: How do I live my One Decision in this moment? In this situation?

And like the heroes of old, the actual attainment of the Quest, or the object of the Quest, isn't what matters in the long run. What matters is the journey of transformation that occurs in its pursuit. While it begins with a destination, it quickly becomes the journey that matters.

The Life Quest and the One Decision

Your Life Quest is your commitment to live your One Decision in all areas of your life, at all times. It is not only claiming your One Decision—to be alive, to stand for truth, to be a creative powerhouse—it is making your life be *about* that decision. When you are on a Life Quest, you consistently orient to your One Decision, supporting others to do the same.

Your Life Quest brings the power of your One Decision into the world. Will you live your One Decision? Will you pursue MORE in all moments? Will you settle for incremental change, or will you completely transform the fabric of your life? This is the choice of your Life Quest: What will your life be about?

The Nature of a Quest

> When you are inspired by some great purpose, some extraordinary project, all your thoughts break their bounds. Your mind transcends limitations, your consciousness expands in every direction, and you find yourself in a new, great, and wonderful world. Dormant forces, faculties, and talents become alive, and you discover yourself to be a greater person by far than you ever dreamed yourself to be.
>
> —PATANJALI,
> *yogi and philosopher*

A Life Quest contains in its very nature unique attributes that move you beyond a series of adventures. While the Adventure trains you to take risks, go outside your comfort zone, and go into the unknown, there are those who will engage in the Adventure and new experiences simply for the thrill, rather than a higher purpose. A Life Quest demands commitment. You don't dabble in it or wait to see what happens before you decide if it is valuable or not. On your Life Quest, every experience is valuable, because you can learn from anything. And everything is in the service of your One Decision.

A quest forces you to leave home. Every historical or mythological hero on a quest goes off into far lands, new territory, challenging terrains. You must be willing to leave what is familiar or comfortable. You leave behind your old conditioning and beliefs as you explore and adopt beliefs that fit your Life Quest and your new view of yourself and the world.

With a Life Quest, you must be willing to surrender, risk your current way of living, and let go of the security of sameness. You purposely leave to discover something more fulfilling than what you already know. You don't re-create what you have already done or what the generations before you have done. You use the past as a foundation for you to spring from, to go farther.

The Quest is proactive. You go toward things and experiences, creating something new. It's called a Life Quest because it spans your life, an ongoing journey that grows as you grow—constantly expanding, enlarging, broadening, and filling in. In a Life Quest you may take a detour or stop for a time, but you never give up. You may feel that you have lost your way, or have dark thoughts, but it is all part of the journey.

A Quest is not about having some improvement in one area of your life; with your Life Quest, the entire fabric of your life shifts. A change in one area shifts all areas. It is a total, all-engrossing endeavor.

And lastly, a Quest comes with no guarantees: The Quest for the Holy Grail never resulted in securing its object. The quest itself was its own reward. It is your intention that sees you through.

"Adventure be damned," exclaimed Mark. "Just give me a good paycheck and regular sex." Despite his elite position on a national championship football team in college, Mark's vision of the Holy Grail was really his father's goal for him—graduating with a bachelor's degree in engineering and having no debt. Even though this meant he had no time for courses in his favorite subject, history, and even though it meant sleepless nights filled with anxiety, at least he was on track for the American dream—with a gorgeous girlfriend and a job with a top consulting firm.

A Life Quest was beyond Mark's imagination. His idea of adventure was a good movie and a night of frolicking with his girlfriend. It was not until he began living an Adventure by moving to a big city that his perspective began to shift. He started getting in touch with who he really was—tapping a full range of emotions that he vulnerably risked expressing with his girlfriend. She clearly did not like this new man he was becoming, and they broke up. After a job layoff forced him to rethink his aim and his personal Holy Grail, he chose his first major adventure—traveling to China to teach English. Still, he was not yet questing. His adventure was more escape than quest. It was not until he began to master Chinese and take courses in history at the University of Beijing that his quest really began. He had put the Way of the Heart and deeper truth behind his Adventure, and it was beginning to add up to a life he loved. "I never knew life could be like this. <u>I now know what I want, I am questing for love—love of history, people, language, and work I respect</u>."

Daily, Mark feels like he needs to pinch himself as he says in wonderment, "I love my life. I am determined. I am on a Quest with love as my beacon. This is living!" Mark had learned that love is not static and cannot be frozen but must be renewed. His Quest is guided by that love as he looks to become the best lover he can be, wherever he is.

Transforming, Not Just Growing

<u>With a Life Quest, from the moment you embark on the journey, you begin to shift. You are more you, but you are far from who you will become—bigger, deeper, and with broader reach. You and your life become multidimensional. Rather than merely seeing improvements in limited life areas, or in incremental changes, your entire life transforms. Make no mistake, this is a transformational journey</u>—the most challenging and rewarding way to go. Engage in your Life Quest and discover the destiny that awaits you.

> *The greatest quest in life is to reach one's potential.*
>
> —MYCHAL WYNN,
> *author and educational consultant*

"I tried going to clubs or out on dates, but they didn't seem all that interesting, so I would bail out. I signed up for classes and went to a few, but they didn't do that much for me, so I quit." This is how Amanda, a thirty-something executive, described her single life. After a promotion took her to another state, Amanda was shocked to realize how one-dimensional her life had become. Before the move, she had pretty much depended on her family and the friends she grew up with to fill her time and create her social life.

While Amanda had committed to furthering her career, she hadn't committed to furthering her life. Discouraged, listless, and going through the motions, Amanda asked to work with me. She wanted to learn how to settle into her new job and location, and how to meet people. She was surprised when I told her that none of these issues was relevant. She was simply facing the reality of not living her life as a Life Quest, a journey that would transform every aspect of her life. She hadn't envisioned the possibility of an exciting life. She was going through the motions, waiting for something to happen, rather than committing to her own Life Quest for MORE. Any attempts she made were piecemeal— a stab at creating a single life, focused career enhancement, alternately working out and then pigging out.

But her eyes began to sparkle as she starting seeing not just her single life but her entire life as an exciting opportunity rather than a liability. She knew that she'd be leaving behind her old way of being, that she'd be out of familiar territory, risking her current comfort for a true Quest. But she didn't care. Fueled by her Desire, she was ready to commit to being the person she was meant to be—an engaging and vibrant single woman, a leader, and a manager. She shared of herself more freely, started telling more truths to others, taking more risks on her dates, and expecting honesty in return. And people started responding to her and seeking out her company. As she observed, "I am not playing it so safe anymore, and it feels great. I feel like I am making my life now, not waiting for it to happen." She had embarked on a true Life Quest for meaning and satisfaction.

A Noble Cause

History and mythology are full of heroes and heroines whose lives are a Quest, who consistently break through barriers, overcome challenges, undergo trials, and have magnificent adventures—Moses' quest for the Promised Land, the Knights of the Round Table and the quest for the Holy Grail, Odysseus' quest to return Helen of Troy, Gandhi's quest for justice and independent rule, Mother Teresa's quest to care for the poor and forgotten. In the service of their noble pursuit,

> *A Life Quest must be fueled from a passion deep inside you so that there's a reason to venture into the darkness.*

they were willing to encounter tremendous challenges and obstacles—even wandering forty years in the desert. You, too, will encounter overwhelming odds as well as immense rewards.

It is your deep and profound commitment, your One Decision, which gives you a reason to go through obstacles, to plumb the depths, and to be uncomfortable in the service of your worthy pursuit. You would never go through these obstacles or face them unless there was a higher reason to do so. You would veer around them and wander off the path. Yet it is in these very encounters that the Quest transforms you. You find out what you are made of, what you are capable of, who you can become.

And living your Life Quest is very different from achieving a goal just to achieve a goal. You choose an entirely new way of being because you sense within yourself a greatness that has been waiting to be tapped. It's not the greatness of fame or achievement or external success, it's a greatness of being. And the satisfaction you experience from stepping into those shoes is what drives you on. A quest for quest's sake is simply another adventure. But a Life Quest as a way of being, deeply fueled from your Desire, is your destiny.

And this greatness, this presence that radiates from you, not only transforms your life but transforms the lives of those around you. If your One Decision is for consciousness, it is not enough that you become more conscious. You want it for those around you as well. You take a stand for the essence of your One Decision in your life. You take a stand for the Way of the Heart and feelings, and suddenly it matters greatly to you that those around you are touched by the power of emotions. You choose Truth, and your relationships, family, and community are all affected by the presence of Truth that you represent. Their lives begin to change, and suddenly there is an exponential impact in the world because of your Quest.

My Life Quest has taken me into vast new territories. It has given me a reason to plumb the depths of my psyche, to face my dark side, to heal old wounds, to weather ridicule and even attack. And through this, I have found depths of intimacy I never even knew existed, I have discovered worlds within myself, I have found out what I am made of, and I have found aspects of my character I hadn't known were there. I have become MORE, and the world around me is transforming as well. And as you continue your Quest, you will find that, unbeknownst to you, you are taking part in the transformation of life on earth as we know it.

Life Quests Begin with One Small Step

Many people's Life Quest begins with one small, and frequently unanticipated, step. Your small step may come to you in a victory that expands your vision, a trauma that moves you deeply, a problem you face that galvanizes you, a dissatisfaction you feel, a picture in the eyes of someone holding a bigger vision for you, or simply as a result of making your One Decision.

> *That's one small step for man, one giant leap for mankind.*
>
> —NEIL ARMSTRONG,
> *astronaut, first man on the moon*

Gandhi's quest to bring equality and freedom to India, which struggled under British rule, began in an unlikely way on a train ride in South Africa. Because Gandhi was considered "colored" under the country's apartheid law, he was ordered to leave the first-class compartment he had paid for and move to the third-class cargo area. When he refused to move, he was thrown off the train. He spent the night in a train station thinking about what had happened to him. It was that night that his quest began. He refused to accept racial injustice. Ultimately, his quest led to India, where he inspired millions and championed India's independence.

Most of the people I work with are fueled by one of two motivations. They either want more out of life, or they have a problem to solve. Often, they imagine radical solutions to both career and relationship problems, thinking they must travel far and change much. Soon, they discover that the journey's beginning, middle, and end are right where they are—facing challenges rather than escaping, engaging more deeply and fully, telling truths that had been withheld, learning skills they had avoided, and being fully present in the moment. While their journey begins with one step, it unfolds into a Life Quest—taking them farther, wider, and deeper than they had ever imagined.

William, an attorney and corporate governance consultant with a degree from a top law school followed by a prestigious clerkship, knew he needed to make a change in his life, but he couldn't decide between what he thought were his two options: Should he become an Outward Bound instructor, or should he start his own law firm? To pursue this vision, he came to the Wright Institute for coaching with Bob, who quickly discovered that William was looking for an escape, not a Life Quest. Not only did William have a large cost overrun on a project he was managing, but he was also recently removed from the partnership track at the firm where he worked. He was labeled a "net-taker" who did not generate new business.

A big wake-up call for William came at a leadership training course when a man he respected, the owner of one of the fastest-growing corporate law firms in Chicago at the time, finally confronted him and said, "I wouldn't hire you as a janitor in my firm." And to top it all off, William's wife was leaving him.

William's real choice had nothing to do with what new job he pursued. The choice was to escape, or to reshape the rest of his life—escape to the wild and a new job, or engage with the very real challenges facing him.

William decided to face the challenges. This placed him squarely on his real Life Quest, rather than Outward Bound. He learned to identify his emotions and confront the family issues surrounding his relationship. As his wife embarked on her own personal development, they began learning together how to reconnect and communicate. In time, they not only embraced their life together but also developed a partnership beyond their imagining. They have become a shining example for other couples.

In his career, William learned to really bring in new business, and he was giving so much more that not only was he back on the partnership track, but the top firm in the country—the one he always wanted to work for—recruited him to teach *them* how to sell and use more teamwork. He took that job so that he could learn to become the best corporate attorney and governance expert he could be.

Starting his own law firm, he sought to bring about meaningful change in how companies govern themselves and assure stockholder value. He knew this would affect his practice, as companies had paid him a lot of money to consult with their executives on governance and other issues; he felt there was still inadequate return from executives to many corporations. He felt that compensation was often too high and that governance and internal controls were insufficient. He went "public" with his concerns about responsibility and governance, putting together a conference with some of the best minds in business and academics, including a Nobel laureate. William wrote a breakthrough book, giving interviews to major media outlets and testifying before Congress. He did lose much of his business with CEOs, but his board business is booming.

Today, William is working with boards of some of the largest companies in the world, helping them with governance and compliance. He ensures that the investors really get what they are paying for.

> *On a Life Quest, you are seeking what was there all along—yourself, the precious gift you are.*

He's working with powerful people who look to him for guidance. And he and his wife have a beautiful daughter and are now both pursuing doctorates—his in education in corporate governance and hers in health care.

How's that for a Life Quest?

The Tools of the Quest— Vision, BHAGs, and Assignments

In order to live the Life Quest and fulfill your One Decision even more powerfully, you must learn to use the tools of the Quest. There are three core tools that will help keep you on your Quest—Vision, BHAGs (Big, Hairy, Audacious Goals), and Assignments.

Vision

Vision helps you create the impossible. If you can see it, you can do it.

To create a vision, you imagine your One Decision as it will manifest in the future. Vision is your purpose projected onto your life. It is a future reflection of what it is that you really desire in your life, identifying a conglomerate of impulses. Vision puts a form or a picture on your Desire, and represents your highest Truth, your Heart, and Presence.

> *The most pathetic person in the world is someone who has sight but has no vision.*
>
> —HELEN KELLER,
> *author and educator who was blind and deaf*

When you're in touch with your vision, you can feel it; it opens your heart. You can either think that you have to lose ten pounds, or envision being supple and light, flexible and strong. The first is a thought. The second is something you can feel in your heart. Vision opens your heart and mind, beckoning you beyond imagined limits. Goals are achieved with steps and plans, but vision creates the impossible. Goals are the stuff of the head, but vision is the stuff of the heart.

Your vision is like seeing a mountain and heading toward it. You climb the mountain, a major milestone in your life, as a result of orienting toward your vision, because that's as far as you could see. At the mountaintop, you

> *No matter how far a person can go, the horizon is always way beyond you.*
>
> —Zora Neale Hurston,
> *African-American folklorist and author*

look out, and you realize you're just in the foothills and there's a bigger mountain in front of you, one that you feel excited and compelled to climb. That's what happens with vision. Your vision shifts, because you see things that you didn't even know existed before. Without a vision you cannot dream. You will only fantasize.

My vision is constantly expanding—I frequently glimpse new, as yet unseen possibilities. Being married to Bob, I am constantly challenged to raise my sights through the influences of our life—the new possibilities he brings, my own emerging desires and opportunities, the curves the world throws us that demand creative thinking, and the examples of our friends and associates that constantly stir the waters of what is possible.

Through it all, my One Decision guides me to continually envision new aspects of myself—my strengths, needs, and gifts. In relationship to Bob and our mutual life purpose and respective One Decisions, I have discovered possibilities in relationships far beyond my original family and community programming. I didn't know it was possible to have this kind of relationship, partnership, conflict, resolution, and the resulting degree of intimacy that we experience.

I never dreamed that we would merge our businesses as a result of knock-down, drag-out arguments about methodologies, philosophies, and our different approaches. I could not have pictured back then that we would be so aligned in serving people, on sharing such rich lives of service.

I had no idea of the ranges of experience that relationships could offer—from engaging fully, finding creative solutions to problems, being able to cuddle softly, weep together, laugh hysterically, love and fight fully, share common purpose and passion. The same is true of my relationship with friends and colleagues. All of life is an ever-expanding vision of possibilities. Now I experience increasing levels of partnership with Bob and my world, which constantly expand and transform my vision.

Sarah and Gerard fought like cats and dogs. Quick to anger, quick to blame, their relationship was fraught with tension and sparks. As they sought help for problems in their relationship, they also began to see their lives and their relationship as part of their quest. They saw that their ability to engage and fight could be used to fight for something, rather than against each other.

While on a pilgrimage to Israel that I led, they saw their ability to fight as part of their purpose and claimed their vision as: "We are connected to one another, in relationship with each other and with spirit. We open our hearts to one another. We fight for what we want, determined to be satisfied and to satisfy each other."

Their vision is a powerful beacon toward which they orient their relationship. While they certainly forget it at times and spiral back to their old patterns of interacting, they much more easily reorient to their vision and purpose. They have ongoing assignments each week as part of their couples group. In their current assignment, which engages the battle of their strong wills, each person must spend one half hour in charge and the other must follow the lead. The previous week, they completed an assignment where they were competing to see who could hold the other in consciousness in the most creative ways—anticipating each other's needs, checking in on the other, leaving notes, seeking to please, and so on. These challenges remind them of their overall quest and train them to continually engage in learning new skills.

Simultaneously, they are both experiencing explosive growth in their careers and are much in demand in their respective fields. They are expecting their second child, rehabbing their home as a statement in a developing neighborhood, deepening their spiritual life through practices, sacred travel, and a Catholic-Jewish parents group, and continuing their personal development.

BHAGS—Big, Hairy, Audacious Goals

Another way to train for the Quest is with what Jim Collins, the author of *Good to Great*, calls BHAGs—Big, Hairy, Audacious Goals.

BHAGs are generally desires we find so impossible we would not even say them. Choosing the impossible forces you to stretch in the service of something that you really desire. BHAGs run the gamut—becoming CEO of a firm, bringing in $5 million or $500 million in annual revenues,

> *The final goal of human effort is man's self-transformation.*
>
> —LEWIS MUMFORD,
> *historian of technology and science*

losing fifty pounds, doubling the size of your business, creating a remarkable, alive, intimate relationship, and so forth.

Your BHAG compels you to take risks that you wouldn't otherwise have taken, develop new skills, make new friends, and God knows what else. Salespeople find new trends and products by committing to their BHAGs. Companies add and drop lines of business. Couples find new solutions to old conflicts. Parents partner better, and singles have more fun. Your BHAG might lead to seeming failure or you may not totally reach it, but you're going to have more self-respect by having proclaimed it. It reminds you of who you are and what you desire, and invites you into who you can become. It is one of the most useful tools in living your One Decision.

"No way. It's too late. Let's just stick it in a box and deliver it." Paul was the chief operating officer of one of the fastest-growing electronic arts firms in the country, and that was the sentiment expressed by his team developing some new software. Ten million dollars into the project, it had become a stepchild that the development team and management team simply wanted to eliminate.

Like red flags in front of a bull, a worm for a fish, a lamb for the wolf, however you want to describe it, Paul rose to the challenge. What others called impossibilities, he called opportunities. This was one of his BHAGs.

Paul stepped in, challenged the team, and led them to create top-performing software on time. He enrolled them in a

BHAG without ever calling it that. His ability to accomplish his short-term BHAG ultimately led to his being put in charge of the production for the entire company, one of the top software production houses in the country.

Now he has a BHAG over the next few years to acquire several new firms and grow the business even larger. He has already made strategic moves in those directions, and having his BHAG to orient to is what has made the difference. His comment is "We will either be great or be dead." My bet is on an outcome of great proportions.

The Assignment Way of Living

Assignments are invaluable in helping you live your One Decision. They help focus your attention and actions minute by minute and day by day. Assignments help you confront limiting beliefs and develop skills. Assignments serve as mini-quests; they help you focus your activity, act as reminders, and give you samples of real actions to take to live your One Decision every day. You will learn more about the power of assignments if you follow the 30 Days to Your One Decision at the back of the book.

Assignments can be used for a variety of goals from increasing sales to enhancing intimacy and augmenting prayer. They are great for building self-esteem and increasing just about any desired effectiveness.

Assignments range from asking for things to asserting yourself. Skills can be developed with assignments such as identifying one feeling an hour, identifying your likes and dislikes, getting positive attention, purposefully making mistakes, or any other behavior you want to develop. It is useful to report your assignments to coaches or friends.

Couples use assignments to learn to communicate and individuals use assignments such as identifying likes and dislikes to increase communication and self-esteem. In sales, they can include everything from asking for referrals to setting a goal of getting a certain number of rejections a day, which forces them to make more sales contacts. Ironically, the rejection assignment always yields more sales. Assignments become a way of living, focusing ourselves on learning and growing in everything we do.

A Responsibility to Live the Quest

You have a responsibility to find out who you are supposed to be, why you came to earth, and what God had in mind or heart when you were breathed into existence. It is your sacred duty to live your life so that you will become the most you can be. This is your divine destiny, the pursuit of which is encoded within you, and it is never too late to begin.

Like most people, unaware of your divine programming, you may have mistakenly applied your natural urge to Quest or pursue. Rather than pursuing the greater MORE, you may have invested your energy searching for the quickest solutions, the cheapest prices, or the fastest and easiest way to do something. The creativity, determination, and resources are directed toward these solutions but not toward MORE in your life. You misinterpret your urges and pursue magical solutions, Soft Addictions, and the "mistaken more" to try to find meaning. You end up with appealing distractions from a real Quest, which is ongoing and very personal.

But shift your focus and you will discover a Life Quest that

> *You are not here merely to make a living. You are here to enable the world to live more amply with greater vision and with a finer spirit of hope and achievement. You are here to enrich the world. You impoverish yourself if you forget this errand.*
>
> —WOODROW WILSON,
> *twenty-eighth president of the United States*

fulfills your One Decision. You will seek Truth. You will seek your heart's desire, and you will discover the precious, powerful, unique gift you are. You discover yourself as a child of a loving universe, placed here to find the richness of your heritage and the gifts that lie within you and others— while using these gifts in the service of humanity. On your Life Quest, you discover the truth that you and all of creation are magnificent and vast. You become an imaginative, creative visionary. You discover that you are gifted, that you're blessed and worthy.

This, then, is your Life Quest: to become and to know yourself through heaven's eyes, beloved and worthy and magnificent. And then to behold other children of the universe as your playmates. You're given the implicit job of helping them find themselves most fully. As you live your One Decision, your Quest means that you honor your natural inclination to help others. Those you help see themselves bigger than they've ever seen themselves before. Your support inspires them to dream bigger dreams and accomplish more than they ever dreamed possible. The beauty of your care translates to the flourishing lives of those you touch.

It is now for you to discover the dreams that God had for you when you were created. Possibilities or destinies have been held for you and prepared for you and offered to you—if only you will open yourself, risk, and seek the only prize worth winning. Go forth and pursue your Life Quest.

You have a destiny. Avoid it and you will experience less. Follow it and it leads to MORE. On the Life Quest, you discover who it is you really are at your core, your most essential, most sparkling self, whom God had in mind when you were made. Your life of MORE surpasses your wildest dreams, not your magical solutions of imagined financial gain or retirement bliss, but the greatest service and satisfaction of uncompromisingly

being yourself, a unique force of nature, part of God's plan. You become the hero of your life journey. This calling is a noble, sacred duty. It is inspiring and daunting, but that's what brings forth courage, and that is what makes life worth living. It is powerful, humbling, and awe-inspiring.

The Keys to the Kingdom

Encoded within you are the Keys to the Kingdom, powerful tools that will allow you to open the gates to heaven on earth. With these keys you will discover a treasure trove of possibilities and a richness beyond your imagining. The Keys to the Kingdom are a unique set of principles that can help you live your One Decision—bringing satisfaction and value to everything you do. Unlocking meaning in every moment, they will inspire you to live a life of joy. The Keys to the Kingdom are yours to use, anytime, anywhere, with anyone and in any circumstance. Learn to use them and open the door to MORE.

It was here all along—the secret to happiness and satisfaction. Locked away, awaiting your discovery, are the means to create heaven on earth. Now it is time to discover the keys encoded within you to unearth this buried treasure and reveal its bounty.

The Keys to the Kingdom are a set of tools that will aid you in remaining true to your One Decision each and every moment of each and every day. A set of powerful Principles, these Keys can open the door to satisfaction in everything you do and bring meaning to every moment. You don't have to wait for ideal circumstances or do things perfectly to live your One Decision and experience MORE. Learn to use these Keys and you can unlock the power of each situation.

Many people think and act in big broad strokes but miss the potential available in every moment. You can use these Keys to unlock the secrets of MORE in any circumstance, at any time. These Principles are the very foundation of life, the source of all meaning, fulfillment, and adventure. They unlock the wisdom within.

Strength, Courage, and Wisdom Within

Encoded within each of us are immense resources of wisdom and power, courage and strength, just waiting to be tapped. And once we have unlocked these resources, life comes tumbling out richer and more abundant than we ever thought possible. We discover everything we need to cope with difficult situations, and to constantly realize our highest potential and our greatest good. No longer lost or adrift, we may finally discover our full magnificence. This is where our true power lies.

> *Strength, courage, and wisdom . . . it's been inside of me all along.*
>
> —INDIA.ARIE,
> *singer and songwriter*

This is a goal of many spiritual traditions. It is what Christ was able to do at the moment of his death: to orient to the principle of love while being tortured and crucified. This is what we are capable of—it is not beyond any of us. All of us have had moments when we have risen to something higher, whether it was to ignore our own needs for the greater needs of another, to find gratitude in our hearts, to align to excellence in the work before us, or to beautify our surroundings. These actions are not merely the province of the saints, they are the province of every human being. It is ours to recognize this vast resource within us and to train ourselves to touch it again and again. But in order to do this, we must constantly align ourselves with the key Principles I call the Keys to the Kingdom.

The Keys to the Kingdom—The Principles

The Keys to the Kingdom are the guiding Principles of MORE. They set the standards for our actions. Orienting to Principles creates a foundation for everything you do, whether it is lunch with your friends, your morning routine, a business meeting, leisure time on a Saturday afternoon, a cab ride to the airport, or dinner with your family. Rather than waiting for something to happen or wandering aimlessly in a suspended state, you orient to a principle and animate that event, creating a sense of meaning and purpose. Living with Principles means that you never have to be in a boring business meeting again, or have an unsatisfying interaction, or lose precious opportunities, or waste an hour or even a lifetime. You can create value and feel satisfaction in everything that you do, with anyone, in any circumstance—a lesson I have learned through my own experience.

> *Live with intention. Walk to the edge . . . Play with abandon . . . Choose with no regret . . . Continue to learn. Do what you love. Live, as this is all there is.*
>
> —MARY ANN RADMACHER,
> *artist*

I used to feel hopeless about ever being satisfied. Bored to tears in my school classes, feeling stuck in interminable business meetings, waiting for a bad date to be over, and succeeding at careers without ever feeling complete, I trudged on in a state of despair. I was forever hoping that somehow the next class, or the next project or maybe even the next guy or the next year would be better and then I would be satisfied.

Then I discovered the power of Principles. Having made my One Decision and marrying my second husband, a dynamic demanding presence, I was forced to learn to assert myself or I would be overrun. Bob had made it clear that he supported my satisfaction and he was more attentive than any man I'd known, but it was still up to me to carve out space with him, whether we were alone or leading a seminar together. Politely taking turns was not his style. I needed to be more alive and engaged to keep pace with him. I found that I could actually disagree with him in front of a class. Truth became our yardstick. Conflict became an inquiry into truth and an opportunity to grow in understanding and personal strength.

My intention to be satisfied guided me into many different situations and helped me choose the principle that would best serve in the moment. A dinner party with my friends was an opportunity to help one another solve problems and pursue our dreams—the principle of beauty and sacredness. My coaching and training activities are exercises in practicing the Principles of compassion, understanding, and the intention to be satisfied. I've learned that my best teaching only happens when I am satisfied, and I am satisfied when I follow the Principles.

Satisfaction, meaning, and love are available for me in every moment of my life when I use Principles—which is why I call them the Keys to the Kingdom.

Principles can drive everything you do. Every action or thought, whether voluntary or involuntary, conscious or unconscious, is animated by Principles. By their very nature, principles are either creative or reactive—and both types are necessary to recognize and take responsibility for as we learn, grow, and develop. Our aim is not to deny reactive Principles but instead to raise our awareness

> *All behavior has an underlying assumption or standard behind it. All of your thoughts and actions are guided by Principles. To the degree you align your thoughts and behavior to positive Principles, you create MORE.*

of which Principles we're orienting to in any moment and to choose our focus consciously.

As you learn to proactively align your thoughts and actions to creative Principles, you experience a powerful compounding effect where one act made in harmony with a creative principle improves your life in multiple areas. For example, when you become more alive at work, you naturally become more alive at home and with your friends. Similarly, when you begin telling the truth more at home and with your friends, you will naturally start telling truth at the office.

The Keys and the One Decision

Since each of us is always living according to some principle, the only question is: Do your Principles guide you powerfully forward or not? Do your Principles attract what you Desire, do they lead you toward your One Decision, do they bring you MORE, or do your Principles limit you and hide the glimmer of what is possible?

The choice is yours: Which Principles do you choose to embrace?

Aliveness or deadness?
Here and now or there and then?
Play or avoidance?
Intent or victimhood?
Truth or deception?
Responsibility or blame?
Choice or circumstance?

To experience MORE, choose to live each moment of your life guided by creative Principles. It is this basic and this profound. When you activate the Principles in your life, you are transformed.

Living a Principled Life

Each of our lives can be characterized by the Principles we hold dearest. Look around you and you will see that the people in your life embody certain principles. My husband, Bob, is a walking embodiment of the Principle of truth. Others I know are characterized by their principles of aliveness, compassion, playfulness, or grace. What Principle or Principles define your life? Ask others what they see strongest in you. Nurture this identity and you will feel a profound shift in your life.

The Principle of Aliveness

Making the One Decision will require a fundamental awareness of what it means to be truly alive, for aliveness is the Principle from which all others spring. Aliveness activates all other Principles, whether it is play, as a mother happily pushes her laughing child on the swing, or intention, as a linebacker hungrily eyes the football before a play. This is the Principle of life in action, the key that unlocks greater meaning, substance, and direction. In each moment, we must ask ourselves: Am I enhancing or suppressing life?

> . . . Ask yourself what makes you come alive. And then go and do that. Because what the world needs is people who have come alive.
>
> —HAROLD WHITMAN,
> philosopher and theologian

When we learn to live according to the laws of aliveness, we are in tune with the world. Riotous laughter, full-blown rage, heated passion, or holding hands watching a sunset and meditating in blissful peace can all be expressions of aliveness. Follow the Principle of aliveness and you will never be bored. You will take risks and become aware of possibilities you never imagined, constantly learning and growing.

Being fully alive means that, in each and every moment, you are the essential you, the you at your very core. Allow aliveness to be your beacon and you will move from fearfully frozen to tentatively engaging, from feeling stuck to speeding forward, from opposition to an open consideration of possibility. Ray Bradbury illustrates aliveness powerfully in *Dandelion Wine* with this scene of a twelve-year-old boy learning about life one summer as he experiences the awareness of being alive:

I'm alive, he thought. . . . Birds flickered like skipped stones across the vast inverted pond of heaven. His breath raked over his teeth, going in ice, coming out fire. Insects shocked the air with electric clearness. Ten thousand individual hairs grew a millionth of an inch on his head. He heard the twin hearts beating in each ear, the third heart beating in his throat, the two hearts throbbing his wrists, the real heart pounding his chest. The million pores on his body opened. . . . "Tom!" Then quieter. "Tom . . . does everyone in the world . . . know he's alive?"

The Principle of Play

To play is to be fully alive in the present moment. In a here-and-now interaction with yourself or someone else, play will encourage you to grow and be nourished. When we are at play, we are curious, experimental, and open to new possibilities.

> *There is work that is work and there is play that is play; there is play that is work and work that is play. And in only one of these lies happiness.*
>
> —Gelett Burgess,
> *artist, writer, humorist*

In fact, just the other day I saw how the Principles of aliveness and play were woven into my experience. At some point in the morning, hard at work on this book, I began to feel drained. Then, I tuned into the stirring piece of music playing in the background, bounded out of my chair, and twirled around with arabesques as the song played. I was a prima ballerina! Then my writing felt like play as I toyed with ways to express these concepts.

Throughout the morning, as I worked, I danced a jig to Irish music pouring through the speakers, read jokes out of a good joke book out loud, lit candles at our home altars, and prayed for my writing.

In the middle of another full session of writing, I took a break, prayed, and did a meditation for the soul of a friend's grandmother who had recently died. After working all morning, I took a magnificent bike ride in the countryside, was moved to tears when thinking about an inspirational story of one of my personal heroes, and went to lunch with Bob, where I read a hilarious passage from a book aloud and we laughed until we cried, attracting the attention of our waitress, who shared our joke and wound up chatting about her upcoming move to another state.

That evening, I shared a luscious barbecue outside on our picnic table while watching the sunset and warmed up with a dip in the hot tub in the twilight.

As I review just a few instances of my play during the day, I am now reexperiencing all the aliveness with myself dancing, with the book, and with Bob. I was truly nourished and believe I grew, and am growing even more, as I write this.

The Principle of Intention

To have intention is to be fully alive to your Desire, to give full expression to all of your wants, urges, and resistances. One of the most vital Keys to the Kingdom, the ability to activate intention in one's life, is a crucial aspect of living your One Decision. Learn to ask yourself, "What is my intention in this moment? Where is my true path?" And very soon you will begin to reap the rewards of this powerful Principle.

As my time with my husband is extremely precious to me, I use the Principle of intention for all of my time with him. In fact, Bob and I attempt to use nearly every moment that we are together meaningfully and well. We make it a point to discuss concerns, address questions, exchange sweet anecdotes from our day, dig deeper into issues, or share some humor or a sense of spirit. Whenever I meet Bob for lunch, I've got an agenda. Sometimes my intent is to solve a problem or get his

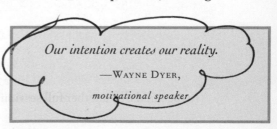

Our intention creates our reality.

—WAYNE DYER,
motivational speaker

input on something so I can move ahead. Sometimes my intention is to share more fully about our days so we feel closer to each other. Sometimes it is to be there for him, to be a sounding board. There is a stated purpose to each of our interactions. And as a result, we both are more nourished, satisfied, and feel closer from our encounters. Magic happens out of these experiences.

When I share this with people, they often judge it as being controlling or lacking spontaneity. But it actually creates *more* opportunity for spontaneity, because we are engaged with each other immediately. We waste few moments and are present in the moment with each other a good part of the time. Once we start the conversation, we don't know where it is going to go or what's going to happen, but we are committed to making it meaningful. We intend to be satisfied, and we are.

The Principle of Responsibility

> With responsibility, you see yourself as the creator, not the victim, in your life.

Responsibility is aliveness in your committed way of being. With responsibility, you see yourself as the creator, not the victim, in your life. You hold yourself accountable for the gaps between your behavior and your stated ideals and desires. You no longer accept excuses from yourself.

Kendra discovered the power of the Principle of responsibility in her job when she took charge of her own career.

"I wanted more career satisfaction, but I expected my boss to be responsible for my development. The result of not taking responsibility for my own professional growth and development was that I did not command the salary, recognition, or leadership opportunities that I desired," she said. "More important, I did not have good relationships with my boss and other people in authority. I avoided resonsibility in many ways. I blamed them for not promoting me and assumed I was a victim of racism, and I blamed the fact that I am black, for my lack of career fulfillment."

When Kendra oriented to responsibility, she began taking total responsibility for her position, her bosses, and the entire company. Her professional development became a necessary tool for her to assure the success of the organization, her boss, other company leaders, her peers, and her employees. Her vision of success shifted from entitlement to ownership. As the owner of her own success, she decided to engage more at work, take on assignments as they came, and discover and define her own leadership opportunities. She actively sought opportunities to partner with her boss to set priorities that were aligned with his, and to recognize problems and commit to their solutions, regardless of whether the problems resided in her functional area or not.

"By orienting myself to the Principle of responsibility, I experienced a remarkable shift, and the results have been tremendous," Kendra shared. "My salary has doubled, I have been promoted three times in four years. I am viewed as a service-oriented problem-solver. I have low staff turnover and I have people who seek me out to work for me. My boss and I partner to create a better department, and I am invested in the success of others."

The Principle of Choice

Our lives are built, moment by moment, through the choices we make, the acts we engage in, and the acts we eschew. And each of our choices is guided by Principles, whether we realize it or not.

> It's choice—not chance—that determines your destiny.
>
> —Jean Nidetch,
> founder of Weight Watchers International

Every reaction we have to our world is determined by choice. Choice and responsibility go hand in hand. To accuse others or turn inward in self-hate or guilt is not to act responsibly. To act responsibly is to simply acknowledge what is so. When I accurately assess situations, my choices are more effective. I make appropriate adjustments. One common misdiagnosis relates to guilt and shame. Too often, we think these are immutable feelings that have suddenly descended upon us, rather than what they truly are: the results of choices we have made.

True power lies within us. It is the power that is released when we use our free will to choose what is life-affirming, life-giving, life-healing, life-celebrating, life-deepening, and which gives meaning to our lives. The true power of Principles is perhaps no more aptly revealed than through Viktor Frankl's story.

In the most hellish of circumstances, Viktor Frankl discovered the power of choice. A psychiatrist in Nazi Germany, Frankl was imprisoned in several concentration camps during World War II. With no control of his external circumstances, in the most dire of situations, Frankl discovered that he still could have control; that no one, no matter what they did, could take away the control he had of his internal state. No one—not the guards, the feared Gestapo officers, or anyone else—could be in command of his attitude and internal state.

Frankl realized that he could choose to reexperience the love and warmth of his wife, even when walking in thin clothing during extreme cold, goaded and beaten by guards. He was shocked at how he could alter his experience by choosing what he oriented to internally.

He then began to study the differences between the people who survived the concentration camps and those who died. They all endured the same physical conditions, the same diet, and the same rigors—so why did some live and some die? He discovered that those who lived created a sense of meaning despite having no control over their circumstances. They oriented to higher Principles of creation rather than victimhood—whether it was helping others, showing dignity, being loving, or by taking other actions. They chose their attitude and their responses. When they operated according to these Principles, they controlled how they guided their lives.

As Frankl reminds us: "We must never forget that we may also find meaning in life even when confronted with a hopeless situation."

Using Principles can literally make the difference between life and death. Even if it isn't our physical death, the Principles make the difference between really living and deadening our lives. Those who find meaning, find life. Those who do not, cannot really live. This is immensely profound wisdom.

> *I am come that they might have life and that they might have it MORE abundantly.*
>
> —John 10:10
>
> *(King James Version of the Bible)*

The real secret to the meaning of life is that it is within us. It is *the* secret that brings us life and brings it more abundantly.

Exponential Benefits of Principles

In any given situation, it doesn't really matter which of these Principles you choose. Aiming toward any one of them will lead you to reap the rewards of all of them. If you orient toward truth, chances are you're going to be more alive and more engaged. If you engage, you'll probably tell the truth more fully. If you're playful, you'll become more alive. You won't ever pick a wrong one; you just have to pick one.

Using the Principles brings you true security no matter what your circumstances. This is new thinking for most people, for whom safety and security mean being in control. When they can't control their circumstances or things feel chaotic, they feel insecure, fearful, and unsafe. They try to control things in their world to feel less scared, more secure, and to have more certainty.

> *Using Principles brings you true security no matter what your circumstances.*

Learn to constantly orient yourself to these or any other life-affirming Principles. And, like Frankl, you will always have control—not of the world, but of yourself. With Principles, you define control differently. Rather than trying to control everything outside yourself, you just control yourself. You can't always make everything happen the way you want on the outside, but you can always choose what goes on inside you. Rather than trying to rein in the universe to feel secure, you go inside and orient to these Principles. And you can always operate according to a Principle, at any time and in any situation. You can orient toward a Principle such as aliveness, truth, or even love no matter where you are and whether your situation is wondrous or hellish or something in between.

Emulating Our Heroes

It is important to have heroes—people who you believe are living according to higher Principles—whom you can strive to emulate. These are the individuals who provide us with examples, who give us glimpses of what is possible.

Yet too often we see the power of the person's life and decide that they are beyond us, that we can't do what they do, that they are exceptional and different from us. We become jealous or hateful toward them because we think they have what we lack. Rather than put the person on a pedestal or, conversely, try to knock them off, we can choose to see how they live and identify the principles toward which they align. Rather than just thinking, *Oh, isn't she amazing,* we can ask ourselves, "How does she live, to what Principles is she orienting, and how can I do that in my life? How did Jesus live and how could I do that in my life? How did Martin Luther King live and how can I do that? How did Mother Teresa live and how can I do that?" When you look at athletes, rather than just admiring their accomplishments and seeing them as entirely different from you, see their commitment to excellence and consider how you might replicate that in your own life.

Whoever these amazing people are, look beyond the person and see the Principles that are at work in their lives. Your heroes didn't come out of the womb fully developed and accomplished; they oriented to Principles moment by moment and created the life that you now admire.

Principles and Life Quest

Principles are fuel for your Life Quest. By orienting to creative, life-enhancing Principles, you are engaging in your Life Quest no matter where you are or what your circumstances. As you pass through different life phases, events, and transitions, orienting to Principles ensures you are living your Quest.

Marie is a Life Quester, a world-class marketing expert in her second marriage with a loving husband and second child on the way. Her life is great and she loves it. But this was not always the case. In the past, her high-powered job was an extension of her thrill-seeking nature. She was easily bored. To feel more alive, she was always seeking excitement and living on the edge—from skydiving to scuba diving to driving fast cars. Her first husband started to look stodgy to her, a bit of a drag. Seeking aliveness in an affair with an older man, she then ended her first marriage. Marie saw herself as a woman on a Quest, yet she was actually a thrill-seeker following limiting or reactive Principles until she sought training—where she was shocked to see herself as an avoider, rather than a Quester.

> *We may be personally defeated, but our principles, never!*
> —WILLIAM LLOYD GARRISON,
> *nineteenth-century abolitionist*

Marie's father dropped out and became a street person when she was four and her little sister was still a toddler. Her mother was promiscuous and brought boyfriends home regularly. Money was scarce, and time with her mother was even scarcer. At a very early age, Marie was charged with going to the store to buy food to prepare for herself and her sister.

Early in her life, she had been as much of a Life Quester as she could be. Her Quest began with both creative and reactive principles. She fought off the pity of neighbors, who looked down on her for her promiscuous mother and drunk of a father, to become a top student, musician, and school personality. Winning full scholarships to the best schools, she became an MBA-level marketer who took her brand from obscurity to national prominence, where it still stands twenty years later. But she had taken her Quest as far as she could, and her vision was limited. She had gone beyond anyone in her family, and at that point, reactive thrill-seeking took the place of real questing and following creative Principles.

Creative Principles did not start guiding her Life Quest consciously until she took responsibility for her failed marriage and learned to live the excitement of aliveness every day of her life. She was discovering the thrill of the Life Quest with full aliveness, play, and commitment. She learned to play and interact fully with her second husband—and she learned to focus her intent into a steel-willed commitment to be the mother her own mother was not and the provider her father was not.

She learned to play with others fully, becoming a valued advisor using truth as her guide, taking her into deep areas of pain and joy that lay hidden, locked away in her childhood attempts at survival.

Marie's Life Quest is truly heroic. There are no simple, beautiful endings, but the results she is creating by living a principled life are remarkable.

Principled Families

I have worked with many families who have learned to live by Principles on their vacations, in relationships, in school, and at home. We introduce children to principled living on weekend adventures devoted to parents and their young children. The kids commit to stand tall, talk true, play hard, do their best, and have fun. The families then evaluate their own and each other's behavior according to these simple agreements. The results are amazing. Not only do children (and their parents!) reduce their pouty, sullen behavior, but also parents excel at work and children thrive both socially and at school.

Some families have family dinners to choose Principles for the upcoming week and report in on how they did the previous week. Other families use Principles to set up communication standards—for example: have respectful exchanges, answer when spoken to, greet one another, take responsibility, don't blame. They give one another encouragement and help one another solve problems.

"It was our best vacation ever!" exclaimed Sharon about their family trip with their six- and eight-year old daughters. "The girls took responsibility to pack their suitcases and pull them wherever they went. Each of us picked our own Principles for the trip: my youngest picked 'fun' and the oldest picked 'courage.' Bill chose 'adventure,' and I selected 'gratitude.' At the end of the day, we reviewed all of our adventures, experiences, and ups and downs. At the end of the vacation, we even did a closing sunrise ceremony! It was so special for all of us."

Sharon and Bill have integrated Principles not just into their vacations but throughout their family life. At the start of the year, each family member chooses a personal Principle and then comes up with goals they want to accomplish using that Principle during the year. They have a great time painting their goals on T-shirts to keep as a reminder throughout the year. They meet weekly to review their Principles and goals, to celebrate successes, and to problem-solve and plan for the next year to go even better. "Our time is more purposeful together, and we have so much more fun!" says Sharon.

Principled Friendships

Principled relating can also bring intimacy and connection between you and your friends. If you follow the Principle of Truth, you would likely hold standards of not gossiping, keeping current with one another, giving one another truthful feedback, and having a vision of what is possible for your friendship and assessing your progress. You take responsibility for your lives rather than having endless "ain't it awful" sessions and blaming conversations that don't go anywhere.

Connie, who is in her early twenties, and her girlfriends meet for dinner at a new restaurant once a week. Instead of going over the week's social plans and who is dating whom, they talk truthfully about what's working and what's not in their lives, and support each other in "winning, not whining and blaming," as they call it.

Even though the women were growing from the evenings, Connie was ready for more. As she explained, "I think we really needed to take bigger risks. We needed to go a little bit further to deepen our friendship and challenge each other to have more success in our lives."

To make that happen, Connie suggested an evening of sharing criticisms, especially in the area of relationships with men. The conversation was painful, but each of them felt she made a significant shift in relating to men.

One friend, Lyn, was not dating at the time, but Connie criticized her as being too easy—Lyn tended to wonder more how men would be in bed than how they would be in life. She set a new standard to stop drinking and getting physically involved on first dates, and discovered how much she was avoiding criticisms of men by sleeping with them so soon. Now she feels that her self-esteem is climbing and the quality of men she dates has improved.

Your Soul in Tune

With creative Principles you are making something new, a new way of being, a new you. You're stepping into the unknown, creating and becoming your higher, essential self—who you really are at the core. You are becoming attuned to spirit. It is like the moments before a great symphony begins—the musicians tune their instruments so that they can harmonize and together create something majestic. When they achieve that initial resonance, when they've all matched the note, you can feel the resolution, the release, and the readiness for something to be created. Then harmony can happen. The orchestra creates magic and music pours forth. Aligning toward creative Principles tunes your soul to a heavenly resonance. Out of this resonance, something shifts. You are inspired. You are in tune with the vibration of the higher Principle.

> *Aligning toward creative Principles tunes your soul to a heavenly resonance.*

When you view it this way, there seems to be no other reason to have a relationship, establish a friendship, or even convene a meeting—why do anything unless you're aligning to higher Principles? If you don't establish a relationship for truth or connection or intimacy, then what would be the point? It would be shared deadness. We relate with others because we want to be connected—we hunger to belong, to be part of something bigger.

And this is the real reason that we have a quilting bee, a dinner party, a community gathering. People come together for more reasons than simply to accomplish something. We use the excuse of having to get something done and to plan something so we can spend time together.

The real reason people come together is that they need a soul tune-up to reestablish resonance. Why do you think you make a dinner date? Why do you think you go to a company to make a sales call? The point is to get people to come together so they have the opportunity to align toward higher Principles, connect at a much deeper level, raise each other up, and create MORE, together.

Unity in Our World

Each of us can align toward Principles and learn to live our lives in their creative expression. Most people have the capacity to hold a higher vision—they just need the invitation to do it. Everyone loves love. Everyone, whether they fight it sometimes, loves and believes in truth. Everyone. If we extrapolate from that, we can see immense possibilities that help us understand the importance of aligning toward Principles today, right now.

> *Aligning to higher Principles makes the seemingly impossible possible: unity in our world. Each of us can take a step. Each of us can make a ripple in the pond.*

It begins with just doing what you need to do in front of you. You have spheres of influence: You are in a couple, or have a family, or a friendship network, or a neighborhood, or a business, or a team at work. As you become aligned toward Principles with the people around you, you experience more unity and more power.

A World Transformed

Imagine what might be possible if we could all harness this power, the power of Principles. This is how the world will change. It is so simple yet so profound. Each of us would have more power, more control of our inner world, and more satisfaction. Imagine families, businesses, organizations, and communities all aligned with life-affirming Principles. As we each become players in the divine symphony of life, our world transforms.

This is how I envision the future: I see families designing their shared lives around Principle-centered living. I see them experimenting with different possibilities of how to have more truth, more engagement, and more connection.

Businesses won't give lip service to some halfhearted or meaningless mission statement. Instead, the whole company conducts business aligned with creative Principles. And everyone knows it—it's not just what the company manufactures and markets, but how truthful, environmentally sensitive, and responsible it is.

Manufacturing and marketing aren't even the point. They are the excuse—the vehicle—for gathering together to share Principles. You may be at the truthful company that makes widgets or the community service company that makes widgets. You're the fun company that makes widgets. You're the playful company that makes widgets. And the creativity flows.

Now we have a transformed business community. And every family is doing the same thing, and every place of worship, and every neighborhood, and every parent, and each individual. What will happen? Peace and love will be the result. It's really that huge. This is the grand design.

Everybody agrees on higher Principles. Consider spirituality and religion: beliefs, dogma, and practices differ, yet all align with higher Principles of spirit, God, Love, and Truth. All religions align to these universal principles.

Imagine if we all aligned toward the higher Principles to unite us, rather than use religion or other differences to divide us. God is infinite, so shouldn't God be expressed in a zillion different ways, through lots of different religions, and in different prisms and aspects? Then through all these different views we can see the alignment toward higher Principles. We focus on what we have in common. Diversity would become a wondrous, kaleidoscopic expression of our common Principles.

Granted, there is much work to do for this vision to be realized. Even if it will take about a millennium, it's time to start.

Co-creative with Life Force

This is what we are put on the planet to do. This is where we are being led. We are supposed to be co-creating something new. If we are made in the image of God, then we are a creator. If we are made in God's image, then we are Truth, and love, and all higher Principles. It's ours to manifest that Truth in everything we do.

Design your world to align with Principles, because you are blessed with the essence and ability to do so—to have life and have it MORE abundantly. This is not for the future or for someone else. It is for you, now.

We are to take the raw material that we've been given on this planet and reform it into creative ways that bring Principles into being. It's not just God's job to be there to intervene for us. We need to intervene for God!

We are not just children of God, we are partners of God. It is our job to align toward Principles and translate those Principles in our actions. It's time for us to take our place in creation and to focus our creativity in these forms that would bring meaningful innovation into being. We have creativity, but without the Principles we make things that are superfluous and meaningless. With the Principles, we'll make magic, beauty, love, connection, and new beauty. And we will also make lots of mistakes, but it will be so much more fun and rewarding because we are aligned with creativity, intention, purpose, and aliveness. It's the only way we'll be the most authentically ourselves. And it's the only way our soul will learn what it's supposed to learn, and it's the only way we'll have the lives that we were meant to have. And then, through doing that, we will make a different path for the future.

It is time to take your place in creation, to align yourself toward higher Principles and find ways to translate them into your life on a daily basis. Take your part in the evolution of consciousness on our planet. You are not just a piece of creation; you are a co-creator in and through your own life every day. That's how big and beautiful this is. You change the world by doing whatever you can that's in front of you. There is room for us all, for each expression, each view of Truth, and each way of expressing the universal Principles that we all embrace: Peace. Love. Truth. Become a principled person making a difference in the quality of your own life and having an impact on those around you. The Keys to the Kingdom will unlock the vast treasure within you and the untold riches of the cosmos. You have the keys within you; you can reach for them and use them anytime, anywhere, and in any circumstance. Open the door to what's possible in your life as you align yourself to the higher principles, and as you claim what's positive, proactive, and creative. You will change, as will those you touch, and eventually you just might change the world.

The Allies

*The universe provides you with Allies for your Quest. You
may not have met them yet, but when you see them, you'll know.
You will recognize them by the gleam in their eyes, the passion in
their hearts, the resonance between their hearts and yours. You will
see the risks they are taking, hear the truths they are telling, and
you will recognize them as fellow questers. Appearing like a nod
of acknowledgment from a supportive universe, these friends will
appear when you least expect them. And you will find that unseen
support arrives from sources that are subtle and often unrecog-
nized, yet nonetheless palpable and even miraculous. Insight, intuition, and synchronicities, will be provided for you; but first you
must commit.*

You are not meant to be alone on your Life Quest. When you
make your One Decision, you open up to the possibilty of immense support. The road to MORE may be the road less trav-
eled, yet all who travel it are bonded in spirit. Aligned to higher principles,
they are brothers and sisters on the Quest. You are meant to be supported
on your Life Quest, yet you must seek it, accept it, and give support in return. You must attract the support to you—allowing your Allies to recognize you through the power of your Life Quest.

In an inspiring scene in the *Lord of the Rings* movie *The Two Towers*,
Frodo Baggins takes up his Quest and the Allies respond:

Frodo: I will take the ring to Mordor, though I do not know
   the way.
Gandalf: I will help you bear this burden, Frodo Baggins, for as
   long as it is yours to bear.
Aragorn: By my life or death, if I can protect you, I will. You have
   my sword.
Legolas: And you have my bow!
Gimli: And my ax!
Samwise: Ha! Mr. Frodo's not going anywhere without me!

You too are on a noble quest, and, as on all noble quests, you shall be joined on the journey, honored and buoyed, by those who have also made their One Decision. It is your duty to hold a vision for one another, provide encouragement, tell one another hard truths, and hold one another accountable; to fuel yourselves with celebration, acknowledgment, and inspiration.

You and your fellow adventurers will become beacons of MORE, attracting still others engaged in their own Life Quests. Together you will present a force much richer and more powerful than you ever imagined possible. Friends merely hang out; Allies share a Quest. Friends merely feel sympathy for you; Allies share the risks with you.

This communal journey is undertaken not only with other people but also in alignment with God, spirit, and nature. Connect with and draw from universal consciousness. Increase your ability to sense connection to higher values and God's will, and act in consonance with the greater whole. Invited to a deeper connection with yourself, others, and spirit, you will become powerful co-voyagers on mutual missions of MORE.

Sidekicks, Sages, Friends, and Allies
on the Life Quest

Consider the heroes of mythology and history, assisted on their quests by friends, allies, teachers, guides, mentors, chance encounters, and new-found friends.

King Arthur drew strength from the Knights of the Round Table—his cohorts in arms—and the wisdom and guidance of Merlin. Throughout the stories of history and myth, there are examples of principled heroes who pursued their Life Quest. For each hero, there are friends, mentors, and guides who showed up along the way.

Allies are essential in living the One Decision and all its aspects. I am learning more and more what it to takes to continually live my One Decision and the huge variety of support we all need to fulfill our missions. I often feel dispirited, and a host of friends and supporters, seen and unseen, reach out to help me do things I never dreamt I could do. I'm realizing it's not only a requirement to live my One Decision but a wonderful reward. Teachers seem to be appearing when I need them, sidekicks are steadfastly supporting me, and I am developing friends in all walks of life. I am even learning to hold those who seem to revile me as a blessing and support on my path. Things have not always been this way for me; in fact my ability to engage and accept the support of Allies is recent.

Allies have always been a facet of the One Decision that I find personally challenging. In my childhood, I made friends but the friendships seemed to go one way. I was terrible at asking for things and most of the kids in the neighborhood were envious that we were more privileged than they.

When Bob and I compare childhoods, there are many more examples of people reaching out to him than me. Similarly, in high school, I had few real supporters while he had teachers and fellows students who made difficult stands on his behalf.

The skill of reaching out and allowing help requires a vulnerability that is very difficult for me to show. For Bob, it is an issue of practicality. He goes into Starbucks and comes out with a new friend. I am shy beyond what most people who know me can imagine. The fear of rejection weighs much more heavily on me. In the coming chapter, I will be working the issues about which I am writing as much or more than

> *No Life Quest or hero's journey is done alone — Han Solo didn't go solo and the Lone Ranger wasn't alone.*

many of you. If you wish, you can imagine me to be one of your Allies in your mind, if not in fact. I hold you as my Ally on the Life Quest—one who is living your One Decision and engaged in your Life Quest along with me.

Allies and the One Decision

When you commit to your One Decision, you recognize and accept that you can't do it all alone. To live your Life Quest you require, and deserve, the support of Allies, fellow heroes on your journey. And you must summon and accept the sources of unseen support that surround you once you've chosen, once you've made your One Decision. Will you accept the bounty of support available to you, or will you attempt to brave it out alone? Will you support others on their journey, or will you hold back? Will you use Allies to help you step into a vision beyond what you could imagine for yourself, or will you play it small? The choice is yours to make.

Comrades of Heart

There is a particular thrill that accompanies the discovery of other people who have made their One Decision and are questing for MORE. There

> *Friendship is born at that moment when one person says to another, "What? You too? I thought I was the only one."... It is when two such persons discover one another, when ... they share their vision—it is then that Friendship is born. And instantly they stand together in an immense solitude.*
>
> —C. S. LEWIS,
> *spiritual author and thinker*

is an almost instant affinity, like meeting a long-lost friend.

Seek out people who have similar visions and who are aligned to similar principles. These people do exist, and they feel just as alone as you may at times. When you meet, the recognition will be powerful. Actively seek out people to serve—people who will also make valuable contributions to your own life and mission. If you are living your One Decision from your heart, and if you are passionate, you are likely to attract people to you on the journey.

Look for enthusiastic, energetic, spirited, dedicated, and caring people who share your sense of purpose. It is also important that they share your sense of humor. They may not be outwardly bubbly, or they may be intense, but what they have in common is a sincere pursuit of MORE, authenticity, and a willingness to take risks. They are people going for MORE and not settling for less. People who are ardently pursuing MORE in their lives are attractive. You want to be with them and feel better after spending time with them. And when you are radiating with enthusiasm, when you have that gleam in your eyes, you will attract people to you who will encourage you and support you.

There is a thrill that you sometimes experience when you are on a sports team, in a competition with your jazz band, engaged in a neighborhood cleanup rally, competing with other creative teams for a prime contract, or decorating a float for homecoming. When you add a higher Principle to that group experience, that group's synergy and excitement is multiplied. Those who are with you believe in you, you believe in them, and you're aligned toward similar Principles. You feel like you matter—that what you are doing counts and is part of the greater whole. Because the stakes are

often high and others are depend-
ing on you, it brings out the best
of you, and you become a better
person through the experience.

> *There is no union more satisfying, no bond more lasting or more powerful, than finding Allies and joining with others toward a greater good.*

There is no greater connection
or alignment than being united in
Principles and sharing the Quest
for life! This is the best possible way to live. It is a significant antidote to
feeling lonely and alone. Relationships based on Principles and MORE
are exciting, intimate, deep, fulfilling, and exhibit the phenomenal bonds
of love and care that we all long for.

Nick was attracted to a sexy, redheaded spitfire, Cathy. She
was intrigued by his Italian good looks, his stable family, and
his potential. While that was enough to keep their passion
alive, it wasn't enough to fuel their Life Quests. Wanting adventure, they moved to Chicago to start a new life.

Soon, they realized that it wasn't going to be all bliss.
With nothing other than a superficial attraction on which to
base their relationship, they grew apart. They saw the trajectory of the course they were on, knowing that if something didn't shift, sooner or later the relationship would end.
They decided to do whatever it took to have the relationship
they really wanted and to invest in their own growth.

They came to the Institute for coaching and then enrolled
in transformation groups to develop more of themselves to

bring to the relationship. Through the Couples Empowerment group, they joined with other couples who were breaking into new frontiers of relationship and partnership. On their Quest, Nick and Cathy grew exponentially—individually and as a couple. As they describe it, "We now challenge each other to grow in areas of conflict, communication, and truth-telling, so that we really enjoy and are satisfied with each other." They committed their relationship to higher principles of truth, aliveness, and engagement.

"We have a relationship beyond our wildest dreams! He knows everything that's ugly about me; he knows everything that's beautiful about me. He knows me. That is one of the things that I hold most precious; that this is a man who loves everything about me and encourages me to be my best, and vice versa," Cathy reflected. "We are constantly truthful with each other, constantly discovering new things about each other, as well as working through the places where it's dark and ugly. I have become a more powerful and womanly woman, discovered my talents, and healed the wounds of my

And whatever happens, remember how good it felt when we were all here together, united by a good and decent feeling, which made us better people, probably, than we would otherwise have been.

—FYODOR DOSTOEVSKY,
The Brothers Karamazov

past. Nick continually develops more mastery in the world, is more conscious, and a bigger and bigger contribution to me, our children, and our community. I keep falling in love with him again and again, as he gives me more facets of himself to love. Now we are teaching and leading other couples, because they want what we are having!"

Strong Friends and Courageous Comrades

In the quest for MORE, you treat your friends and loved ones as resilient, strong, powerful people. You don't coddle them, protect them, or hide things from them. You are in mutual, genuine relationships that are solid and can weather challenges. When you have conflicts, you work things out with one another.

You don't manipulate or compensate for one another. You are bold, forthright, and truthful. Each lets the others know what works and what doesn't, what you need and want. Protecting your friends and loved ones actually conveys to them that you do not think they have their own strength. It tells them that you do not see them as worthy of being treated fairly and openly.

In many relationships, people try to maneuver and manipulate rather than tell the truth. *I'll wait until he is in a good mood*, you think, *then I'll tell him*. Or you engage in politics to get what you want, manipulate the truth, or spend time scheming.

With Allies of MORE, you

> *I do not wish to treat friendships daintily, but with the roughest courage. When they are real, they are not glass threads or frostwork, but the solidest thing we know.*
>
> —RALPH WALDO EMERSON,
> *essayist and poet*

deal things out straight and in the moment. You don't wheedle, connive, seduce, intimidate, or guilt-trip to get your way. Mollycoddling, cover-ups, or insincerity have no place in relationships of MORE. You say directly what you need and want, trust others to do or say what is right for them, and then work it out from there. It brings integrity, spontaneity, and strength to relationships. You become much more real and genuine in your interactions.

It does take skill and commitment to live this way. You may think that this isn't practical for everybody, but it is necessary for anyone who wants MORE out of life. You don't need to be perfect or impeccable, but you must be willing to reorient to the possibility of strong relationships. You must be willing to continually improve your ability and learn the skills that increase the power of your relationships. It is a journey of increasing truth, responsibility, and strength.

Vision Keepers

Allies hold our vision for us, and we for them. They remind us when we've lost sight of our vision, just as we remind them when they've lost sight of theirs. When one of the troops falls down, Allies pick each other up, or give each other a kick so they will get back on their own feet—making it more uncomfortable to stay down than to get back up.

> *Treat people as if they were what they ought to be and you help them to become what they are capable of being.*
>
> —JOHANN WOLFGANG VON GOETHE,
> *German writer, politician,*
> *humanist, scientist, and philosopher*

As a Vision keeper, you see what is possible for your Allies. Holding a vision doesn't mean you judge—it means caring about people, wanting the best for them, and showing them what they are capable of becoming. And it doesn't have to be mutual. You can gain great satisfaction just by calling for the highest from others. It is a great honor to hold a higher vision for the people in your life, to see them as capable of MORE. Everywhere around you there are people you can contribute to—your children, partner, employees, work team, your children's friends, neighbors, and customers—anyone you are in relationship with.

As I walk with Bob from our office to the coffee shop, he checks in on the maintenance man's progress on buying his first house—which Bob helped him see as a possibility. He's inquiring about the doorman's French lessons and he's encouraging me to see my ability to handle a situation I am wrestling with. At the coffee shop, he talks to the counterperson, whom he's been encouraging to go back to school, and checks up on the status of his college application.

Bob is a vision keeper wherever he goes. He has held visions for the parking attendants in the garage to invest in buildings, go to beauty school, stop selling drugs—all of which have happened. He also coaches CEOs and top-level managers to reach for MORE in their work and their personal lives. He has held a vision for managers to become top executives, for entrepreneurs to expand their business plans, for mothers to have complete satisfaction with their children, for single people to have magnificent, independent lives, and for couples to experience depths and heights of intimacy and partnership.

All of us are limited to what we can see for ourselves. Growing up in a factory town, I could only see as far as my experience allowed. I didn't even know some things were possible, and frankly, I was pretty shocked to find that a whole world of possibilities existed beyond what I had glimpsed so far. I have done so many things in my life that I wouldn't even have dreamed of doing without Bob and others holding vision for me— much less thinking I was capable of achieving them. Without Bob's vision, I wouldn't have developed the body of work and mastery from which to write this book, I wouldn't be completing my doctorate, I wouldn't have become a public speaker, I wouldn't know the amazing richness of intimacy and partnership. And it doesn't stop. He continually holds a higher vision of possibilities for me, just as I do for him. He sees potential and invites me and others to reach it.

> *A vision keeper creates and holds your vision until you can keep it yourself. Cherish those who see you as more than you now see yourself. They will open you up to possibilities of MORE.*

There may be times, as a vision keeper, when you are holding a vision for someone who does not choose MORE. At other times, you may hold that vision for someone for years before that person chooses to make it so. And sometimes it takes a life team.

At a weeklong intensive training she attended, Shannon offered to cut and style people's hair, something she had done in high school and college to help pay the bills, but never took seriously. The mother of school-aged twins, Shannon had recently been reconsidering her career options in a difficult job market, feeling lost and unsure.

I saw how happy, alive, and present she was, how her eyes gleamed and she seemed to be having a blast styling and cutting hair. I told her that she had a gift and suggested she go into the beauty industry. She lit up at the suggestion and got excited about the possibility. But then she couldn't quite make the mental leap to working in a salon. It didn't seem like a prestigious enough job to her, and instead she explored becoming an educator, a trainer, and other fields she felt were more esteemed.

For two years, her women's leadership group and I held a vision for her as she wavered. Finally, she took the plunge and went to beauty school. She finished school at the top of her class, won a statewide student championship, is competing nationally, and now works in one of the top salons in Chicago. As Shannon shares, "Each day, I feel the most me I have ever felt, and the happiest I have ever been in my career. I owe this to the women of my leadership group and to Judith. They held a vision for me of something I could not see. Without them, I would have never gone to beauty school and I would never have realized my talents, nor been on this amazing journey of working with some of the most talented hair people in the industry!"

Admitting You Need Others

One of the biggest hurdles many people experience in accepting support is admitting that they need others, or that they deserve them. When I encounter this, my response is always "How would it be possible to do this without other people?" Having other people is not a luxury. It's your right and your duty to be surrounded by other people on the Quest.

Instead of feeling as if you're needy, desperate, or alone, you can admit that you are hungry for connection, to be inspired, to care and be cared about. You're rightfully claiming the support you need and desire as a person on the Quest. In fact, it's your job to claim it!

All of us, to some degree, can read off our laundry list of reasons why we won't be supported: fault, pride, fear, shyness. On your Life Quest, it's time to drop those old excuses and faulty beliefs that don't allow you to accept support. If you don't, then the battle is already over, and you've lost by turning away the people and resources that could help you achieve your dreams.

Commit and Be Supported

When you make your One Decision and commit to a Quest for MORE, support flows to you. Too often, people wait for the support before they decide to take a risk. It is only by committing, however, that the fullest support can come to you. If you aren't getting enough support, chances are you haven't committed to something big enough to draw others in. They have too little to support. What that means is you aren't fully committed yet, you haven't made your One Decision, you are not fully pursuing MORE, or you haven't enthusiastically shared your Quest. Once you commit, the universe aligns and all sorts of resources flood your way that never would have been there otherwise. If they're not there, then you haven't committed.

When I take more risks, I get more support. People I don't even know or have just met have been very supportive of my journey, and it's been quite amazing to me. People have treated me with immense kindness and good wishes.

> *It is probably not love that makes the world go around, but rather those mutually supportive alliances through which partners recognize their dependence on each other for the achievement of shared and private goals.*
>
> —FRED ALLEN,
> *radio personality*

They have helped me find resources, encouraged me, shared their stories, and inspired me.

For example, while I was traveling on a jam-packed book tour, my plane was delayed and I arrived at a hotel in Nashville in the wee hours of the morning, tired and drained. I struck up a conversation with the desk clerk about why I was in town and about my book. We kept chatting as he escorted me to my room. When he opened the door, I saw that he had given me the presidential suite—this magnificently appointed, multi-roomed respite above the city. He had noticed my fatigue and had decided to upgrade me to this beautiful room at no charge. I just cried. It was a lovely, kind, supportive gesture.

People with whom I outwardly have little in common have supported me. Where we align is on higher Principles. When they respond so kindly and supportively, I know I am getting a huge nod of encouragement from the universe.

As I am wrapping up these chapters of the book to submit to the publisher, I am blessedly surrounded by the love and support of my Allies. Before me is an altar with candles lit to remind me of the forces unseen, but nonetheless very powerful. I have reminders of spiritual experiences from travel to sacred sites, aspects of divinity to pray to and to bless this writing. The women's organization I founded has assigned themselves to pray in shifts for me and my team as we work throughout the weekend.

Students from our Institute are coming by to support me and to be part of this process. People volunteered to bring meals, do proofreading, check sources, give back rubs, even share some good (and bad) jokes to keep us nourished in our work. They have prayed over these pages, lent their stories to be shared with you, and most important, are committed to pursuing MORE through their One Decision.

Bob is editing each chapter, suggesting stories, interpreting our work in a way for me to include in the book. He is supporting everyone who is working, staying up all night with me, telling me how proud of me he is.

I just got an e-mail from my niece asking me how the writing is going. A friend called to share something, saying she didn't know why, but that somehow I was to hear this story she shared. It turned out to be an amazingly serendipitous moment, because the story related directly to what I was struggling with when she called. And there is MORE.

The more I share what I am doing, the more I include people in my Life Quest, the bigger my commitments, the more enthusiastic I am, and the more support that pours forth. And the more support I have to give.

If You Build It, They Will Come: A Life Team

The requirement and the reward of MORE are that you create a life team—a team to support your Life Quest. You cannot make lasting change in your life without people who really know you, without people who can consistently give you the same feedback over and over until you finally hear it. Without this level of support, you will never hit your potential, because you're actually avoiding the most powerful source of development there is: input from the people around you. Years of weekend workshops and seminars will mean little without the continuity of a life team pulling for you.

> To fall in love is easy, even to remain in it is not difficult; our human loneliness is cause enough. But it is a hard quest worth making to find a comrade through whose steady presence one becomes steadily the person one desires to be.
>
> —ANNA LOUISE STRONG,
> *journalist*

This may seem obvious and logical, but most of us have no clue what it really means. We have little training in thinking about our relationships this way, and have little to no experience in doing it. We accept easy friendships that come our way. We aren't trained or raised to think that Allies are people we seek and choose.

Learn to seek out people because their skills, gifts, or way of being is a good fit for you. Look for those who can coach you in an area you're weak in, or can provide a model for you, or a connection to other tools and resources that further your Life Quest.

Creating your team means actually looking for, meeting, and soliciting people to be friends—people who have influence, connection, life experience, perspective, and other qualities that contribute to you. You consciously gather the friends, mentors, teachers, guides, and resources needed for your Quest. And the power and gift they each bring to you will be vastly different, person by person. You may need a hard-edged, driving friend who will hold you accountable to your sales goals for your business. You might seek a softer friend who has the gift of being able to comfort you when you feel raw. You need someone who sees clearly and speaks the truth without censoring, another who is accepting. You need different people for different purposes, and your needs change throughout the course of your lifetime. As you need different things, needs for your team change. Thus, you need to be prepared to outgrow members of your life team at different times, or for them to take a different direction.

The very concept of creating this life team runs directly contrary to what many of us are comfortable with. In our society, it is against the rules to evaluate friends. You think it's "wrong" somehow to say what you want from them. It is against some unwritten protocol to move on when you don't get what you need from your friends. You must break these rules, because these are the rules of mediocrity. To live your One Decision, you must stretch beyond the beliefs about relationships that no longer serve you.

A good-looking, single, and popular twentysomething, Leo counted scores of people among his friends. He had an active social life, but as time went on he found himself connecting with only two or three people out of his larger social group.

"When I made my One Decision, I started evaluating my life more closely and looking at what I really wanted out of my relationships with others. I realized that I was wasting a lot of time hanging out with some people I wasn't connecting with and, in some cases, didn't even like."

By making his One Decision, Leo got the motivation he needed to start evaluating his relationships, and he started slowly changing how he engaged in his friendships. He started by not going out with large groups as much, but rather spending quality time with the two or three people he cared about most. He realized he still wanted a larger social network—and more than just friends, he really did want to build a life team.

He started doing new activities, like joining a volleyball club and taking a comedy improvisation class, where he could meet new people. As he focused on his new life team, his entire purpose in dating started to shift. He began meeting all kinds of people. Rather than spending time only with women who had the potential to be his future wife, he had a blast getting to know a huge variety of people, some of whom ended up being new friends, and some of whom just ended up being great resources in different areas of his life.

He was delighted to discover that the world was filled with an abundance of people who could contribute to him and to whom he could contribute. Rather than staying in a rut with his same old routines, finding a life team has opened up worlds of possibility for Leo.

The Power of the Unified Field

When you are with other people who are focused on higher Principles, magic happens. It is as if there is a force field that is created, bringing each person to a higher level than he or she could possibly go by themselves. When members of a team are operating in extreme harmony, they can generate results that are significantly greater than would be expected simply by adding the parts. We call this the Unified Field.

Imagine a higher state of group consciousness. It builds in strength and scope as more people commit to and align toward higher Principles. At the most unified end of the continuum, there is a discontinuity, a leap to the Unified Field. There is a point where the group seems to jump to the Unified Field—much as the fabled starship *Enterprise* jumped to warp speed.

You can actually sense and feel the Unified Field. It is the collective consciousness of people aligned to higher principles. It is an amazing, palpable force. You can see its mysteries revealed as it works in us and through us. The baseline of each person's performance rises. What had been hard gets easier, what had been coming easily brings more depth and creativity. There is a sense of group flow. Problems get solved. Answers come readily. There are unexplainable synchronicities; what you need is instantly provided by someone without your asking. It's like someone showing up with a glass of water just as you realize that you are thirsty.

We get a glimpse of what life should be and will be as more and more of us make our One Decisions. This wondrous design leads us to think, "What else is possible?" As we learn to live our lives this way and create this powerful force with others, the possibilities are endless.

Allies Seen and Unseen

Allies do not stop with the team you have gathered. You are always loved, supported, and guided by spirit if you allow it in. You have team members beyond this world, and forces on your side beyond what you can see or touch.

Reach out to the Divine. Ask for help, guidance, and inspiration. Offer your fears, hopes, your gratitude and thankfulness. Let God see your open heart, hear your concerns and offer you solace, support, love, and guidance. Walk in partnership with the Guiding Spirit. Dedicate your Life Quest to spirit and listen, really listen, for the guidance. Seek input from the heavenly realms.

Whether you believe that angels exist or not, consider this at least metaphorically: Angels cannot help you unless you ask. If you ask, then the angels will rush in. In stories about angelic intervention, usually someone prays for support, and when every option is exhausted, they come. I fantasize that the angels are always hovering above us, calling, "Give me something to support. Pleeeease, something to take on!" They walk over to the other guardian angels nearby and say, "Well, my human's not doing squat—just sitting there whining. So I don't have jack to do. I'm bored. I can't go anywhere else. Why did God give me that one? Not going for MORE. Oh, wait, I hear something . . ."

And then the voice is raised—asking, seeking, and praying, "I need something . . . I need help . . . I want MORE." Then the angels rush in. . . .

If this is not literally true, it's certainly metaphorically true. There is a lot of help available, but only if you're going for something. If you don't ask or give permission for someone to support you, they can't get in.

Recognize Signs of Support

Support comes in many ways. It could come through someone else listening to their intuition, or being "nudged" to offer a prayer for you, to reach out to you, to give you something. It can come through inspiration, synchronicities, signs, and signals.

When I am writing, I ask for help. I pray and ask for the forces to come through me and to use me as their instrument. I am sometimes amazed at what flows from my fingers when I am in that space. Things beyond my conscious knowledge seem to flow through.

I have had many synchronicities just in the writing of this book. In the midst of the Adventure chapter, I was vacillating on the importance of a section I was writing called "The Illusion of Security." When I picked up a book and opened to a page with the header "The Illusion of Security," I knew then that it was important.

Another time I was writing about how you have to pursue MORE, it doesn't come to you, and I opened a book to a quote that expressed that sentiment perfectly. And just as I typed the header "Strength, Courage, and Wisdom Within" in another chapter, the song "Strength, Courage, and Wisdom" by India.Aire came over the speakers.

Be aware of the support that comes your way, and offer gratitude in return.

The Melchizedek Effect

Abraham is one of my heroes. A man on a Quest for God, he believed in the One God at a time when people believed in multiple gods. It was a very long, lonely path, because he was going against the prevailing beliefs at the time. As the story goes, after a battle, Abraham and his weary men were greeted by Melchizedek, who presented Abraham with bread and wine, demonstrating friendship and religious kinship. Melchizedek bestowed a blessing on Abraham in the name of the God Most High, the One God. Abraham was greeted by another who believed in the One God! I like to think about how Abraham would have been heartened by this, knowing that he was never alone, that his Quest was honored and blessed.

Now it is your job to be the Melchizedek in others' lives. Do not wait for someone to affirm you or let you know that what you are doing is okay. Instead, be the Melchizedek. Find other people who are on a Quest for MORE, who are orienting toward a Principle and higher purpose. Go out, find them, and encourage them. Share lessons and best practices with them. Bless their Quest.

There is magic in this. In search of their spark, your pilot light is on. By looking for their spark, you activate your own. It's really true: In giving, you receive so much more.

On the subway, stuck in traffic, at a business meeting, in your neighborhood, or at your church, look for sparks and glimmers of possibility. When you see someone doing an unsung-hero deed, sing it. When you see someone cleaning up a neighborhood when no one else seems to care, what do you do? Sing it. When you see someone stand up in a business meeting and say a necessary truth that was hard to say, sing it.

Be a source of inspiration. Celebrate the victories and share the losses of your Allies, and they will share yours. Reward acts that are done in the name of the MORE—a truth told, beauty expressed, a risk taken. You are a sustainer of questers, an encourager of souls, a rekindler of spirits. By sustaining, you are sustained.

Albert Schweitzer said, "In everyone's life, at some time, our inner fire goes out. It is then burst into flame by an encounter with another human being. We should all be thankful for those people who rekindle the inner spirit." You can be a rekindler of the inner spirit for others. And by doing that, you'll rekindle your own.

And all you need to do is step into it. Engage. Get on the field and commit, then ask for assistance, command the resources provided for you, and reap the rewards.

You are not alone. All you need to do to get support is simply to ask. You ask and the gates of heaven spring open. Untold resources and support—seen and unseen—rush to your aid. You find new friends, unexpected gifts, synchronistic moments, and acts of extreme kindness and generosity. Your flame is rekindled, knowing that legions march with you. Your Quest is yours alone, but you are not alone in the pursuit of it. Other Life Questers are at your side, supporting you, mentoring you, and cheering you on—just as you provide support and encouragement to them. You give what you would receive, and receive what you would give. Welcome the support all around you, actively seek and engage it, and respond with gratitude in kind. You need others—the dedication of friends, a company of Allies—just as they need you.

The Good Fight

Unleash your passion, your courage, and your determination to live the life you were meant to live. Fight the Good Fight. Do not be swayed by your doubts or by the naysayers who are threatened by your dreams. Yet do not underestimate the enemy: the internal and external forces that rob you of MORE. Fight for your One Decision—for what you Desire, for Truth, for Presence and consciousness. Fight to follow the Way of the Heart. Celebrate your victories. Rebound from your defeats. Discover the true joy of living life as a passionate warrior. Sound the trumpets, pound your chest, and proclaim your battle cry, MORE!

When you make your One Decision, you throw down the gauntlet and the Good Fight begins. The time has come to wage the battle that your heart asks of you, to fight in the name of your Principles, in the defense of your dreams, and in the service of your Life Quest. Fighting the Good Fight means living in constant pursuit of what you care about.

It is not just the spoils of the battle or the results of the engagement, but the investment in yourself that yields the reward. Discover

> *The good fight is the one that we fight because our heart asks it of us.*
> —PAULO COELHO,
> *Brazilian novelist*

the thrill and power of engaging in the Adventure of MORE, the willingness to fight for MORE, no matter what.

A Warrior for MORE

One of the reasons we experience so little MORE is that we are under the illusion that it should just come to us rather than us having to fight for it. With movies and television ads celebrating the quick fix, the magical solution, or the purchase that will satisfy all of our desires, it can be difficult to realize that the engagement in the journey is the point, the MORE is in the pursuit! The prizes we can put on a shelf or deposit in the bank are never the real wins—it's the contest itself. We must engage, we must make con-

> *Satisfaction lies in the effort, not in the attainment; full effort is full victory.*
> —MOHANDAS K. GANDHI,
> *political activist and human rights leader*

tact with life, discover it, pursue it, wrestle with it; this is the Good Fight. This is how we become the hero of our own life—a warrior for MORE.

What Are You Fighting For?

The Good Fight is fought on many battlefields, both internal and external. It is fighting for what is true, keeping yourself honest even when you fear that your honesty could bring you rejection or loss. It is fighting for what is right—in meetings, conversations, and even in your own prayers.

Sometimes it is easy to miss some of the most important battles. We often think that the real fights are only about big issues—the environment, human rights, poverty. However, the smaller battles, the everyday defeats and challenges, can be just as important. If you are sitting in a

> *Few of us will do the spectacular deeds of heroism that spread themselves across the pages of our newspapers in big black headlines. But we can all be heroic in the little things of everyday life. We can do the helpful things, say the kind words, meet our difficulties with courage and high hearts, stand up for the right when the cost is high, keep our word even though it means sacrifice, be a giver instead of a destroyer. Often this quiet, humble heroism is the greatest heroism of all.*
>
> —WILFRED A. PETERSON,
> *author*

room and people are saying things you don't agree with, or that are untrue or offensive, the battle is to find your voice and speak up. If you see your friends making the same mistakes over and over again, you no longer sit by and watch them suffer. You overcome your fear of interfering or hurting their feelings or making them angry. The Good Fight is to be a good friend and insist they do better for themselves.

When we fight the Good Fight, we take more stands and speak up more often. Even when we fail to speak, or are defeated when we do speak, we still learn and grow and keep on fighting. If you don't agree with what is happening, don't allow yourself to just sit back and complain about something. Fight the Good Fight and try to change it.

Shelley was proud of her friend Ashley, who had four children under age twelve and was an executive in a fast-growing company. Yet Ashley constantly complained about her nanny, who sometimes missed picking up the children, didn't communicate about school events that Ashley was supposed to attend, and had friends over without permission.

At first, Shelley tried to support Ashley, listening, even commiserating with her. Finally, Shelley realized that this was not in service of her friend, and so she waged the Good Fight. She told her, "Listen, you've been complaining about your nanny for months. We've talked about it repeatedly and come up with solutions, but you haven't done anything about it. I can't see how I'm supporting you if I continue to just listen while you complain. Something has to change. I don't want to talk about this again until you tell me what you are doing about it. In good conscience, I can't call myself your friend and allow you to continue like this."

Ashley was stunned at first, and even taken aback by Shelley's abruptness. But she recognized the truth in her friend's words, the love behind the firm message. Shelley's willingness to fight the Good Fight, to speak up for what she believed was right, helped Ashley shift from complaining to responsibility and to take the necessary steps to hire a new nanny.

Fighting the Good Fight can also mean fighting with others for what is right or fighting yourself and your own doubts. It can be turning down dessert as you are trying to stick to a diet to lose weight, admitting that you were wrong in a fight with your partner, insisting that your children share in family responsibilities, being willing to take a stand for your relationship to be the way you want, applying for the job you are nervous about, resisting temptation, or effecting social change. It can be anything from fighting your own inertia to battling self-doubt to fighting a social injustice.

The Battle Within

We often look at fights as being only something we engage in with another person. Yet the biggest battle is the one that takes place within us. Mastery of one's own mind is perhaps the greatest challenge we face and the key battlefront. From an evolutionary standpoint, the primary role of the brain is keeping our bodies safe. As a result, hundreds of thousands of years into the human journey, our minds struggle to maintain this primary function, keeping us from reaching beyond our experience to tackle bigger and greater feats. "You have been safe until now, so let's keep it that way," we are programmed to tell ourselves. But we must fight and challenge these unconscious mechanisms that thwart change. These mechanisms of the mind include defensiveness, minimization, and rationalization, all geared to keep us from doing anything unpredictable and dangerous to our unconscious mind.

> *We have met the enemy, and he is us.*
> —WALT KELLY,
> *cartoonist*

If you compare the conscious and unconscious minds, the unconscious mind is like the largest part of an iceberg that is under water. Most of our mind functions outside of our awareness. It is automatic and hidden. It often operates in opposition to our stated values without our awareness. Our conscious mind has great values and lofty aspirations that are often undermined by our unconscious mind, which values the status quo.

The journey of the Good Fight involves being willing to live in a state of readiness to defeat anything that would stand in the way of living a life of MORE—including the battles we fight within ourselves against self-doubt, victimhood, and fear. We must overcome our natural inclination to maintain the safety of the status quo, the known and comfortable. We think we are reasoning when we, in fact, are defending, minimizing, and rationalizing to justify avoiding the Good Fight.

We kill our desire for MORE because we are afraid to fight the Good Fight. We pretend that un-decisions are One Decisions. And so we lose both the battle and the war. If we are living with the Way of the Heart, however, we are willing to face our fears, get the support we need, learn the skills we need, and engage in life fully. We do not need to avoid the fight. In fact, getting support and learning the skills *is* the Good Fight.

> *A Native American elder once described his own inner struggles in this manner: Inside of me there are two dogs. One of the dogs is mean and evil. The other dog is good. The mean dog fights the good dog all the time. When asked which dog wins, he reflected for a moment and replied, "the one I feed the most."*
>
> —GEORGE BERNARD SHAW,
> *Irish playwright and Nobel Prize winner*

Excuses and Rationalization

Because we are afraid of change, we make excuses and rationalize our choices of safety, avoiding the Good Fight. We complain of not having enough time to do something different, or of being too tired. We judge other people who are passionate and work hard for what matters to them as being workaholics or being misled, brainwashed, or obsessed. Or we put them down and make fun of them.

We plan fantasy escapes rather than doing something effective to change the situations we are in. We look for magical solutions—from winning the lottery to a new job. We indulge in Soft Addictions. We justify to ourselves and others why we aren't living up to our potential

> *Time is a created thing. To say "I don't have time" is like saying "I don't want to . . ."*
>
> —LAO-TZU,
> *sixth-century Chinese philosopher*

and making the moves we know we should. These are not justifications or minor diversionary thoughts—these are dream killers. These are the enemies of MORE.

I can't help but think back to all the times that Bob encouraged me to write my first book and supported me to do so, and how often I resisted by saying, "I don't have time. I am too busy. How am I supposed to do that on top of everything else I am responsible for?"

I acted as if there were something wrong with him for suggesting the idea, not as if there was something wrong with my thinking. It appalls me now to realize that I was killing my own dreams by ignoring the messages they brought. I was scared, unwilling to pursue my dream, my MORE. I wanted to convince myself that the truth was that I didn't have enough time.

What I found was that if I were willing to fight the Good Fight in the service of my dreams, I would make time and make my dreams come true. I rearranged my priorities, found the support, and garnered the power to tell the truth of how scared I was. I received the encouragement and help I needed to plan and succeed. Everything I needed was there once I engaged in the battle and stopped accepting my excuses. Thankfully, Bob fought the Good Fight with me or I may never have written my books.

I was at a conference where I met the CEO of a fast-growing creative company who had a contract with a major publisher for four books—but was more than a year and a half late in delivering his first manuscript. He kept saying he was too busy, he couldn't run his company and write this book. He rejected every suggestion I gave him for getting it done, saying again and again he didn't have time.

In reality, he was smothering his dreams with excuses. And I realized that could have been me—if I hadn't had Allies who told the truth and helped me follow my heart. My Allies were the holders of my One Decision and insisted I overcome my excuses and rationalizations. They forced me to open myself to the support and experience of MORE.

We say we don't have time and yet we say we still want MORE. This contradiction shows that not only are we killing our dreams, but we're also saying that we want the results without the effort. Yet MORE does not exist without effort, without quest; MORE is your Quest.

MORE isn't delivered like takeout food that shows up at your door thirty minutes after you place the order. MORE will only come from engaging in your Life Quest, fighting the Good Fight, and staying true to your One Decision.

Rewards of MORE—More Challenges, More Fights

Most computer games become increasingly difficult and complex as you progress—with each subsequent level requiring you to develop more skill in order to advance even further. This increase in difficulty and challenge is where the Adventure is, bringing new opportunities for success and excitement. And it is also how you get better at playing the game and experience the satisfaction of improving, while still having new challenges ahead of you. How boring to keep playing at the same level, yet that is how many people live their lives.

> *The greatest reward for doing is the opportunity to do more.*
>
> —JONAS SALK,
> *developer of the polio vaccine*

Students often come to the Institute wanting us to help them find better jobs. We ask them if they have earned an A+ in their current situation.

How can they imagine that life will open up the next level of the game if they have not mastered their current challenges?

"I don't like the job. It's not me," they say at first. When they become honest with themselves, they realize that they have been avoiding fighting the Good Fight—not saying the truth in meetings, not preparing, making excuses for not doing their best, and on and on. When they take on these challenges they develop more skill and more satisfaction. Then the next level of the game opens up, taking them into their next career move.

When you are not fighting the Good Fight, and not receiving increasing challenges, you are losing ground. You're not frozen, and you haven't hit a plateau. You're actually going backward. There is no neutral gear in the Good Fight—only forward or backward.

Once you begin fighting for MORE, you will discover the wonder of the electronic games in your own life. Life brings ever-increasing challenges. You will then find the real reward by fighting the Good Fight— win or lose, you are being true to yourself.

Engage!

You don't know what is possible until you engage in the Good Fight. You don't have to know all of your dreams, or see your vision clearly, to fight for MORE. You don't need to know the object of your Life Quest. All you need to do is follow your urges appropriately as they point to your deeper Desires, be present, and live your Adventure. As you fight the Good Fight, you will find your dreams, develop your vision, and see the possibilities for MORE.

As you engage in the Good Fight, you start to see more choices and possibilities to make things work. Rather than giving up because you feel overwhelmed or hopeless, you will find alternative steps and possibilities. Rather than kill your dreams, you can find ways to move toward them even if it is a small step. You find resources to make things happen. You are more conscious and more creative in finding solutions where you couldn't see them before.

If you are not engaged in the Good Fight, you don't see the value of it. All you see are the problems, the defeats, the downside. You miss the joy of the Adventure drumming in the warrior's heart, the sense of pride and purpose that radiates from his face, the sheer excitement that pulses through his body at just fighting the Good Fight. Beware of those you call friends who do not and will not hear the drum and fight the Good Fight.

Greg landed an exciting and much-coveted yearlong internship in videography. He took on extra assignments to take advantage of this fantastic opportunity. There were many nights that he didn't get what he called his "eight hours of beauty rest," yet he was thriving.

He knew he had the opportunity of a lifetime, and he was excited and thrilled to be learning all he could. Others ridiculed him for working too hard and not getting enough sleep: "They're taking advantage of you. When are you going to get a real job? You're doing another late-night gig, are you nuts? You're working too hard." They could not understand Greg's excitement and passion. In fact, it frightened them. They couldn't see that he was fighting the Good Fight—that he was alive, engaged, in great shape, and enjoying himself immensely.

Greg realized that while he fought the Good Fight to take

on the challenge of the internship (including resisting his own victimhood and stinking thinking about not measuring up, working too hard, and so on), he hadn't taken on the Good Fight with his detractors. He didn't share how excited he was about what he was doing and didn't counter their seemingly caring but disempowering statements of limitation. He failed to invite them to join him in the Good Fight.

He said, "It occurred to me that if they really had a great life, they probably wouldn't be worrying about my sleep. They'd be sharing in my excitement and be proud of me. I missed an opportunity to talk to them about what was going on with me and also to ask them what was going on with them. I'll have another opportunity—every time I engage in the Good Fight."

Fighting the Battle on Two Fronts

If your approach to the Good Fight is only looking at an external win—the object of your Quest—it's not a big enough win. You can gain a great deal on the outside, but if it doesn't transform you on the inside, it isn't MORE. In order for it to have any true meaning for you, it must be an internal win.

The real issue is what you conquered inside. Did you shift or change? Did you overcome your doubt and find courage? What demon did you fight internally? What temptations did you avoid? Did you overcome stinking thinking to accept a new challenge? What's the triumph within your own psyche? What big barriers did you break down inside? Did you access your fear or your anger rather than avoid your feelings?

> *In the Good Fight, there are no small battles, and no small victories.*

Internal wins include greater awareness, greater Truth, self-esteem, personal honesty, intimacy with self and others. Internal wins manifest as discipline, compassion, giving, and receiving. They are personal and you define them by overcoming your own barriers, meeting your needs, and dealing with your circumstances.

In fact, the outside results only matter as mirrors for the inside. It's nice to win the outer battle, but it's not the big battle. Engaging in the Good Fight means that you got yourself out on the field and fought. That you win a prize isn't what matters. You've already won when you've transformed yourself by engaging.

Fighting For, Not Against

The Good Fight is fought *for* something, not against something. You're fighting for yourself, for your dreams, Principles, your heart, aliveness, consciousness, life, manifesting what you were put here to do, purpose, deeper Desire. These are the things worth fighting for.

Mother Teresa fought for something. Her mission was to honor the sanctity of life. Every human life had dignity for her. If people had not experienced that dignity—the gift of the blessing they were while they were living—she made sure they understood it while they were dying. She did not fight against death, nor did she fear it. Rather, she fought for life, while tending to and honoring the dying.

> *Life is life—fight for it.*
> —MOTHER TERESA,
> *Roman Catholic nun and humanitarian*

The Good Fight means choosing to engage in life and belong rather than escaping. If you're not fighting for greater aliveness, you're not living your life fully. You are like a race car driver just cruising to finish the race and not really trying to win. Experience your life, live full out, see how far, fast, and deep you can go. That's what we're here for. Get out there. Do it!

The Challenges and Adversaries of MORE

As a warrior of MORE, you are called to stand up for your Principles, values, beliefs, and your purpose. You must defeat doubt, trounce temptation, and weather hardships. You must get up after you fall down. To do this, you must rein in your stinking thinking, cultivate courage, and vanquish victimhood.

As on any hero's quest, there are adversaries and temptations on the path to MORE. In the fables, you must slay dragons and conquer enemies. Yet in the path to MORE, these adversaries lie beneath your own skin, haunt you within your own mind, reside within your own household, confront you in your daily life, and are embedded within the fabric of modern life. The distractions from the Good Fight are legion: too much television, superficial values, peer pressures, stinking thinking, mistaken beliefs, people pleasing, and so much more. I have treated these in depth in my previous book, *There Must Be MORE Than This: Finding More Life, Love, and Meaning by Overcoming Your Soft Addictions.*

To pursue MORE, you must be aware of these adversaries and develop the vigilance and skills to continually resist and overcome them.

> *to be nobody but yourself in a world that's doing its best to make you somebody else, is to fight the hardest battle you are ever going to fight. never stop fighting.*
>
> —E. E. CUMMINGS,
>
> *poet, painter, essayist, and playwright*

At first glance, Claire, a former homecoming queen and pompom girl, is an unlikely warrior. Her bubbly personality belies the battles she wages against many adversaries—her need to please; her upwardly mobile, striving upbringing; her mistaken beliefs, societal influences, and expectations— as she claims MORE in her life. Her Good Fight has caused her to evolve into a potent, powerful woman of substance.

But it wasn't always that way for Claire. First, she followed her family conditioning, societal influences, and her own mistaken beliefs and got married in her twenties. As she said, "I had a marriage that everybody thought looked really great. I had a smart husband with a lot of money, a nice car, and a nice condo downtown, and we took fun vacations in Europe. We had the same background and we seemed to be really compatible."

It seemed too perfect, a magical solution for happiness. Yet the reality was that Claire was bored and unhappy. At first she blamed her husband. Then she made her One Decision. She decided to be genuine and live a satisfied life. She began to fight for MORE and resist her victimhood. Through a transformations lab and coaching at the Institute, she discovered that "I had never worked on myself and hadn't figured out who I was and what I wanted. I went for a magic formula that looked like it was going to get me what I wanted and what I needed to be happy. And I found out that the formula was *not* working."

She took a huge risk to engage in the Good Fight for MORE in her own life, for her own power, and to confront her marriage. "I finally had enough sense of myself to say, 'Listen, this marriage is either going to transform into a phenomenal marriage or we're not going to be together.' It was one of the scariest things I've ever done, but I knew that that was just how it was going to be and I had the support and the encouragement. So I said this is how it's going to be, one or the other."

The outcome was that Claire and her first husband did divorce, but they did it in a way that was responsible and that allowed them to face much truth and mutual responsibility. By taking that risk, she opened up new realms of possibilities. She fought against settling and learned how to become single again, and then learned how to be in a relationship again.

When she met and married her second husband, Collin, who is on his own Life Quest, they formed a quest together, in a relationship very different from her first marriage, forged of truth and genuineness.

Not only was Claire fighting the Good Fight in herself and her relationship, she was fighting to transform her career. She had been raised to take it easy, to avoid risk, to depend on a rich husband, not to tax herself too much. Working for a government agency, Claire loved the contribution she could make there, but knew she didn't have a lot of room to grow. Again, she took big risks and fought against stinking thinking that tried to hold her back, and ended up joining a major world financial institution as an assistant vice president. Soon she was promoted to vice president and was supervising more than fifty trainers and managing the professional development training for 70,000 people across the country.

She later chose to risk again, fighting her conditioning, which would have her settle for security, and joined the Institute staff as an entrepreneurial business coach and trainer.

She fought some internal battles and faced some dark fears and past traumas in order to become a mother. Courageously facing them, she just became a mother for a second time at age forty-one.

As Claire reflected: "I feel like a real person, not just a cutout paper doll going through the motions of what I thought I should do to have a 'good life.' Now I am authoring my life, creating a satisfying marriage after divorce, and mothering two lovely children. I am adding depth to my career by risking leaving the corporate world to work in an entrepreneurial environment where I am learning to sell and live a more robust lifestyle. I am making a difference in the world by touching and teaching others—one person at a time. I no longer use caffeine to pump myself up all day. I stopped watching television and now fill my evenings with meaningful activities with people I care about. I am grateful to be creating a life that is satisfying, true, and uplifting— far beyond the empty picture I thought I should live in my twenties."

Fighting the Wrong Fights

Most of us fight stupid fights, not the Good Fight. We react against others. We fight to maintain the status quo. We scramble so someone doesn't find out we've done something wrong or we don't know what we're doing. We fight to be right. We fight defensively to fend off being revealed and seen with all our flaws. And when we do that, what are we really doing? We are failing to fight *for* things. We miss our opportunities to be creators, masters of our universe.

And our defensiveness is just the beginning of the wrong kind of fights. We fight to get everybody to like us, a ridiculous use of resources. We fight the Truth. We fight to keep things the same. We fight to protect our ego. We fight for money. It's not that we shouldn't have money, but fighting for that alone misses the point.

Think about some of the fights you've had with your spouse, friends, sisters, or brothers. You were fighting to keep them down, fighting to be right, fighting to win. You've been fighting dumb fights for as long as you can remember.

Sometimes you won't even be that straight about your fights.

> *If this life be not a real fight, in which something is eternally gained for the universe by success, it is no better than a game of private theatricals from which one may withdraw at will. But it feels like a real fight.*
>
> —WILLIAM JAMES,
> *philosopher and psychologist*

You invest all of your energy in fighting straw dogs or being brave inside but cowardly out—to make up battles where you're the only one who knows you're in a battle. You avoid a fight, and then act like you're fighting against someone in your mind alone. You punish someone by withdrawal or giving them a hard time and don't even let them know what it is they did wrong. You complain about something or someone rather than talking to him. Or you carry out your fight with revenge fantasies.

This all takes a lot of energy, strategy, and cunning. And it takes a lot of tools and weapons. But it's the wrong fight. These are false fights. You're fighting covertly and manipulatively, using your weapons and resources in ways that aren't going to take you anywhere. These are the unfought battles.

But for many people, fighting misguided fights would actually be an improvement. Many of them lose with the very first adversary, because they don't engage at all. That's the first loss of the battle. Or you lose the battle, because you see an outside adversary where there isn't one. Or you envision the adversary outside of you even bigger than it actually is.

Know what you're fighting, and make sure it's a Good Fight.

The Weapons of the Good Fight

A warrior is constantly training and keeping his skills sharp. He is constantly improving his ability to fight. To fight the Good Fight, you must both enjoy your life and continually train, so that it becomes second nature to choose conscious activities that refresh and rejuvenate you. After all, how can you keep your edge without continual training and support? It's all part of your conditioning. A warrior continually pushes for higher levels of performance and fitness in all areas of life. Battle readiness and vigilance require living a life you love and loving the life you live. Your One Decision demands it. And even the act of engaging in the training itself will bring you MORE.

> *I know that every good and excellent thing in the world stands moment by moment on the razor-edge of danger and must be fought for.*
>
> —THORNTON WILDER,
> *novelist and playwright*

Continual training is much more than developing aggressive skills. It includes developing surprising, counterintuitive weapons of the Good Fight such as self-care, nourishment, and much more that will surprise and delight you.

Compassion, especially for yourself, is a powerful tool in its own right. You don't stop stinking thinking with stinking thinking. It is not about beating yourself up. It is about being able to treat yourself with understanding and compassion. Develop compassion and understanding to identify the conditioning that has led you to think and believe in certain ways that limit you. Do not accept, however, the propensity to continue to operate in accordance with those limiting beliefs. Being able to face the truth and tell the truth requires compassion.

A sense of humor is a phenomenal weapon to disarm your stinking thinking and allow you to see the ludicrousness of your stances, to put some light into your thinking. To laugh at yourself, to disarm the lies, is to fight the Good Fight.

Learning to care for yourself and nourish yourself is a critical skill. You must tend to your emotional and spiritual needs as well as your physical needs to fortify you. Then you are strengthened. You reinforce the message that you are loved, that you are worthy. You are more resilient and less susceptible to the thoughts of your unworthiness when you are treating yourself as worthy and precious. Self-care and nourishment means monitoring your victimhood and acknowledging and expressing your emotions.

To the Victor Go the Spoils

The Good Fight exposes you to scrutiny, judgment, and ridicule. It may cost you friends, you may be attacked, and you may be hurt. Isn't that what happens to any hero?

All these things have happened in my life. I have been judged, attacked, and ridiculed. I have lost friends. I have been humiliated, hurt, and slandered. And if you are not fighting the Good Fight, that is all you see. But my fellow warriors of the Good Fight see the gleam

> *From the moment you make your One Decision, you are on your way to becoming a hero.*

in my eyes, the passion in my heart, and my transformation as a person. Warriors of the Good Fight recognize the passion in the pursuit of one another's Life Quests, the thrill of engagement, the sublime satisfaction in living a life they love and being people they respect. Because with the hurts, or perhaps because of the hurts, they have MORE.

This is your path, the path of the warrior fighting the Good Fight—in spite of the costs. Yes, you will be hurt and suffer losses, but with the Way of the Heart, you need not protect yourself from pain. You must take care to minimize wounds and heal rapidly. You are a warrior. You can take it;

you invite it. You will feel your life. You will experience all of life. You will have MORE.

Enduring some hurt or loss is nothing compared with the possibility of gaining your heart's desire. You will reap rewards for the risks you take and the moves you make as a warrior of MORE. You get MORE—the object of your fight—by the very act of engaging in the fight.

These, then, are the rewards of fighting the Good Fight for MORE. This is what you are fighting for. This is what comes to a warrior of MORE. You are genuine, authentic, and real. You will feel unsatisfied and want MORE, as you should, yet you will be more at peace with the self you see in the mirror. You are a force of truth and light, and life flows through you. You are fulfilled, satisfied in your dissatisfaction as you are engaged for even MORE. You find peace, endless creativity, and love. You can feel all of your feelings and express them powerfully.

You know conviction, commitment, and dedication. You have made a life-guiding One Decision to orient your life to something MORE. You fill your days with meaning, guided by Principles. Your Heart leads you to more connection, spontaneity, and expression. You test yourself, always stretching, learning, and growing. You become MORE than you imagined possible. You develop self-respect, integrity, intimacy, and deep bonds of friendship. You feel everything in the panoply of life. You access spirit and commune with nature. The rewards are consciousness, overcoming the dark, enveloping the light, developing your character, becoming yourself, becoming whole, experiencing intimacy beyond anything you thought possible. You have limitless resources—friends, networks, and creativity. You love! And you are loved. You have life and have it MORE abundantly!

You have entered the Kingdom, and you have the Keys. The warrior arrives, triumphant.

Thy kingdom come. Thy will be done on earth as it is in heaven. . . .

This is the prayer of the Good Fight; this is what beats in the heart of the warrior. The rewards of the Good Fight are heaven on earth. That is worth fighting for. It is the only thing worth fighting for. It is at the heart of all Good Fights—for freedom to be yourself, human rights, freedom from hunger, disease, and tyranny. That is why we left Eden—so that we could create heaven on earth in partnership with God.

Fight the Good Fight! Live your One Decision and take your place as a warrior in the battlefield for MORE. Take up the weapons of compassion and Truth and love. Arm yourself with the radiance of spirit. Raise your flag. Sound the trumpet. Lift your heart. Let your spirit soar. Rally the troops. Lead from your Heart. Do not listen to anything other than that which quickens the Desire in your heart. Be the warrior you were destined to be. Fight the Good Fight. Engage in the battles, for you are a warrior of MORE. This is a holy mission, and these are your holy orders. That is the Good Fight, the challenge and the reward. And so it is . . .

30
Days
to Your
One
Decision

30 Days to Your One Decision

M aking and living your One Decision can be one of the most important and powerful steps you take in your life. Now that you have read *The One Decision*, use this thirty-day guide to prepare to make your personal One Decision (or deepen it if you have already made it) and to begin to learn how to apply it. By making your One Decision, you proclaim what is important to you and use that powerful declaration to guide your life. No matter where you are on the path—whether you have already made your One Decision, are ready to make it now, are just curious, or want to consider making it—reading the book and using this guide will serve you. The timing of your One Decision is a personal choice, but by deepening your understanding of and applying the concepts, you will move toward making your One Decision to live a life of MORE.

Like a diamond, the One Decision has many facets, and the most powerful have been described to you in each chapter of this book—the Adventure, the Desire, and so on. Through each day's reflections and exercises, you will become more aware of how these facets are currently manifesting in your life, how you might like to use them, and how to create a vision of what is possible for you in the future. As you discover more about the One Decision and its many facets, you will begin to create action steps that you can take to shift your life and realize your vision.

You will begin to see how you can use your One Decision as a guide for your everyday choices, a beacon to remind you about what matters when you are in doubt, and a touchstone to evaluate your life choices. Rather than living your life by rigid rules, you will discover that your One Decision provides a lens through which to view and evaluate your choices: Is this in alignment with my One Decision or not? If it is, then go on. If not, you can readjust your course. As you work through the 30 Days, you will solidify your idea of how you can shape your life of MORE, one little decision at a time.

Fully living your One Decision takes a lifetime. Yet by dedicating yourself for the next thirty days, you will develop a solid foundation to maximize the benefits from this life-altering commitment. Through a simple process of reading, reflecting, experimenting, and analyzing, you will discover the power and freedom that a One Decision can create in your life.

At any point that you feel moved to make your One Decision, use the forms provided in the Appendix to commit, signify, and share your commitment. You can also go to my website, www.judithwright.com, where you will find other exciting tools for registering and celebrating your One Decision.

Awareness, Action, and Application

The 30 Days are divided into three stages of ten days each: Awareness, Action, and Application. In the initial ten-day stage of Awareness, you are preparing for your One Decision using the key skills of self-observation and awareness. In the Action stage, you experiment with concrete exercises to make shifts in your life that reflect the One Decision. In the last ten days of Application, you will apply what you've learned and use the reflection and exercises to envision your life in a new way.

In each stage, you will revisit the ten facets of the One Decision— each time with a different emphasis and different exercises. Combined, these three stages give you a foundation of the skills of MORE that will help you deepen and clarify your One Decision throughout your life.

Ten Facets of the One Decision

As a reminder, the ten facets of the One Decision are:

1. The Adventure
2. The Desire
3. The One Decision
4. The Truth
5. The Way of the Heart
6. The Power of Presence
7. The Life Quest
8. The Keys to the Kingdom
9. The Allies
10. The Good Fight

As you go through the exercises in the next thirty days, be aware of which facets resonate the most with you—which speak most powerfully to you, touch your heart, or inspire you. In fact, many people dedicate themselves to Truth, or the Way of the Heart, or one of the Keys of the Kingdom, or Desire, and so forth, *as* their One Decision. Once you make your One Decision and begin living it, you will discover all of its facets—by living one, you live them all.

Daily Lesson

Each day's lesson consists of a Morning Reflection to read and contemplate, a Daily Life Assignment to do an activity to implement the lesson during the day, and an Evening Reflection to review and analyze your day to get the most value from your efforts.

Morning Reflection

Each morning, read and reflect on the day's lesson and the questions. Set aside some quiet time to read and reflect on the lesson to prepare you for the Daily Life Assignment, whether in contemplation, prayer, or meditation. Set a timer and allow at least five minutes and up to twenty minutes of quiet time, meditation, or prayer to envision your day going forward. Or if you do not want to invest that much time, at least close your eyes and envision a scenario in your day where you will apply the lesson.

Daily Life Assignment

During the day, do the Daily Life Assignment to apply the lesson to your everyday life and increase your understanding of the facets of the One Decision. Doing the Daily Life Assignments gives you a way to focus and to make powerful changes in your life. It also teaches you a skill of the Life Quest, the assignment way of living.

Evening Reflection

Each night, review and summarize your activity and insights in the Evening Reflection. Reflect on what you have *learned* and how you have *grown*. *Learning* is about knowledge. It means that you know something today that you did not know yesterday. *Growing* is about behavior. It means that you do something or behave in a way that you could not have done or would not have done previously. By reviewing in this way, you are getting the most out of your day, and consciously guiding and assessing your life.

I have included three different ways you can choose to do your Evening Reflection to record how you're learning and growing. In our work with students, we have found that some enjoy journaling and some do not, so we have provided several ways for you to reflect on the lessons at night. Choose the form that you are most comfortable with, or alternate if you wish. You can do your review through a Daily Reflection Chart with a short summary of what you have learned, by journaling, or by using the

Responses, a sentence-completion exercise. Feel free to tear out or copy the blank Checklist, Journal, or Responses and keep them by your bed to use to review and reflect at the end of the day. You might also want to use the online versions at www.judithwright.com.

Understanding and changing your behavior are keys to a life of MORE guided by your One Decision. Use any one or all of these tools to help you as you learn to live your One Decision.

Resources and Support

You may want to complete this guide with others, as most of us learn and grow more easily with the support, companionship, and example of others. Join others in a One Decision group that meets weekly for support and encouragement. Invite your friends, family, colleagues, coworkers, church members, or neighbors to participate with you to form your own group. Remember, everyone wants MORE out of their lives, and others may appreciate the opportunity to have support to make a deeper personal commitment in their lives, too. We have prepared a Group Guide with weekly discussion questions and other support to assist you. If you would like help to form a group, or to join an ongoing group, be part of an on-line community, or get a One Decision Buddy, log on to www.judith wright.com or call us at 1-866-MORE-YOU and we can help you connect with others on the journey. Visit www.judithwright.com for additional support, inspiration, and tools to make and live your One Decision—from an online journal, registry of One Decisions, inspirational stories of people living their One Decision, a free e-zine of inspiration and tips, to forums and many other interactive and downloadable tools—as well as a special limited-time offer. There are endless resources and support to help you in this guide and elsewhere. Your job is simply to open yourself up to building the life you want—a life of more.

May you embrace these thirty days to have MORE of every-thing you desire. May you discover the exponential benefits of the One Decision that give you the life you always yearned for—a life of love, fulfillment, purpose, abundance, contribution, inti-macy, and spirit. With each of the facets of the One Decision, you have been given the tools, the wisdom, and the secrets you need to create a satisfying and meaningful life. Now it is for you to choose. Have MORE, be MORE, live MORE! Blessings on your journey.

Awareness
{The First Stage: Days 1–10}

In this initial ten-day stage, you will prepare to make your One Deci-sion with a series of lifestyle exercises that focus on strengthening the key life skills of self-observation and awareness. Do not underestimate the power of awareness. Simply being observant brings about change by pro-viding you with clues to the specific types of behaviors, actions, desires, and decisions that will support you in living your One Decision and im-proving the quality of your life. Even if you have already made your One Decision, deepening your skills of observation and awareness will help you apply it more powerfully.

Day 1
Awareness of Adventure

Morning Reflection
Your life is meant to be an Adventure—full of surprises, new experi-ences, and opportunities to learn and grow. Each moment is an opportu-

nity to take the fork in the road—to newness or sameness, challenge or avoidance, expression or withholding. You are meant to experience the full range of life; highs and lows, successes and defeats—all of these are part of the Adventure of being fully human. There is no wrong feeling, no true failure if you learn the lessons available. Adventure often begins with curiosity or awareness. Be curious as you live your life. Wonder: What will happen next? What will I create out of this situation? What can I do with this circumstance? How can I best deal with the hand I've been dealt?

Think of a public, historical, or literary figure whose life is/was an Adventure. Who do you know personally who lives life as an adventure? What makes these people adventurers? How do you feel toward them?

Now ask yourself: How will I live my life today? Will I live my life as an adventure, or avoid the possibilities in a series of familiar ruts and routines?

Daily Life Assignment:
Notice Adventures Taken and Not Taken

Awareness is the aim today. Notice when you take the exciting, challenging, risky path and when you choose caution. Take note of Adventures taken and not taken. As you make choices, analyze which ones move you into Adventure or away from it, into rote behaviors and numbness or into excitement and possibility. Do you take risks, try new things, and embrace all of your experiences? Or do you settle into comfortable ruts and routines of Soft Addictions, or sink into self-pity or suffering?

There are times when being cautious is appropriate, but there are also times you avoid risk by numbing out, operating instead on automatic pilot. When you do this, you are waiting for Adventure to happen to you and living your life defensively, rather than engaging. True Adventurers embrace life, take risks, and live to maximize their potential.

Sometimes when things don't go the way we'd like, we suffer and feel sorry for ourselves. You can learn to reframe these experiences by viewing them as necessary aspects of the Adventure of being human. Your One Decision will help turn those frustrating roadblocks that before seemed impossible to overcome into the exciting challenges you must face to truly live life as an Adventure.

Evening Reflection: Learn and Grow

What did you learn about yourself and Adventure today? Did you grow, and if so, how?

Record your thoughts in your Evening Reflections Journal, Responses, or Chart.

Day 2
Awareness of Desire

Morning Reflection

You are meant to desire MORE. Just as you were given physical hunger to prompt you to nourish your body, you were also given spiritual hunger to guide you to feed your spirit.

No matter how much money, happiness, social position, or even love you have, you are still meant to desire MORE. True abundance means that there are always MORE blessings for you to receive as well as MORE opportunities to serve. Desire springs from the deepest longings of your soul and the hungers of your heart—the hunger to be affirmed, touched, seen, and heard, to love and be loved, to express, belong, learn, connect, to matter, to make a difference, to be one with the greater whole of life. These Desires are the universal hungers of every human heart, which lead you to everything that is powerful, meaningful, and loving in life. As you activate your Desire, heed and interpret your true urges, ignore false wants, and follow your genuine yearning, you will create MORE.

Bring to mind people who live guided by their deeper Desires. What words would you use to describe them? How would your life be different if you lived more this way?

Now ask yourself: Will I recognize, follow, and fulfill my Desires or will I ignore and numb them?

Daily Life Assignment: Notice Your Desires and Diversions

Be aware of your Desires today, whether you fulfill and express them or not. Your Desires manifest as feelings, thoughts, and urges to speak and reach out. They are generally subtle, so you will need to be vigilant to notice them. Surface wants mask true Desire. Most people are far more familiar with their wants than the deeper Desires of their heart. Notice how often you ignore or numb your deeper hungers by indulging in surface cravings, such as too much food, gossip, surfing the Internet, and other distractions. What did you do more of today: Checking out, or having a nourishing rest? Watching TV, or engaging actively in your own life? Going to a bar, or being intoxicated with the love of life? How in touch are you with your deeper hungers? If you are really aware, you will begin to notice more and more urges by the hour.

INSIGHT FOR THE DAY

We have been conditioned to ignore and repress our urges in order to conform and fit in. It is more socially appropriate to numb your urges with Soft Addictions than to follow them.

Evening Reflection: Learn and Grow

What did you learn today about your urges and Desires? How did you grow?

Record the answers to these questions in your Evening Reflections Journal, Responses, or Chart.

Day 3
Awareness of the One Decision

Morning Reflection

Your One Decision will be your beacon to guide you to a life of MORE—more of everything you truly desire. With your One Decision, you make a conscious choice about how you want to live your life; you choose between opposing ways of being—to be or not to be, to live life as an adventure or let your life pass you by, to live the Way of the Heart or ignore your feelings and your intuition. While the choice may seem obvious when you see it in stark contrast, most people have not made this powerful, definitive choice to change their life for the better. They lack a positive guiding philosophy to help them make choices in their lives. When you make your One Decision, you will be committing to a life of MORE, however you choose to describe it. This personal commitment is a dedication to a positive way of being, a quality of life, a higher principle, or a higher power. You use your free will to choose the kind of life you will lead. This powerful commitment will be a guiding light for all of your life choices, leading you to a life of MORE.

Think of a public, historical, or literary figure whose life is or was committed to something higher. Whom do you know personally who has made a One Decision? What makes their lives different from other people's lives? How do you feel toward them? What do you admire about them?

Now ask yourself: How will I make choices in my life? Will I live my life guided by my One Decision?

Daily Life Assignment:
Notice How You Make Choices

Be aware today of how you make your choices—from what you wear, what you eat, who you spend time with, how you interact with others, and how you structure your time, to how you engage in a project, what you do, where you go, even what you think. Do you make choices based on convenience, pleasing others, trying not to get in trouble, avoiding the fear of rejection, trying to avoid pain, or following the path of least resistance or familiar routines? Do your choices seem random, rote, or unconscious? Or do you make choices that seem to be in alignment with a higher decision— what do I desire, what is most truthful, what feeds my heart, how will I best learn and grow?

INSIGHT FOR THE DAY

Most people are not truly aware of their motivations and how they make choices. Awareness at this level is a skill. We are faced with innumerable choices every day, some more important than others. Catching your choices and realizing how you make them is a demanding skill that you are probably just beginning to learn.

Evening Reflection: Learn and Grow

What did you learn today about yourself and how you make choices in your life? How did you grow?

Record these observations in your Evening Reflections Journal, Responses, or Chart.

Day 4
Recognizing Truth

Morning Reflection

Living a life of Truth is a powerful and ever-evolving journey. The journey is personal because, as you become more genuine with yourself and others, you will find that there is always a deeper level of Truth. You continually learn to discern Truth from illusion, notice your impulses to avoid Truth, and tell the truth even when you are uncomfortable doing so. And with each step you take into Truth, you become more real, more authentic, more you. You become, as one of our students said, "Free to be me!"

Who do you know who lives genuinely? What words would you use to describe them? How would your life be different if you lived more this way?

Now ask yourself: Do I choose Truth or illusion? Will I choose to be genuine or disingenuous?

Daily Life Assignment:
Awareness of Truth

Today, be as truthful as you can with yourself as you look at your life. There is no need to express anything you would not normally. Simply be aware of when you tell the truth and when you hide or sidestep the truth. Do you stop short of full expression, or do you follow your Truth into uncomfortable territory? Do you make excuses, blame the traffic for lateness, or tell white lies? Do you tell lies of omission, space out, play dumb, tell blatant lies, engage in cover-ups, or give false or incomplete reasons?

Notice in what situations and with whom you move more toward Truth and where you move away from Truth. In what situations and with whom were you more genuine? And when were you more fake and with whom?

Be aware of the times you reveal a difficult Truth and note how you decide to take the risk.

Insight for the Day

One of the reasons we do not tell the truth as much as we like to think we do is that we feel ashamed or guilty of what is true. We fail to recognize that telling the truth all the time is an accomplishment. Be gentle with yourself in this. You have the remainder of your life to learn to live Truth at this level.

Evening Reflection: Learn and Grow

What did you learn today about yourself and Truth? How did you grow?

Record responses to these questions in your Evening Reflections Journal, Responses, or Chart.

Day 5
Awareness of the Way of the Heart

Morning Reflection

In living the Way of the Heart, you tap the wisdom of your emotions, the power of your deep caring, and the truth of your intuition. When you lead from your heart, you bring the full richness of your experience to bear. Not dependent on the rational alone, you form a powerful alchemy of thoughts, feelings, and intuition. Your feelings flow more freely. You become less guarded. You are willing to be revealed, open, and available to others—powerfully presenting and sharing your deepest and wisest self. You allow yourself to care more deeply. You open your heart to immense possibilities of intimacy and profound connection with yourself, others, and spirit.

Think about people who you think live with Heart. What words would you use to describe them? How would your life be different if you lived more like this?

Now ask yourself: Will I live a heartfelt life or a heartless life? Will I honor and express my feelings? Will I share more of myself? Will I trust my intuition? How will I live my life today?

Daily Life Assignment:
Heart Monitor—Notice Your Feelings and Caring

Be aware of where you live with Heart and where you don't, and think about why. Today, observe when you experience your emotions and when you numb them or avoid them. Are there times that you feel anger, sadness, fear, joy, or love? Are there times when you are out of touch with your emotions? What are the activities, behaviors, or thoughts that move you more toward the Way of the Heart and those that move you away from your heart? Were there times today when you are more caring and loving? Or times you felt unconcerned, uncaring, shut down, apathetic, or numb? Just simply notice and note your experiences.

Insight for the Day

Blending the wisdom of the heart and the reasoning of the brain is an art. You may notice today that you tend to discount one versus the other rather than learning how to blend them.

Evening Reflection: Learn and Grow

What did you learn today about yourself and your feelings and your heart? How did you grow?

Record these in your Evening Reflections Journal, Responses, or Chart.

Day 6
Awareness of Presence

Morning Reflection

You tap into the Power of Presence when you are fully present, pulsating with aliveness, with your senses acute, your consciousness expanded, and with your awareness active. You are poised for action, on alert, scanning, or deeply immersed in your experiences. You are *in* your experiences, not merely observing them. You participate in life more fully, sensing more, and tuning in to yourself and those around you. You are alert, conscious, awake, aware, and available. Experiencing this quality of "being with" is where you feel connected to yourself, others, and spirit. Your gifts flow freely, your creativity soars, you are in touch with your emotions, you are in your body, and your senses are heightened. You are able to experience a deep connection with yourself, others, nature, and spirit. You experience MORE, you become MORE, and you bring MORE to others.

Bring to mind people whom you consider to have a powerful Presence. What is it about them and their way of being that is so powerful? How are they present?

Now ask yourself: How present am I right now? Will I notice myself and others being present throughout the day today?

Daily Life Assignment:
Notice When You're Present

Notice how present you are throughout the day. Be aware of when you are present and when you are not. How often are you checked out, in a zone, only half there? How often and when do you feel awake, alive, and energized? In what situations are you more aware and more available? What words describe the various times that you feel more present? What thoughts, feelings, and actions move you away from being present? Which ones seem to help you be more present?

Often we act present but we're really not home. We think that because we're talking, interacting, and physically moving around that we are there, but often it's not the case. With the Power of Presence, you start to catch yourself and notice when you're acting like you're present and you're really not. And having a sense of humor while you're catching yourself is definitely a plus!

Evening Reflection: Learn and Grow

What did you notice about being present today? What did you learn about the Power of Presence? How did you grow?

Record these observations in your Evening Reflections Journal, Responses, or Chart.

Day 7
Awareness of the Life Quest

Morning Reflection

Through your Life Quest, you become the hero of your own life. You leave behind what is familiar and embark on the worthy pursuit of MORE in all aspects of your life. Guided by your One Decision, you engage in the Adventure of following your Desire, becoming more Present, following the Way of the Heart and the path of Truth. You are on a Quest for MORE—seeking new vistas and possibilities in your relationships, career, growth, spirituality, and higher purpose.

Think of people whom you consider to be living or having lived a full Life Quest, whether someone you know or a public, historical, or literary figure. What makes their life a Quest?

Now ask yourself: Will I notice how I limit the possibilities for my life and become aware of the ways I could be living my life as a Quest for MORE? What is possible in my life?

Daily Life Assignment:
Notice: Vision of MORE or Resigned to Less?

Be aware today of when you sense that there may be larger possibilities for your life and also when you feel like you have given up or resigned yourself to less.

Notice if you have a vision or goals—or even a glimmer—of more possibilities for your relationships, work, for yourself, your spirituality, or higher purpose. Where are you questing for MORE or settling for less? Watch today for places where you have resigned yourself to how things are, where you have become hopeless or settled for less. Be aware of where you may have a vision for MORE, for powerful goals—or wish you did. Where do your actions seem to have a sense of mission or purpose and where do they seem more purposeless? Simply note what is so and the feelings you have about how you lived your life today.

INSIGHT FOR THE DAY

Living a Life Quest is a major accomplishment. It requires you to make your One Decision and to dedicate yourself to the pursuit of your vision. Developing a vision of MORE takes skill. Just as your vision of MORE will continually grow, so will your ability to pursue it.

Evening Reflection: Learn and Grow

What did you learn about yourself today? What did you learn about how you view possibilities in your life? What do you see about the possibilities of your Life Quest for MORE? How did you grow today? Record these thoughts in your Evening Reflections Journal, Responses, or Chart.

Day 8
Recognizing the Keys to the Kingdom

Morning Reflection

The Keys to the Kingdom are the principles—such as aliveness, engagement, intention, play, or responsibility—that can unlock the treasure, or potential, of any situation at any time. By orienting to the power of Principles, you create, find, or even generate purpose in every moment. You will be moving with the core power behind your One Decision, even if you have not identified it yet. With Principles, there are no wasted experiences, no situations that can't be mined for deeper value, no circumstance that can't yield productive surprises and be worthwhile. Using the Keys makes satisfying experiences even more meaningful, and unsatisfying and difficult situations more purposeful.

Reflect on the characteristics of those you deem to be living lives guided by higher creative Principles. What words would you use to describe them?

Now ask yourself: Will I recognize and live according to these Principles or follow a life of random, unguided acts?

Daily Life Assignment:
Watching Principles in Action

Watch today to see what Principles you are operating from. Are they creative, such as aliveness and engagement, or lower, such as deadness and disengagement? All of our actions are guided by Principles, whether creative or limited, and whether we are consciously aware of them or not. In all we do, we orient unconsciously to aliveness or deadness, intention or drifting, engaging or disengaging, play or boredom, creating or destroying. Note which Principles you gravitate toward today. Which ones would you like to operate from in your life?

INSIGHT FOR THE DAY

Principles determine all we do. Live toward higher Principles and live a life of MORE. You will find it easier to observe yourself if you accept that learning to live a principled life is a challenge and takes a lifetime of striving to achieve.

Evening Reflection: Learn and Grow

What did you learn today about yourself and living with the Keys? How did you grow?

Record these new pieces of wisdom in your Evening Reflections Journal, Responses, or Chart.

Day 9
Awareness of Allies

Morning Reflection

When you commit to your One Decision and live your life as a Quest for MORE, you need and deserve powerful support. You are meant to be surrounded by people who believe in you and your Quest—who encourage you, buoy you, train you, give you straight feedback, expect more from you, hold you accountable, hold a big vision for you, help you strategize, celebrate your victories, and support you through your defeats.

No one person can provide all of that; for a life of MORE, you need a life team. Some of your Allies will be aligned with you on your purpose; others will be helpful on your path even if their lives do not run parallel to your life purpose or One Decision. And your support goes beyond the seen to the unseen—to the presence of spirit and powerful forces that guide and protect you. Allies and sources of support can include friends, coworkers, peers, and coaches, and also the power of nature, beauty, and other resources. And in turn, you are a teacher, mentor, support, guide, and encourager—one who serves others.

Think of people in your life who create teams of support, who use Allies to live their Quest fully. Whom have they gathered around them? How have they gone about building their team?

Now ask yourself: To what extent am I supported by others and supportive of others?

Daily Life Assignment:
Notice How You Give and Receive Support

Be aware today of the support you give and receive. Be conscious of the people in your life. Do they try to contribute to your Life Quest—and do you allow them? Did you reach out for support today, to whom and for what? Do you surround yourself with people who hold a high vision for you? Did you give support to others? Did you pray, meditate, or engage in spiritual disciplines today as a way to draw upon unseen resources?

INSIGHT FOR THE DAY

Giving and getting support is a life skill to be developed. It may come naturally to you or it may feel awkward to enroll those around you to support you in the things you care about. Whatever point you are at in building your life team is fine. Awareness is simply about noticing where you are and where you want to be.

Evening Reflection: Learn and Grow

What did I notice about getting and giving support? What did I learn about Allies and how did I grow?

Record these reflections in your Evening Reflections Journal, Responses, or Chart.

Day 10
Awareness of the Good Fight

Morning Reflection

The Good Fight is the fight for your dreams, the fight for MORE, the fight to live your One Decision. When your One Decision guides your daily choices, you will make moves and take stands that are unpopular and require you to face resistance and sometimes even attack.

In the Good Fight, you recognize the internal and external forces against your pursuit of MORE and you are willing to face and overcome them. Each time you choose to follow your urges, tell the truth, be more conscious, express your emotions, be genuine, or align toward a principle, you have fought the Good Fight. And each time you wake yourself up when you have been unconscious and out of touch with your heart or you ignore the negative thoughts and temptations that take you away from MORE, it is a victory in the Good Fight. There is no battle too small to be celebrated. The Good Fight is fought both within yourself and in the world around you. Engaging in the Good Fight, you become a victor by having the courage to fight for a bigger, better life of MORE.

Fighting the Good Fight isn't always a blazing battle. Fighting the Good Fight is often taking the unpopular stand, risking telling the truth, trying what you've been told can't be done throughout the day. Think about all the little skirmishes you could have engaged in yesterday, last week, last month. What would it have been like if you had been willing to fight those fights?

Now ask yourself: Will I fight for what I need to live my One Decision today, or will I watch my life happen? Will I sleepwalk through my day and not even notice, or will I pay attention to all the ways I could engage in the Good Fight?

Daily Life Assignment: Notice Where You Do and Don't Fight the Good Fight

Be aware of the challenges you face in living your One Decision and a life of MORE. Observe today where you fight the Good Fight and where you do not. Be aware of the times that you step up to challenges or shrink from them. Do you withhold Truth, ignore your Heart, and diminish your Presence? When do you succumb to unconsciousness, sit through boring conversations without speaking up, avoid offering a new idea that might be shunned, or listen to your stinking thinking that tries to talk you out of your Quest? Today, notice successes and notice avoidances of fighting the Good Fight.

INSIGHT FOR THE DAY

Sometimes fighting the Good Fight means learning to face your own errors head-on. No athletic contest is won without dropped balls and mistakes. When you deny your errors, you cannot learn. You can learn equally from successes and failures. As you live your One Decision and fight the Good Fight today, consider every step of fighting the Good Fight as an important learning tool to pack in your bag for future adventures.

Evening Reflection: Learn and Grow

What did you notice about where you fight the Good Fight and where you avoid it? What did you learn about your own Good Fight? How did you grow?

Record these in your Evening Reflections Journal, Responses, or Chart.

Action

{The Second Stage: Days 11–20}

In this stage of the guide, you will have ten days of experimentation. Each day, you will apply the observations you made in the first stage by doing concrete exercises that will help you make small shifts in your life that reflect aspects of your One Decision. You will also be developing the building blocks you will need during the final ten days of this guide, the Application stage.

Day 11
Experiment in Adventure

Morning Reflection

As you live your life as an Adventure, you will learn, grow, evolve, and even be transformed. The full blessing of being human requires you to risk and reach out—to continually discover more and more about yourself, the world, and what is possible. Becoming an adventurer means exercising the muscle of Adventure. Your personal evolution takes place one step at a time, and each step takes you further into your potential. Adventure is essential to evolution, transformation, abundance, and a life of MORE.

Think about one person you respect who lives life as an Adventure. What words characterize that person's way of living life as an Adventure?

Now ask yourself: How would my life be different if I lived my life more like that person? To what extent will I step into the Adventure that awaits you?

Daily Life Assignment:
Take at Least One Conscious Risk

Adventurers face fear. They take risks. Take at least one risk today and break out of some familiar routine. You might ask a question you have been afraid to ask. Send in your résumé for the job you've been wanting to pursue, ask that person that you have been afraid to approach out on a date, make a request for something you want from a loved one, speak up at a meeting, or, at the bare minimum, take a different route to work, order something different for lunch, wear something out of the ordinary for you. If you are part of a One Decision group, gather "evidence" to take back to your group. Share what you did and learned, and learn from what the others have done, too.

Insight for the Day

Adventure leads to new experiences, and new experiences mean risk to your unconscious mind. As a result, risk evokes fear as well as excitement. Remember to embrace the excitement by recognizing and facing your fears. Don't push it too far today, but risk.

Evening Reflection: Learn and Grow

What did you learn about yourself and Adventure today? How did you grow?

Record these observations in your Evening Reflections Journal, Responses, or Chart.

Day 12
Experiment in Desire

Morning Reflection

Our lives are defined by how we deal with and express our Desires. Your Desires can be a magnificent expression of who you are, or you can repress your Desires and limit who you are. Even though these Desires are the same for every human being, we are often reluctant to express them to one another, to share our yearning, and to act on them directly. We fear rejection, being too revealed, or being judged as weak or needy.

Following your Desire empowers you to live your One Decision. Notice your hopes for retirement, money, status, fame, time, energy, or material goods. What do you hope those things will bring you? Perhaps it is freedom, security, respect, acceptance, or love. If so, then claim these as your deeper Desires—what you truly hunger for. For only then can you truly express who you are and fulfill your Desire.

Desires have motivated all that is magnificent in human expression—art, poetry, architecture, scientific discovery, and spiritual expression. Desire has also led to connecting deeply in relationship with those you care about. Notice your Desires, and separate those that flow from deep inside you from those that are surface cravings, which you realize will not genuinely meet your deeper yearnings.

Now ask yourself: What do I Desire right now? Am I willing to claim my Desire today?

Daily Life Assignment:
Act on a Desire

Sense your urges today and follow them. See where they lead. Perhaps you will feel the urge to share an endearment, ask for a hug, pray with passion, compliment a coworker, tell your boss about something you want changed in the office, blurt out something you meant to say to a friend, bring out your inner rock star and sing as you play air guitar with the music playing loud, buy flowers for no reason. By following your urges, you can start to notice the deep Desire underneath them—the Desire to know and be known, to love and be loved, to make a difference, to matter, to exist, to know spirit. Pay attention to this deep Desire. Learning to fulfill this Desire directly is what leads you to a life of MORE.

INSIGHT FOR THE DAY

Beware of counterfeit desires. If you really tap into your Desire, you will probably be surprised by what you find. Most of us confuse surface wants and Desires. For example, wanting money is fine, but is it security that you really yearn for? Did you want food when you really craved nourishment for your soul?

Evening Reflection: Learn and Grow

What did you learn today about yourself and Desire? How did you grow?

Record these findings in your Evening Reflections Journal, Responses, or Chart.

Day 13
Experiment with the One Decision

Morning Reflection

Living a life of MORE requires a definitive act—you must make your One Decision. You can prepare for this commitment by awakening your deep yearnings for something greater—for MORE in your life. Allow yourself to dream—what do you want MORE of? What do you truly Desire—MORE love, intimacy, satisfaction, fulfillment, peace, belonging, connection, mattering, contributing? What is the highest good that you yearn to be identified with, or to dedicate your actions to—love, truth, service, higher power, spirit, God? Now take a look at the facets of the One Decision to find clues. These facets—Adventure, Desire, Truth, Heart, Presence, the Life Quest, Principles, Allies, and the Good Fight—can become building blocks of your One Decision. Which of these aspects resonates most with you? Which feels most important to you? What will bring you the quality of life you desire? The answers to these questions will form the essence of your One Decision.

Accept that you yearn to have and be MORE. Let yourself feel your Desire for MORE. What might be in the way of making your One Decision for MORE?

Now ask yourself: How will I live my life today? Am I willing to make my One Decision? Will I live my life in accordance with a greater commitment—my One Decision?

Daily Life Assignment: Test-Drive a One Decision

If you feel inspired and moved to make your One Decision, remember that you can do it right now or any time throughout this guide. You can commit and seal your commitment by using the forms at the end of this appendix. But you don't have to commit fully to your One Decision right now. You can try one out or take it for a test-drive. As if you were dating on the way to "going steady" or becoming engaged, you will claim a personal One Decision to explore today and for the next seven days. If you have not already made your One Decision, choose one from the list below, or adapt or make up one that feels right for you—one that resonates with your heart or speaks most powerfully to you. (You can also try a different one every day to see which feels most right to you.) This begins a trial period for you to explore a One Decision by acting as if you have committed to it. Use it to guide at least one of your decisions today and every day for the next seven days. If you are participating in a One Decision Group, share it at your next meeting.

- I live my life as an Adventure.
- I pursue my deepest Desire.
- I live my life with Heart and feelings. I care!
- I choose to care and engage.
- I am truthful and genuine.
- I am conscious and Present, fully participating in my life.
- I choose to live as if every moment matters and to be a vessel for spirit.
- I choose to act as Jesus would today.
- I choose to live a life fully lived.
- I choose, once and for all, to be alive, awake, and engaged.

Learning to use your One Decision to guide your life choices is like exercising a new muscle. It may be hard at first, but it gets easier with practice. Be gentle with yourself, knowing that you are beginning to cultivate a complex skill. Do not be surprised if you do well today and break down tomorrow. This is common—breakdowns are part of the journey.

Evening Reflection: Learn and Grow

What did you learn today about yourself and your sample One Decision? How did you grow? Did you make decisions any differently by using your sample One Decision?

Record these observations in your Evening Reflections Journal, Responses, or Chart.

Day 14
Experiment in Truth

Morning Reflection

Only with Truth can you share yourself. Only with Truth can you know others and be known. And only with Truth can you discover the very real abundance around you. Experience the freedom of Truth—the relief of being revealed, open, with nothing to hide. Imagine a life in which you take steps each day to unburden yourself of illusion, your false self, cover-ups, and untruths. Begin to walk the path of Truth.

The path of Truth leads to your most essential self. Whom do you know who embodies this expression of Truth in a way that inspires you? What words describe them?

Now ask yourself: What illusions must I overcome and what barriers must

*I face to tap my most essential self? Will I commit to living this way? How will
I support this commitment?*

Daily Life Assignment:
Tell the Truth

Today, tell the Truth, whether it is big or small, at least one time. Find
an instance in which you normally would have withheld your thoughts and
communicate your Truth. Acknowledge a dislike you would have withheld.
Deliver a compliment you would have kept to yourself. Ask a question you
might have avoided. Or admit a weakness you would have covered up.

Be more of your true self today—as genuine as you can be, wherever
it is easy. Today is not about stretching yourself—just one small step will
be sufficient. If you start with too high a level of difficulty, you will likely
break down and begin to rationalize why this is unachievable. Don't forget the vast possibilities for being truthful with yourself; see if you can find
truths you would not even have allowed yourself to notice, let alone
express.

INSIGHT FOR THE DAY

As you develop your vision of a life of expanding Truth, remember that Truth comes in degrees of difficulty and risk. Truth
can be very personal. It often begins with awareness. Will awareness
of Truth lead you to act and express it? We must remain vigilant to
stay on the only safe path, the path of Truth and genuine expression.

Evening Reflection: Learn and Grow

What did you learn today about yourself and Truth? How did you grow?
Record these discoveries in your Evening Reflections Journal, Responses, or Chart.

Day 15
Experiment with the Way of the Heart

Morning Reflection

Living from your heart, in your heart, and with your heart open, you will discover the rich treasures of your emotions. Your feelings—fear, hurt, anger, sadness, joy, and love—are your vehicles and guides to the Way of the Heart. Your wondrous emotions contain immense information—they let you know what you care about and what matters to you, they warn you of danger, provide the impetus to move from pain and toward pleasure. Your emotions are your conduit to the depth of your being, to the hearts of others, and are a pathway to spirit. It is through feeling and expressing your feelings fully and responsibly that you become real, spontaneous, and vibrantly alive. Open the pathway to the Way of the Heart and discover your creativity, intuition, and your ability to sense rightness—the Heart's wisdom. Sift through your urges to discover your true Desire, and follow it to deeper satisfaction. The Way of the Heart is the pathway to intimacy—the ability to connect with yourself, others, and spirit in a deep and profound way.

Think about how you may have hardened your heart, shut off your emotions, and lost touch with the wisdom of the Way of the Heart. Consider what it would be like to open the channels of your heart, to fill it with all that is good.

Now ask yourself: Will I go on the journey to discover more about my feelings and learn to express them more thoroughly and responsibly? Will I experience my feelings more deeply and engage more in life? Will I honor my emotions, valuing them as a powerful force in my life? How will I live today with Heart?

Daily Life Assignment: Feel!

Today is a day for the Way of the Heart. Touch the longings and feelings inside your heart—your anger, sadness, hurt, fear, joy, and love. Give yourself permission to feel. Allow your feelings to bubble up and express them with another person today. Share your feelings as fully and responsibly as you are able at this moment. Let someone know how you feel—hurt, angry, afraid, joyous, or even loving. If you are able to have the feeling wash across your face as you share it, then do so. If you are only able to guess or report on what you might be feeling, then share that. Do this face-to-face if you can—and if you can't do that, then do it by phone, e-mail, a poem, or a card. Whatever it takes, see that you express yourself with another person today. Do it at least once.

Insight for the Day

Most of us ignore many of our emotions and, in so doing, become separated from the Way of the Heart. You may find at times that you are afraid to express your feelings. You even rationalize why you shouldn't express them, sometimes bitterly defending a position contrary to what you truly feel.

Evening Reflection: Learn and Grow

What did you learn today about yourself and your emotions? How did you grow? What did you do differently in relation to your Heart and feelings?

Record these observations in your Evening Reflections Journal, Responses, or Chart.

Day 16
Experiment in the Power of Presence

Morning Reflection

Putting the Power of Presence into action brings enormous benefits. You'll find that your energy, productivity, and intimacy with others all increase when you tap the Power of Presence. You orient to the new FAT:

Flow, Aliveness, and Truth. You initiate conversations, take a risk to be the first to raise your hand or speak up in a group, say the next thing that's on your mind when you'd normally stop talking, allow your feelings to come into your awareness, express them, and keep telling the truth to the best of your ability. Or you might Presence yourself in a more quiet way. Perhaps you let your caring show toward someone by offering them a word of encouragement rather than pretending things don't matter. Maybe you share with someone how you're really feeling rather than curtly replying that you're "fine" when someone asks. The ways in which you express your newfound sense of Presence will vary. What's important is that you are allowing your life force to course through you.

You hold the Power of Presence in your hands. Think of a time when you said something, did something, or acted in a way that made you feel like you were more alive, more awake, more engaged. What did it look like? How did you feel?

Now ask yourself: Am I willing to put the Power of Presence to work in my day?

Daily Life Assignment:
Be Present—Show Up!

Today is the day to show up! Use your senses, access your emotions, and be conscious, awake, and alive. Your life assignment is to be as present as you can with yourself and another person today—a loved one, a coworker, an acquaintance, the doorman, the waitress at lunch, or whomever you choose. Make genuine contact with this person—really be with them. Share something you might previously have been afraid to share. When you do this, it will help to stay in your body, to sense your aliveness, and to use your senses: smell, touch, look, taste, hear. Open your heart and access your feelings, and let them flow. For extra credit, make real contact with more than one person. Share your thirty-day guide toward your One Decision with another person today.

Insight for the Day

You may be blind to your Power of Presence, having consciously or unconsciously made up stories and excuses as to why you are missing that power. You may think that you aren't substantial enough to command attention. Or you might think your ability to be present is dependent on the situation at hand: that you are checked out because you are tired, or someone is boring, or you think if you are fully yourself someone won't like you. These types of justifications are what limit the Power of Presence. Watch for their possible emergence as you address today's assignment.

Evening Reflection: Learn and Grow

How did you put the Power of Presence into action today? Where did you try something new to be more available or more conscious? Where did you avoid it? What did you learn about Presence? How did you grow?

Record these findings in your Evening Reflections Journal, Responses, or Chart.

Day 17
Experiment in Life Quest

Morning Reflection

When you follow your Life Quest, it will lead you unerringly to MORE. On the Life Quest, you discover who it is you really are at your core, most essential, most sparkling self. You discover the person God had in mind when you were made.

Your Life Quest is the realization of your vision for your life. It is your One Decision in action. Imagine what is possible on the unknown frontiers of your life—for your relationships, your career, your spirituality. Dream big, expand your horizons, and imagine your life as a noble Quest for MORE.

Think about the ways you may have avoided the unavoidable—your destiny—in the past. Consider how you may now consciously engage in your Life Quest to discover and fulfill this destiny.

Now ask yourself: What could be possible for me if I lived my life as a Quest for MORE? How will I live my life today? Will I live this day as a Quest for MORE in my life?

Daily Life Assignment: Quest for MORE

Be on a Quest for MORE today. Begin to think of and create a vision of MORE in an area of your life and do something to pursue it. Make it something that fulfills a deeper Desire, something that flows from your Heart and from your Truth. Do you dream of more intimacy in your relationships, more satisfaction at work, greater self-esteem and self-respect, greater connection to Spirit? Envision a possibility and write a statement of your vision as if it has already happened. Be grateful for it.

Now go into your day and do something in the service of the vision you have written—actively pursue MORE at least once today. Share a sweet moment with your beloved, have an impromptu picnic with your children on the living room floor, ask for feedback at work, give a friend a compliment, or take a purposeful walk in the woods and commune with spirit. Actively seek MORE today in at least one area of your life.

INSIGHT FOR THE DAY

Avoid the obstacles on your Life Quest that would cause you to stop reaching, to stop searching. Look at every step on your Quest as a reason to celebrate. Whether you do something foolish and you're humiliated or you do something great and you feel wondrous, revel in the challenge and opportunity of life.

Evening Reflection: Learn and Grow

What did you learn today about yourself and your Life Quest? What did you learn about vision? How did you grow? What did you do differently today in the service of your vision that you might not have done before?

Record these observations in your Evening Reflections Journal, Responses, or Chart.

Day 18
Experiment with Keys to the Kingdom

Morning Reflection

Coupled with your One Decision, the Keys to the Kingdom add even more power to all you do. Every moment and every situation holds the potential for MORE if you can unlock the possibilities with the Keys. When you use these powerful Principles, situations that looked bleak gain the possibility of new meaning, conflicts can be resolved, gridlocked circumstances open up. Celebrations become more meaningful, time becomes better used.

There is no problem or situation immune to the power of Principles. You can always choose to orient toward a Principle, whether it be love, truth, responsibility, aliveness, play, intention, engagement, or any other Principle of your choosing.

Think of people you know who use the Keys well in their everyday life. What Keys do they use and how do they use them?

Now ask yourself: What is the one Key that I can best use to guide me most effectively today? How could I use it?

Daily Life Assignment:
Choose a Key, Any Key, and Use It

Choose at least one situation today in which to apply a Principle of your choosing. It can be as simple as being more alive in a meeting, interacting and engaging when you normally would have withdrawn, or noticing how you created a situation in which you feel victimized.

You can use Truth to resolve a thorny conflict or add value to your day. For example, rather than resenting your car pool duty, you can use the Principle of responsibility or intention to reframe the duty as an opportunity to talk to your children and get to know their friends better. You can also use the Principle of engagement and presence in your morning routine—really smell the coffee, feel the warm water splashing against your skin in the shower, sing a morning wake-up song. Orient to aliveness to keep your energy flowing throughout the day. Encompass the quality of beauty today as you pick out your clothing, put on your makeup, straighten your desk, or set the table. Choose one Principle and apply it to at least one situation today. See how it can enhance your experience.

INSIGHT FOR THE DAY

Learning to use the Keys requires experimentation and mastery. Persistence will be one of your most valuable tools in learning to use the Keys. Willingness to fail, analyze your results, and envision new behavior will make your persistence pay off.

Evening Reflection: Learn and Grow

What did you learn today about yourself and the Keys? How did you grow?

Record these findings in your Evening Reflections Journal, Responses, or Chart.

Day 19
Experiment in Allies

Morning Reflection

You are never alone on your Life Quest. You may sometimes feel lonely, or you may feel that others don't understand you or are threatened by changes you are making in your life. Yet there are always fellow travelers who walk this path, who are engaged in the quest for MORE, who have made a One Decision, whether they call it that or not. Reach out and invite others to join you on the path. Support others on their Quest and allow yourself to be supported. Even those who travel a different path are likely to support you.

For this to happen, you must welcome this support, actively seek and engage it, and respond with gratitude and your own support. No one can fight the Good Fight alone.

You need help. You need support. You need others, just as they need you—the company of allies, the comfort of friends, a League of Your Own.

Every moment, you are surrounded by Allies, whether you recognize it or not. Think about the people you've encountered this week, last week, last month. Did you miss opportunities to support others or be supported by others?

Now ask yourself: How can I create the support I need to live my One Decision? How have I rejected or failed to accept and use Allies in my life, and how might I do it differently in the future?

Daily Life Assignment:
Support and Be Supported!

Solicit support from one or two people today. You may ask someone to help you with a problem, fix your computer, advise you on a project, provide critical feedback, mentor you on your career path, or be an ear for you as you share your feelings about something. Ask a friend to work out with you, commit to making your quota of sales calls today, or ask someone to check in with you to hold you accountable, or have a buddy meet you for dinner to explore your dreams together.

In addition to asking for support from someone, you will also give support to one or two people. You could reach out to someone you know who is struggling, lend an ear, encourage someone to take a risk in the service of their dreams, offer to baby-sit for a single mom, or even help someone carry a heavy package.

Insight for the Day

Don't be surprised to have your request for support denied or your offer refused. Remember that it's all part of the Adventure. If you never ask for or give support, you will never receive it or experience the profound pleasure of giving it. So keep asking and keep giving.

Evening Reflection: Learn and Grow

What have you learned about reaching out to give to others or to receive from them? What have your risks taught you about building a team of Allies? How have you grown?

Record these discoveries in your Evening Reflections Journal, Responses, or Chart.

Day 20
Experiment in the Good Fight

Morning Reflection

The Good Fight means fighting for what matters to you, whether it's consciousness, love, truth, or awareness. It is the battle to stay on course with your One Decision. Fighting the Good Fight means that you face up to the conflict between light and dark that exists within you and in the world around you. You recognize the push-pull of opposing forces and fight for the light.

To be engaged in the Good Fight means you have recognized that MORE doesn't simply come to you—that you must fight for it and fight hard. And by engaging in the battle, you are saying that there is something that you want that is worth fighting for.

Unleash a little more of the passion, courage, and determination you were born with each day for the rest of your life. Become a warrior of MORE, a knight of the Heart.

We have all experienced times in our lives when we've allowed ourselves to become unleashed, to step outside our normal behavior, and to take risks. These times often become turning points in our lives. Can you think of a time when you've stepped outside your normal way of being and taken more of a risk, been more passionate, or fought for something you cared about?

Now ask yourself: Am I willing to experiment with fighting the Good Fight today? Am I willing to see the opportunities that open up before me as invitations to do something different?

Daily Life Assignment: Fight the Good Fight!

Look for an opportunity to fight the Good Fight today—a temptation to resist, a truth to tell, a risk to take. Fight at least one battle. For example, you could tell people what matters to you, take an unpopular stand for something important to you, or tell a family member something you've been avoiding talking about. Or, just for today, you could resist a temptation and turn down an enticing offer that would take you off the path to Truth. Resist the temptation to gossip or zone out. Instead, have a meaningful conversation or teach yourself something new.

INSIGHT FOR THE DAY

Notice where you are swayed by your doubts or the naysayers who are threatened by your dreams. Never underestimate the enemy—the internal and external forces that would rob you of MORE. Fight a little more for your Desire. You may fight for Truth, consciousness, or to be Powerfully Present. Celebrate your victories. Rebound from your defeats.

Evening Reflection: Learn and Grow

How many fights did you fight today? Were they internal or external? Are there areas of your life where you avoided the Good Fight? Are there other areas where you're more comfortable risking? What did you learn today and how did you grow?

Record these in your Evening Reflections Journal, Responses, or Chart.

Application
{The Third Stage: Days 21–30}

The focus of this last ten-day stage is application. You will revisit each facet or skill area of the One Decision, this time applying the skill as fully as you can to your daily life. Each morning you will envision using one particular facet throughout the day. Then, during the day, through the assignment, you will bring this vision to life. In this final ten-day period, you are learning the mechanics of using your One Decision to guide your everyday choices. Even if you do not make your One Decision during this final stage of the guide, you will come that much closer to living a life of MORE.

During these last ten days, you will face your biggest challenges. You will revisit the same topics, only this time you will be invited to envision even greater possibilities for your life in relationship to others, to your health and well-being, to your work, and to spirit.

Day 21
A Day of Adventure

Morning Reflection

You are becoming more aware of what matters to you and why it is worth taking risks to achieve MORE in life. Living your life as an Adventure means taking risks in the service of your One Decision. There is no MORE if we live each day the same. MORE means something new, additional, different from what we have already experienced. Stretching beyond the familiar into what is new can make us feel out of control—but be assured that this is a natural part of the Adventure.

Remember, the gift of life can only be claimed if you are willing to live your life as an Adventure, calling upon your deepest faith and trust. Your One Decision guides you to explore worlds of awe and wonder—to experience all that life has to offer, to feel every feeling, to take risks and be challenged, to learn and grow, to develop, to become the most you that you can be.

Live every day of the remainder of your life as an Adventure, and build your vision of what is possible. You will be reborn; you will reconceive and re-create yourself. As you step continually into the unknown, you become your most magnificent, sensitive, courageous, and creative self.

Think of people you respect who have lived lives full of Adventure. How did they sustain and develop themselves throughout their lives? How did they continually reengage in the Adventure? Was there a vision guiding them? What else characterizes them? Start envisioning your own life as an ongoing Adventure.

Now ask yourself: What would my life look like if I lived it as an Adventure? What is my ideal vision of my life as an Adventure in relationship to my self-esteem, relationships, work, health and well-being, and spirituality?

What risks might I take at work, in my relationships, in how I treat myself, in my spiritual life? Will I see myself as an adventurer, explore possibilities in all areas of my life, stretch my limits, and experience life fully?

Daily Life Assignment:
Live a Day of Adventure

There are two parts to today's assignment, engagement and vision building. Today, you are to live the Adventure of MORE as fully as you can, applying your One Decision in at least two areas of your life. Follow it into at least two risky situations in at least two different areas of your life—from career, to relationship, to spirit. Build your vision of a life of Adventure by talking to others about your Adventure and sharing your evolving vision—how you can continue to grow by living your One Decision the rest of your life. You can begin to practice building your vision as you picture the ways you will make your choices as you live your One Decision today and throughout the rest of your life. What risks do you want to take in the service of your One Decision?

INSIGHT FOR THE DAY

Even adventurers rest. Remember that the task of adventuring demands that you rest and recreate, express and receive, create and deploy to advantage throughout your life. The journey is never ending.

Evening Reflection: Learn and Grow

What did you learn today about yourself, Adventure, and vision? How did you grow?

Record these observations in your Evening Reflections Journal, Responses, or Chart.

Day 22
A Day of Desire

Morning Reflection

Guided by your One Decision, your Desires lead you to your life of MORE. Learning to recognize and follow your urges and fulfill your Desires is, indeed, a lifelong job. And, as you continue your journey, you will find that your old patterns of fulfillment cease to satisfy you and new skills are required. Learn to continually tend to your inner urges, and they will lead you to fulfillment. Open your heart to the wonders that await you as you kindle your Desire for MORE. It is only through activating your deeper urges that you will pursue your heart's Desires and unfold the treasures in store for you throughout your life. Your Desires are the fuel of your One Decision. The more in touch you are with your heart, the more your Desires will be your trusted guide in partnership with your One Decision.

To honor your Desires is a skill you will develop throughout your life. But the most important thing you can do is follow the Desire that's right in front of you at any moment. There is no "later" when it comes to following a Desire. Now is the time to act.

Now ask yourself: What are my deepest, most essential Desires right now? What is my ideal vision of living my life, guided by my Desire in: relationship, work, self-esteem, health and well-being, and spirituality?

Daily Life Assignment:
Live Your Desire

Today is about following as many Desires as you can. A child runs from one thing to another delighting in each experience, but with a limited attention span. You can honor this veritable geyser of Desire emerging within you while still keeping the focus of an adult if you develop the discipline. Sense your urges and act on them. When faced with a choice, ask yourself, *What do I Desire?* Be willing to experiment—jump in the mud puddle, buy flowers, ask for help, speak up, spend time with someone you really enjoy, say no to someone you don't.

This day is dedicated to developing your vision of a life guided by Desire—a life guided by your One Decision. First, follow as many Desires as you can. Second, envision the possibilities of your life as if it were directed by your Desire.

INSIGHT FOR THE DAY

In any given moment, there is a Desire to be followed right in front of you. As you begin to live your entire day directed by Desire, you'll begin to discern true Desire from false temptation. Remember that it's all part of learning and growing. At any moment you can ask yourself, What is my deepest Desire in this very moment? Wherever your answer takes you is simply another adventure to explore.

Evening Reflection: Learn and Grow

What did you learn today about yourself and living with vision and Desire? Have you begun to imagine what your life would look like if it were fully directed by your Desire? How did you grow?

Record your observations in your Evening Reflections Journal, Responses, or Chart.

Day 23
Day of Deciding: Your One Decision

Morning Reflection

Claim the magnificent life that awaits you—a life of MORE satisfaction, fulfillment, feelings, intimacy, purpose, abundance, and contribution. Make your One Decision and use it to powerfully guide your life to MORE. No longer will you float without purpose and meaning, flitting from one magic solution to another. Through your One Decision, you will discover your purpose and live with greater meaning. You will begin to see results beyond what you thought possible, in all areas of your life.

Your One Decision affirms your essential Truth—I am alive. I am engaged. I am conscious. I am a child of God. I am a vessel for spirit. I choose Truth. I choose love. I feel my feelings and experience all of life. The most powerful and usable One Decisions assert these powerful truths—claim them as your own.

With your One Decision, you become the creator of your life. With it, you draw a line in the sand—from this point on, I live a life of MORE.

Your One Decision unites you with the powers of the universe in new and powerful ways.

Review your experience with each day's assignments. Which facets resonate most with you? What qualities do you relate to most powerfully—truth, consciousness, engagement, feeling, presence, love, service, aliveness? Think about what you Desire, what you want MORE of. Listen to your heart and allow it to express your One Decision. What are the words that best reflect your One Decision?

Now ask yourself: What is my One Decision and how will I live it in my life? If I don't know yet, or am not ready to make my One Decision, how will I live my life "as if" I have made my One Decision? What will my life look like as I live into my One Decision? What will my work be like? What will my relationships look like as I live according to my One Decision? How will it impact my sense of myself, how I see myself, how I feel about myself? What will it mean to my health and well-being? What is possible in my spiritual life?

Daily Life Assignment:
Live Your One Decision

Deepen your commitment to your One Decision today and develop your vision of how it will look in your life. Whether or not you choose to make your One Decision today, you can at least move toward making it. Take a moment and create a special space—light a candle, take a walk outside, play an inspiring piece of music, say a prayer, or even dance. Now choose the wording for your One Decision that feels right to you—the simpler the better. Remember, the wording isn't what matters—it is the heartfelt sense you have when you say it that matters. Now write your One Decision. Use the pages provided in the appendix to claim it, record it, celebrate it, and share it!

Try out your One Decision as fully as you can. It is your beacon; let it shine. Today, before you even encounter situations in which you will have choices to make, plan to use your One Decision. Apply it as fully as you can today in all areas of your life—your work, relationships, within yourself, your spirituality. Perhaps you will engage and invest more fully in a work project, take a risk in a relationship and ask for what you want, counter some negative self-talk within yourself, or do a spiritual practice more fully today—whether it is deepening your presence in prayer, reading something inspirational, journaling, or walking in the woods. Keep envisioning its power in your life from this day forward.

INSIGHT FOR THE DAY

One Decisions aren't just about determination. There are many exemplary people who have dedicated themselves to being the best at something—whether athlete, or musician, or scholar—but that isn't a One Decision. Your One Decision defines all of your life, not just one area. And remember, your One Decision is not something you use to indict yourself or beat yourself up. It isn't about being perfect or doing things right. It is about committing to a quality of being that matters to you. By committing to it you galvanize your activities toward that quality of being.

Evening Reflection: Learn and Grow

What did you learn today about yourself and your level of readiness and commitment to your One Decision? What did you learn about you and your One Decision? How did you grow? How did you do things differently by applying your One Decision?

Record these in your Evening Reflections Journal, Responses, or Chart.

Day 24
A Day of Truth

Morning Reflection

Your One Decision gives your life more meaning and direction built on a foundation of Truth. The Truth shall set you free; however, freedom requires courage and risk. Tell the truth to free yourself from limiting convention and to experience MORE. Truth is a personal journey. Your ability to discern Truth, admit it, receive feedback, and to share and deliver Truth to others develops over time. It is the most intensely personal and rewarding path you can take. Open your mind and your heart to Truth and you shall be free.

Truth beckons you, just as the fear of its outcome frightens you. The push-pull will always be there as you learn to use increasingly deep truths to guide you deeper into your potential.

Now ask yourself: Am I living as if I am a magnificent child of a loving universe that offers me constant opportunities to reveal myself and be fully known to others and orient to Truth? If not, then why not? What do I think it will take to live an ever-deepening life of Truth in relationship to: my health and well-being, work, relationship, self-esteem, and spirituality?

Daily Life Assignment: Live a Day of Truth

Challenge yourself to tell the truth as fully as you can today, both to yourself and to others. By tuning in to yourself, you will be able to express thoughts and feelings you would normally withhold, and tell yourself truths you normally would avoid. Be as genuine as you can. Today's challenge is twofold: to express Truth more fully and to develop an expanding vision of Truth throughout your life.

What avoidances, lies, and half-truths do you cling to as an excuse or a rationalization for falling short of the potential of your One Decision? You might choose to confide this Truth to a trusted friend, a mentor or adviser, or a fellow warrior in the Good Fight for MORE. Shine light on your dark places and align yourself with Truth.

INSIGHT FOR THE DAY

Negative self-talk can be very seductive and alluring, a web of self-generated deceit that may start out as a little self-abuse or self-pity but soon becomes a snare that entangles you. Treat yourself with gentle and loving Truth. When a negative thought or self-doubt challenges you, remember that it is stinking thinking and that your true self is much greater than your excuses, self-criticism, and other limiting thought and speech patterns.

Evening Reflection: Learn and Grow

What did you learn today about yourself and Truth? How did you grow? Record these in your Evening Reflections Journal, Responses, or Chart.

Day 25
A Day of Heart

Morning Reflection

Living with Heart brings you MORE. You feel your feelings more vividly and savor the richness, power, and depth of life. You enter into your feelings and discover their vast wisdom, rather than merely observing or denying them.

When you live the Way of the Heart, you unleash the power of your emotions, intuition, creativity, and passion. You begin to trust that who you are and how you feel at the deepest and purest level are the very things that are most lovable about you. The most powerful way to live, the Way of the Heart, is also the most vulnerable. Through the Way of the Heart, you realize the strength of your vulnerability. When you remove your armor and reveal your Heart, you open yourself to love and be loved, to feel, to be intimate, to be spontaneous, genuine, and real. You will feel blessings of abundance flowing to you and through you, leading you to the life you were afraid to wish for. Take a risk, reach out, drop your guard, and put down your shield. Find true security instead as you freely give and receive love. Experience being real, genuine, potently authentic—who you really are and were always meant to be.

Your One Decision is in the service of your Heart. Envision living the Way of Your Heart—full of feelings, open, revealed, available to love and be loved. Picture your life as lived from the genius of your heart.

Now ask yourself: What would my life be like if I lived what was in my heart? How will my relationships transform as I live the Way of My Heart? What will my work life be like as I tap my emotions, intuition, and creativity more fully? Who will I be and what will it be like for me to become more genuine? What will it be like to have an openhearted relationship with God or spirit in which I can be totally open and revealed, with my emotions flowing? What will it look like for me to be open to love and to be loved?

Daily Life Assignment:
Live the Way of the Heart

Today, follow the dictates of your heart as fully as you can in each area of your life—relationship to yourself, others, work, and spirit. This may include expression or listening. You could share your feelings with someone at work, put your heart into a work project, let someone know how much you care about them, pray with a full heart, laugh out loud, reach out to someone who needs a shoulder to cry on, act on your intuition.

Continue to focus on building your vision of a life guided by the Way of the Heart. How will you apply this to your life going forward? Think about how you will apply Heart in areas of your life—your work, relationships, spirituality, your relationship with yourself. What skills do you need to learn to be able to live more in your feelings to integrate Heart into your life?

INSIGHT FOR THE DAY

Heart is not necessarily soft. Frequently, doing things by the Way of the Heart is like tough love. Remember that the heart is amazingly resilient; don't sell it short.

Evening Reflection: Learn and Grow

What did you learn today about yourself? How did you grow?
Record these in your Evening Reflections Journal, Responses, or Chart.

Day 26
A Day of Being Powerfully Present

Morning Reflection

Your Power of Presence is yours and yours alone, but it is a heritage you must claim and develop. The secret is to be yourself, conscious and aware, alert, alive, and in touch with what is going on inside you, *your* feelings, and the sense of being with *yourself.* It is also expressing your Presence genuinely. Your Power of Presence is based on your commitment to your One Decision. Through the strength of this commitment, you will be able to use your senses and your feelings to genuinely manifest who you really are, wherever you are. You have a lifetime to tap this precious resource of boundless opportunity, of exciting adventure, new experiences, and MORE. Simply said, the Power of Presence is when you are most you. At any time during your day, you can ask yourself how present you are. You can check your emotions, awareness, and Truth. When you see that you are falling short, you can adjust and bring yourself back into full presence and, thereby, into fulfillment.

To be powerful is to be able to act or to effect change in something. To what end do you want to manifest your Power of Presence? What work do you want to get done in the world? What acts do you want to perform and what do you want to effect?

Now ask yourself: Am I willing to put the Power of Presence to work in my day and throughout my life? What is my ideal vision of living powerfully present in: relationship, work, self-esteem, health and well-being, and spirituality?

Daily Life Assignment:
Live Powerfully Present

Today you will make the Power of Presence your own. In previous days, you have raised your awareness of your Presence and you've taken some steps to try to be more present in your day. Today you will scan each life area: relationship to your self, others, work, your body, and spirit. What if you were entirely Present in your life? What would your life look like now? At home? At the office? In your spiritual life? With yourself? What could it look like in five years? Ten years? Twenty years? Your assignment today is to practice living "as if." Picture that Powerfully Present person in five years and act today as if that had already come true. Try out being that person. You don't need to do it perfectly or sustain it forever. Do things that you would do if you were living that vision. Limit activities that numb you or put you in a zone. Be as Present as you can, as often as you can, today.

Insight for the Day

Powerlessness is the other side of power. If you do not stretch into your powerlessness, you will never fully experience your actual power and your Power of Presence. So often we try to avoid situations where we feel powerless. We limit our risks, play it safe, or avoid situations where we feel like we're beyond our capacities. In order to tap your Power of Presence, you must be willing to stretch into areas where you feel powerless, where you go beyond what you've done in the past.

Evening Reflection: Learn and Grow

What have you learned about having a life in which you are Powerfully Present? Are there certain areas of your life where you feel you are Present and others where you are not? How have you grown from painting a vision for yourself, from acting "as if" it were already true?

Record your answers in your Evening Reflections Journal, Responses, or Chart.

Day 27
A Day of Life Quest

Morning Reflection

In the Life Quest, you will begin to realize how vast the One Decision really is. You'll realize that it encompasses your entire life and, in fact, defines all of your life. There is no end to your Life Quest. Here is where the deeper challenges reside and the greater rewards arise. All of your days, seek to live the Adventure guided by your Desires, expressing deeper Truths, and following a path with Heart in the partnership of Allies for the betterment of all. Remember, you are meant to be the hero of your own life, embarking on a Quest that is yours alone—to seek, discover, and create.

Can you redefine yourself as a Life Quester? Few really prepare for a Quest. They prepare for career, marriage, to "get by" in life, or even to suffer. What will you need to see yourself as worthy of and responsible for a Life Quest?

Now ask yourself: Will I live my life as a Quest for MORE? Will I see myself as a hero of my own life? Will I accept that my failures are just as valuable as my successes on the journey to MORE? Will I leave behind what is comfortable and familiar to explore the frontiers of my life and live the noble Quest? What will my life look like when I live it as a Quest? What will it look like to Quest in my career? What is possible in my relationships? My spiritual life? My own potential?

Daily Life Assignment:
Live Your Life Quest

Today, build your vision of your life as a Quest and live your Quest as fully as you can. Here is where you build the vision of your One Decision as it manifests itself in your Life Quest. Remember, every area of your life is the territory of your Quest—your relationships, your work, your health and well-being, your spiritual life, your relationship with yourself. Think about the possibilities available in each area and see yourself as a person going for a greater goal, a bigger vision in each area, and actively pursuing MORE.

Envision this day you are about to live. Ask yourself how each person you will encounter and each thing you will do today fits into your Life Quest. Ask yourself what living the Quest fully would look like today. Let the answer to that question guide you into this day as completely as you can.

This is not just a day to "get through." This is a day to live as a Life Quester would live—and see this as a template for your vision for the rest of your life.

Insight for the Day

Tour de France champion Lance Armstrong needed to keep himself in good shape for three weeks of grueling competition. He was a champion because he knew how to conserve his energy and at the same time stay within striking distance of his competition to win. Your Life Quest requires conservation and exertion. Prepare for a very long journey. Know there will be good days and bad, that you will learn on the way, and that you must strategize for the whole race, not just a burst. Plenty of people win for a day. Few engage in the Life Quest as magnificently as possible.

Evening Reflection: Learn and Grow

What did you learn today about yourself and your Life Quest? How did you grow? What did you do differently today as you lived your life as a Quest today?

Record these in your Evening Reflections Journal, Responses, or Chart.

Day 28
A Day of Principles

Morning Reflection

Your One Decision is impossible to realize without using the principles.

These Keys do more than open doors. They are also tools that will guide you in the darkest times. Your One Decision activates and directs your Life Quest. Your Life Quest requires you to face dangers. The weapons with which you fight enemies and clear the way on your journey include Truth, Presence, and Heart, but common to these, and always at the ready, are the Keys. In the darkest times, the Keys can help—as courage is fading and the object of the Quest is unclear.

When things are going well, the Keys maximize benefit and progress. They guide you at high velocity and help you stay on the path. They work as a homing device to help you avoid sidetracks and unnecessary trouble and provide common points of focus to which you and your Allies can orient.

Gyroscopes keep planes and rockets upright. Compasses keep travelers oriented. The Keys to the Kingdom keep you true to your One Decision when you do not know where to turn, when your Heart is troubled and you are working out your deeper Truths.

Now ask yourself: How will you remember to use the Keys when you most need them? What would your life be like if it were directed by the Keys in work, relationship, self-esteem, spirit, and well-being? You are building a vision of that possible reality. Keep up the good work.

Daily Life Assignment:
Live a Principled Day

Live in consonance with as many Principles as you can today You could use the Principle of play as you pick up your children from school, singing in the car; or use intention to complete the project that's been hanging over your head; or apply the Principle of connection for your family dinner tonight and have each family member report on a highlight and lowlight of their day. You are probably already using Principles a lot more than you know, but if you intend to use them for the rest of your life, be aware of the Keys and how you use them. Develop a vision of living with the Keys each and every day.

INSIGHT FOR THE DAY

Have you ever thought you lost something and discovered it was in your pocket or on your person the whole time, like the person who can't find his glasses, only to discover that they are perched on the top of his head? You will experience something similar as you learn to use the Keys. You will feel lost and hopeless, confused and at wit's end, only to rediscover that you had the solution available to you the whole time. The Keys were in and with you.

Evening Reflection: Learn and Grow

What did you learn today about using the Keys? How did you grow?

Record these in your Evening Reflections Journal, Responses, or Chart.

Day 29
A Day of Living with Allies

Morning Reflection

Building a life team of Allies is not an overnight task. It's an ongoing journey of seeking, searching, engaging, being supported, and supporting others. As you build your team of Allies throughout all areas of your life, you will have the opportunity to see the best and the worst in yourself and others. But with your One Decision as your guide, you will be more willing to see others more clearly and to reveal yourself.

Allowing one another to see all of the ups and downs, and to share in the victories and failures, is what it means to be an Ally. You are vision keepers for one another. No matter what circumstances may bring, you hold a vision for one another, provide encouragement, tell one another hard truths, and hold one another accountable. You are willing to coach and be coached, to mentor and be mentored, to give and receive—to create a powerful network of support as you live your One Decision.

Think of a time when someone has held a vision for you just when you needed it most. Or perhaps when you've stepped in to provide the encouragement that someone else needed.

Now ask yourself: What will it take for me to live every day as if I am surrounded by Allies? What training, classes, or coaching will I need to create the support I need? How can I recognize the Allies I have in people who are nothing like me? What is my ideal vision of living my life with a team of Allies who support me in living my One Decision in: relationships, work, self-esteem, health and well-being, and spirituality?

Daily Life Assignment:
Live Knowing You Are Surrounded by Allies

Scan your life for Allies on your life team. Collaborate with as many people as you can on as many things as you can today. Do not think you must always *do* things to support others. Simply listening with caring can also be a gift. Similarly, unburden your heart about what matters to you. Consciously build your vision of a life full of Allies today and for the rest of your life. Keep track of how many possible Allies you have through your life: At work? In relationships? For your health and well-being? In your spiritual life? At home? As you collaborate with people today and create your list, pay attention to areas where you'd like more support. Imagine what you'd like your support team to look like in five years, ten years, or twenty years. Live today as if you have that team of support.

INSIGHT FOR THE DAY

Remember that living a One Decision is not an overnight thing. This 30 Days guide will give you experiences to live your One Decision, but it really takes a commitment to continual learning and growing to step into the life you were destined to live. That means seeking out coaching, courses, training, and other development for the continual support you deserve.

Evening Reflection: Learn and Grow

What was it like living a day with Allies? What did you learn about your vision for your life team? How did you grow out of giving and receiving support at this level?

Record these in your Evening Reflections Journal, Responses, or Chart.

Day 30
A Day of Fighting the Good Fight

Morning Reflection

Heroes fight the Good Fight. You become the hero of your own life when you make your One Decision and choose Adventure over suffering, Quest over complacency, Heart and Presence over numbness. In fact, the very act of choosing is a battle of the Good Fight.

You would not have made it to this lesson if you were only choosing complacency, or to bide your time or just get by in life. Through these thirty days, you have explored living your life as an Adventure, following your Desire, pursuing Truth, living with Heart and Presence, practicing Principles, and gathering Allies. Each time you pursued a challenge in the service of your One Decision, you have fought the Good Fight. The Good Fight takes place one engagement at a time, one commitment at a time, and one encounter at a time. Each day of your life presents challenges—opportunities to take responsibility for your life, to tap your personal power in the service of your One Decision. Without the Good Fight, you would probably never taste the full sweetness of life available to you—it is in the Good Fight that you tap your potential. And without your One Decision, you would probably avoid the Good Fight.

Now, on this thirtieth day, and in all the days to come, you have a choice: MORE or Less, Abundance or Scarcity, One Decision or indecision. Which do you choose, and will you fight for it?

A life of MORE guided by your One Decision requires you to unleash your passion, your courage, and your determination to live the life you were meant to live. Do not be swayed by doubts and the internal and external enemies that would divert you from your destiny and rob you of MORE. Fight for what you desire, for truth, for consciousness, to be present, to follow your Heart. Discover the life you were meant to live. Claim it now!

Now ask yourself: What is my ideal vision of living my life, fighting for what matters in: relationship, work, self-esteem, health and well-being, and spirituality? How will I assure my reengagement when I drop off, as we all do from time to time? Will I develop and use a powerful vision to help me reorient and empower myself when I am feeling unmotivated and not conscious? Affirm to yourself: I fight the Good Fight in the name of my One Decision—to have the life I have always desired, a life of MORE!

Daily Life Assignment: Claiming Your Good Fight!

Congratulations! You are completing your 30 Days and today is dedicated to visioning and celebration! If you haven't yet made a One Decision, this would be a great time to do it. Remember, you don't need to do it perfectly. Simply write your One Decision as you envision it at this time. It can evolve as you do. Remember, there are forms in the appendix to claim it, record it, celebrate it, and share it. If you don't feel ready to make your One Decision, today is still a day to revel in your victories so far. Remember, you have fought a Good Fight simply by getting to this lesson. Today you will celebrate that you engaged in battles—took on assignments, challenged yourself, tried new things—whether you won or lost. You have taken risks, deepened your awareness, and learned lessons in using your Desires to fuel your Good Fight—the things that really matter to you. Use these victories and lessons to move forward with even greater effectiveness.

Your assignment is to choose at least one way to celebrate the Good Fight in service of your One Decision—host a dinner party and share your battles, toast your successes and glean the lessons of your defeats, write yourself a congratulatory note, raise your cup in salute, honor yourself with a sacred ceremony of your own choosing, say a prayer of thanksgiving for your journey, or invite your Allies to live a life of MORE with you. Celebrate your thirty-day journey.

Now develop and record your vision of a life fighting the Good Fight from what you have done, would like to have done, and seen others do. Do you see rest, recreation, diet, fitness, Allies, Truth, and Heart in your battle? Do you see acknowledging and celebrating your willingness to live according to your One Decision and fight for MORE? Your assignment from here forward is to live a life engaged in the Good Fight, delighting in the engagement, honoring your defeats, and reengaging. Fighting because it is the right thing to do, because it is the path with Heart.

INSIGHT FOR THE DAY

Remember that the Good Fight can only be fought with a sense of delight and personal responsibility. You are losing the battle when you minimize your efforts, ignore your victories, or blame others for your shortfalls. Honor your Journey. Reach out for assistance if you need to adjust your attitude—enlist the help of Allies both seen and unseen. Reorient to your One Decision and celebrate your victories. You are a warrior for MORE!

Evening Reflection: Learn and Grow

What have you learned in these 30 Days about the One Decision and fighting for the things that really matter to you? How have you grown from creating a vision of a life guided by your One Decision and fighting the Good Fight? In what ways have you changed through these 30 Days? And in what ways do see that you would still like to change?

Celebrate your gains by recording these observations in your Evening Reflections Journal, Responses, or Chart.

Days to Come:
Living Your One Decision
All the Days of the Rest of Your Life

Living your One Decision is a lifelong journey, a noble Life Quest. Just as a hero on a Life Quest continually sharpens his skill, may you continue to learn and grow. May you have the courage to live your One Decision, make mistakes, learn, and live a life you love. Life is not loved by preoccupation with avoiding mistakes; rather, it is loved by risking and venturing. May you experience your life as a Quest for Adventure with Heart, Desire, Presence, Truth, Principles, and fighting the Good Fight with the support of Allies.

And from this day onward, may nobility, honor, and love be the values that define your life. And may you experience caring, serving, and compassion—the natural outcomes of any true One Decision. May you experience blessing, grace, and loving embrace. May your life be blessed with MORE.

Thank you for the honor of sharing this journey with you.

Judith Wright

30 Days to Your One Decision
APPENDIX

In this appendix, you'll find a variety of forms that will help you use the thirty-day guide and make your One Decision. First are forms that give you three different ways to do your **Evening Reflection**. You'll find a completed sample as well as a blank form, which you can copy to use throughout the thirty days. Choose the form that you are most comfortable with, or alternate if you wish.

With the **Journal**, you simply write free-form and mark plus (+) and minus (−) to track thoughts and behaviors that moved you toward or away from your One Decision. With the **Responses** form, write in your responses to each of the statements provided. The **Daily Reflection Chart** is another option; use this checklist to track your assignment each day and to jot down a few thoughts about it. Any of the forms is fine. Just pick the form or the combination that works best for you.

After the Daily Reflection Chart, you'll find a few pages to help you in making your One Decision. The first pages offer four simple steps to claiming your One Decision, and the page that follows is a form to officially record and claim your One Decision. Again, choose the options that you feel will help you in making your One Decision. Blessings on your journey!

Contents

Journal
(sample)

Journal on your day. To help you become more aware, you can place a plus (+) next to the thoughts, actions, and situations where you were moving toward the facet of your One Decision and a minus (−) next to where you moved away from it.

Day 15: Way of the Heart

I was surprised to see that I resented today's assignment. I looked at paying attention to my emotions as a pain. I guess I think paying attention to my emotions is not important, what's new? Dad was always angry and Mom cried. I did not like either. Escaping to my room seemed better. I guess that's what I did today. Watched TV most of the night and didn't call Peter to talk. − I'm still not sold on this. I can see some use but, wow, this seems extreme.

I'm going to have to talk to my Ally group about this. + At least I did tell my assistant how angry I was about the new policy of getting sign offs on messenger service use. + Big deal, ugh.

Journal

Journal on your day. Place a plus (+) next to the thoughts, actions, and situations where you moved toward the facets of your One Decision and a minus (−) next to where you moved away from it.

Responses
(sample)

Complete the sentences below nightly for each day's exercise.

1. The most difficult aspect of today's assignment for me was:

I don't really believe I should always tell the truth. I did take myself to task a bit and talk to Sandy about how I think she is being used by her boyfriend and she was really put out, at least I think so.

2. The lesson about living my life and my One Decision that I want to keep in mind and apply in the future is:

I do believe that this can be useful and I can do it more but I'm not really sure how. I know I want to be able to tell my boyfriend more and if we are going to get married, I don't want a life like my Mom and Dad's, where they don't talk and hide things from each other.

3. My vision of my life with this assignment is:

I'm not really sure. I'm going to have to talk to a few friends and my Allies about this.

4. My *Learns*—What I learned today is:

For sure, how hard it is for me and that I am not anywhere near as honest as I thought and I don't think anyone else is either, certainly not Sandy.

5. My *Grows*—The things I did differently today are:

I did say a lot more than I usually would. I think a lot of this for me is really just talking more. I think I am more truthful than a lot of folks but I need to talk.

Responses

Complete the sentences below nightly for each day's exercise.

1. The most difficult aspect of today's assignment for me was:

2. The lesson about living my life and my One Decision that I want to keep in mind and apply in the future is:

3. My vision of my life with this assignment is:

4. My *Learns*—What I learned today is:

5. My *Grows*—The things I did differently today are:

DAILY REFLECTION CHART (SAMPLE)

DAY	READ LESSON	REFLECTED	LIFE ASSIGNMENT DONE	
1	X	X	X	When I look at things as an adventure, I suffer less.
2	X	X	X	I have desires all the time . . . I just never take the time to notice them!
3				
4				
5				
6				
7				
8				
9				
10				
11				
12				
13				
14				
15				
16				
17				
18				
19				
20				
21				
22				
23				
24				
25				
26				
27				
28				
29				
30				

DAILY REFLECTION CHART

DAY	READ LESSON	REFLECTED	LIFE ASSIGNMENT DONE	
1				
2				
3				
4				
5				
6				
7				
8				
9				
10				
11				
12				
13				
14				
15				
16				
17				
18				
19				
20				
21				
22				
23				
24				
25				
26				
27				
28				
29				
30				

MAKE YOUR ONE DECISION

Congratulations! You are now ready to make your One Decision. Here are a few simple steps you can follow to honor this important moment.

1. Claim it

Claim your One Decision as your own. Make it a personal reflection of your vision for your life. Your One Decision may have come to you as you read the book or were working on the 30 Days guide or sometime thereafter. The timing isn't important. What is important is that you choose words that feel powerful for you and state them in the present tense as if they have already happened. Once you've claimed your One Decision, move on to the second step and declare it.

2. Record it and Declare it

On a page that follows, you will find a space to claim your One Decision. You can photocopy it or write directly in the book. Simply fill in your name at the top of the page, write your One Decision in the space provided, and sign and date the bottom of the form. This document then will be a reminder for you to stay inspired on your journey.

3. Celebrate it

Celebrate your One Decision! You have just committed yourself to a life of MORE! This is a big step and an important event—a celebration of the new you . . . the real you. Mark the occasion—you could throw a party, create a spiritual ritual (set up an altar, light a candle, pray about it, and share it with your higher power), declare it out loud, make a special dinner and toast to yourself, share with close friends, take yourself out on a date, spend quiet time in nature, or announce it from the rooftops. You can choose to celebrate it in any way that feels right to you. What is important is that you celebrate yourself for taking such an important step.

4. Share it

One important way to make your One Decision real is to share it with others. You can share it with your friends, family, coworkers, and mentors. What is important is that you include your Allies or people that you know will help remind you and keep you accountable. One of the best places to share it is on my website, www.judithwright.com. Enter your One Decision, read other people's One Decisions, and take advantage of the great tools and resources to keep you inspired. We'll help you remember your One Decision by e-mailing it to you at intervals. Include your friends in your celebration and share it with them. And share it with yourself—put it on your desktop, on your mirror, in your wallet, or on an altar, or frame it. Keep it in front of you to remind you of your new way of being.

My One Decision is . . .

I, _____, hereby dedicate myself to
(name)

living my One Decision.

I swear upon this day, _____, in the
(month and day)

year of _____.
(name)

_____
(signature)

Acknowledgments

This book is a reflection of my One Decision, and it has been one of the most challenging and wonderful adventures of my life—challenging because of the demanding content and tight deadlines, wonderful because it has been like riding a wave with teamwork that has inspired and deeply touched me. I could not have done it without the loving, competent support of the many caring and dedicated Allies who partnered with me to bring it into being. Some of their names are listed here and some are not, but they are all inscribed deeply in my heart for everything they have given to me and all that they have shared of themselves to bring MORE to the world.

To my husband, Bob, the loving force of Truth, for modeling commitment and dedication and for opening me up to infinite possibilities. It is his lifework that is reflected in this book, and I am deeply grateful to be sharing it. In gratitude for everything—from developing this powerful work and for support in writing, editing, story crafting, and business guidance, to kicking my butt, soothing my soul, inspiring and encouraging me, and for loving and believing—all when I need it.

To our students who have made their One Decisions, dedicating themselves, and who are living models for what it means to embrace lives of Adventure with Heart, Truth, and Presence—whose real lives inspired this book and whose stories grace its pages.

To our dedicated staff, who constantly stretch beyond what seems possible with immense goodwill, bighearted enthusiasm, diligence and hard work, deep dedication, wild creativity, loving support, conscientious care, and continual inspiration. To Barb Burgess for her partnership and for applying her many gifts, from marketing to editing and so much more; to Liz Mansfield for creativity and wordsmithing; and to both for doing whatever it takes and sharing amazingly creative all-nighters/all-weekers with fun, focus, and grace—I am privileged to have you as my team. And to Angie Calkins, Gertrude Lyons, Beryl Stromsta, and Kathy Schroeder for countless tasks and acts of kindness and support, from odd projects, late-night deliveries, and last-minute packing, to loving support and graciously picking up the slack.

To Patricia Crisafuli for her enthusiastic support and editing acumen, and to Barbara Bohn, Marilyn Pearson, Ela Booty, and Bruce Wexler for their help in editing, proofreading, and sharing ideas. To our design and Web team, Christina Canright and Collin Canright, for their caring, creativity, and generosity, and for their stalwart support of MORE and One Decision trainings.

To the phenomenal and inspiring team at Tarcher/Penguin: To Joel Fotinos for his breadth of vision, depth of spirit, and dedication in sharing his love of his work with the love of our work to birth this book. To Sara Carder, for her diligence, grace, and eloquence in editing. And to Terri Hennessey for her marketing support, and to the entire sales, publicity, marketing, design, and production teams for making this book possible.

To Stephanie Kip Rostan and James Levine of the LevineGreenberg Agency for their continued dedication and caring and for shepherding the process.

To the Wright Institute Summer Training Participants for breaking the limits of what is possible in productivity, fun, and teamwork, for demonstrating that work is play, and for providing a living model of what it is like to build a community of people who have made their One Decision. Special thanks for the One Decision stories, audio, design, photos, brainstorming, and ongoing support and inspiration. And to our marketing support and creativity think-tank, Jennifer Stephen and Scott Stephen, for their caring contribution.

To our adjunct faculty, the Wright Institute advanced students, who are living amazingly successful lives and now teach what they have learned so they can serve and learn even more—student leaders who coach, lead labs, and conduct trainings—for sharing their precious time, successful lives, and vast gifts so that others may learn to live lives of Adventure on their Quest for MORE.

To the women of SOFIA, the Society of Femininity in Action, and especially for my Women's Leadership Training Group, for believing, and for your selfless service, support, camaraderie, and living demonstration of the power of a community. For gracing everything with your presence, from magical meals, back rubs, and late-night laughter, to your stories generously shared in this book—for being models of feminine power and support and for carrying the torch and lighting the world around you. And to those women leaders not yet named: Michele Gustin, Wendy Manning, Edda Coscioni, and Denise Delves.

To all the other Allies seen and unseen—and to Prairie Spring Woods—for nourishing my spirit and inspiring my journey.

And the greatest thanks to the Divine Spirit that flows through us all.

ABOUT THE WRIGHT INSTITUTE, INC.

The Wright Institute helps people discover, vision, and live successful lives of purpose, meaning, and fulfillment. You can recognize Wright Institute students and consulting clients by their results—they have potent and powerful relationships that last, families that work, and businesses that contribute to staff, industry, and their communities. Wright faculty and students not only serve at the highest levels, but they also transform the companies and even the industries in which they serve. The stories shared in this book are their stories, only a small selection from the thousands of people who have transformed their lives with their One Decision and Wright Institute programs.

Anyone can have MORE in life, but few have learned the skills to lead these lives of greater meaning, satisfaction, and purpose. It takes commitment, training, and support to live a life of MORE. So, over the years, the Wright Institute has developed and offered our students and clients the practical and life-transforming skills they need for success in every life area, from self-esteem and relationship to career building.

Our educational methodology features our unique accelerated learning model that integrates three core developmental elements: *coaching, laboratory learning,* and *classroom training*. In our *trainings,* students develop vision, learn philosophy, use concepts, and engage in powerful experiential exercises. In the *learning labs*, they learn, apply, and practice actual life skills with group support, and in *coaching* they develop their personal strategies and individual skills. Mutuality is at the core of all we do. Our faculty are constantly learning and growing alongside our students, living with greater effectiveness, consciousness, and love. Our faculty walk the walk, continually developing and even transforming their lives along the way. Faculty and coaches have spent at least three years in additional training before delivering services to students.

Coaching in our model has many applications. It teaches people to live their One Decision in all life areas. Our leadership coaching is used by top executives across the country. Career, couples, family, and singles coaching are delivered along with subject- and goal-specific coaching like weight, financial management, self-esteem, and others. We are especially proud of our unique MORE Intimacy Training (MIT) and vision coaching.

Students employ the assignment way of living in our *groups or learning laboratories*—demonstrated in the *30 Days to Your One Decision*. Assignments are like small experiments in thinking, acting, and relating. By engaging in assignments, students challenge limiting beliefs and develop new skills. *Laboratory learning* takes place in ongoing group interaction using facilitated interaction: in- and out-of-lab assignments; and in regular progress assessment, including in-depth feedback.

In addition to the One Decision, all elements of our curriculum include developing vision, challenging mistaken beliefs, identifying and responsibly expressing emotions, applying insight to effect behavior change, and developing practical skills. Our *courses* and *classroom trainings* are generally highly interactive, using experiential exercises to help participants develop powerful visions of future possibilities and the skills to make their visions reality. Students come from all over the country to our trainings and participate by phone in our labs, coaching, and classes. We also have a robust array of publications, tools, educational products, teleclasses, and online materials to support people to live lives of MORE.

Through thousands of examples and success stories, we know that there is no one perfect formula. And a perfect formula isn't the point. Our passion and mission is to support people through any means and resources available to live full, exciting, engaging, successful, satisfying lives. Our curriculum has developed in response to our students' expanding vision of living life to the fullest. Descriptions of a few of our introductory courses and services follow.

The One Decision Training

Charge your life and jump into your greatest possibilities. Experience the facets of the One Decision in a powerful, supportive, inspiring environment. Whether you're just deepening the concepts or would like to make a One Decision or more fully commit to a One Decision you've already made, this powerful training brings you the experience you need. This book introduces you to the One Decision, but it's only with experience that your One Decision will become your own. Invest in yourself, your life, and MORE. You'll be inspired, meet Allies to share your journey, and discover more tools and concepts you can use to have MORE of everything you desire.

Special Offer for Readers Only

Visit www.judithwright.com and follow the information on the One Decision. Click on "For Book Readers Only" and enter the code: 774748Q for information about a limited-time special offer.

For questions or more information, contact us by phone at 1-866-MORE-YOU or 312-645-8300, or e-mail us at contact@wright learning.com.

Year of MORE

Turn the corner to a life of MORE of everything you desire. Build the foundation for a life of greater satisfaction and fulfillment, financial and relationship success, as well as enhanced self-esteem and personal potency. Spend a year developing your most valuable asset—yourself. This proven one-year program gives you the life skills and tools to bring about dramatic transformation in every area of your life. Participate in this training from anywhere in the country by phone (or in person if you live in the Chicago area). The Year of MORE is composed of four quarters, each with a different focus: self-care and nourishment, personal power, family and intimacy, and life purpose and spirituality. (Whatever your faith, you will learn to live it more fully.) The curriculum includes a weekly meeting (by phone or in person) and four in-person weekend trainings, one for each different focus, throughout the year. You can start the program at any quarter. Don't just make a few small changes in your life. Transform yourself into your most sterling self and live a life you love and are proud to share. For more information, visit the Wright Institute online at www.wrightliving .com, or contact us by phone at 1-866-MORE-YOU or 312-645-8300, or by e-mail at contact@wrightlearning.com.

Coaching

Make more money, have better relationships, overcome challenges, love your work, achieve goals, and get MORE of what you want from life— with the backing of your own personal coach, someone who is always in your corner. The Wright Institute has been training and developing world-class coaches since long before coaching was a household word. Our coaches have experience and expertise in a wide variety of areas—from individual goal achievement, to relationships, to business strategy and career success. We have a personal coach who will help you live your dreams. The beauty of a coach is that you can work with them from anywhere in the world by phone and schedule your coaching meetings at times that are convenient for you. Whether you want to enhance your performance, engage in high-level problem solving, or have more meaningful living while living your dreams—don't hesitate, schedule a vision assessment and planning session today. Call the Wright Institute at 1-866-MORE-YOU or 312-645-8300, visit us online at www.wrightliving.com, or e-mail us at contact@wrightlearning.com.

SHARE YOUR STORY

Thank you for sharing the journey of the One Decision with me. I hope you have found it as powerful, insightful, and inspiring as I have in my own life.

Please stay in touch with me as you explore the concepts of the book and progress toward making your One Decision. In fact, I would love for you to share your story with me—how you made your One Decision, or any success or challenge stories along the way. I can then share your story with others and they can benefit from your experience.

Visit my website and submit your story and your One Decision. And, if I use your story on my website, I'll send you a special bonus gift. Simply log on to www.judithwright.com or e-mail us at contact@judithwright.com, or call 1-866-MORE-YOU. Reading others' stories and sharing your own is a great way to create more Allies on the journey.

Best wishes as you create MORE of everything you desire. Stay in touch!

Judith Wright

ABOUT THE AUTHOR

"One of the most sought-after self-help gurus in the country" the *San Francisco Chronicle* hails Judith Wright, a world-class educator, coach, lifestyles expert, inspirational speaker, best-selling author, and corporate consultant.

Judith cofounded the Wright Institute in Chicago, with her husband, Bob, to help individuals, couples, families, and corporations get more out of everything they do: more meaning, fulfillment, and success in relationships, career, parenting, and finance—all the areas of their lives.

After receiving a B.A. in psychology and an M.A. in education and counseling, Judith rose to national prominence in academia, where she designed cutting-edge programs to help adults with disabilities attend college. Next she was recognized nationally for her innovative model programs to support children with disabilities and their families. A trailblazer in human development, she has since been revolutionizing the personal-growth industry, developing transformative couples, leadership, women's, and communication trainings.

Judith demystifies what it takes to lead a great life as she teaches proven, time-tested perspectives on how to have it all through her writing, teaching, coaching, and public speaking. A media favorite, Judith has appeared on more than three hundred radio and television shows, including *The Oprah Winfrey Show*, *Good Morning America*, and *Today*. Magazines and newspapers across the country feature her work, including *Marie Claire*, *Fitness* magazine, *Health*, *Better Homes and Gardens*, *Shape*, the *New York Daily News*, the *Chicago Tribune*, the *Boston Herald*, and the *Detroit Free Press*.

A powerful speaker and coach, Judith inspires women's groups, couples, community leaders, and corporations alike. Her talks on lifestyles, feminine power, productivity, communications, and relationships educate, inspire, and entertain groups such as the Mega Success seminars, Bank One, AC Nielsen, the International Association of Junior Leagues, the Miss USA Women's Power Summit, and many more.

To book Judith as a speaker for your company or organization, to learn more about her trainings and seminars, or for more information on a personalized coaching curriculum with Judith, visit her website at www.judithwright.com. Or contact her by phone at 1-866-MORE-YOU, 312-645-8300, or by e-mail at contact@judithwright.com.